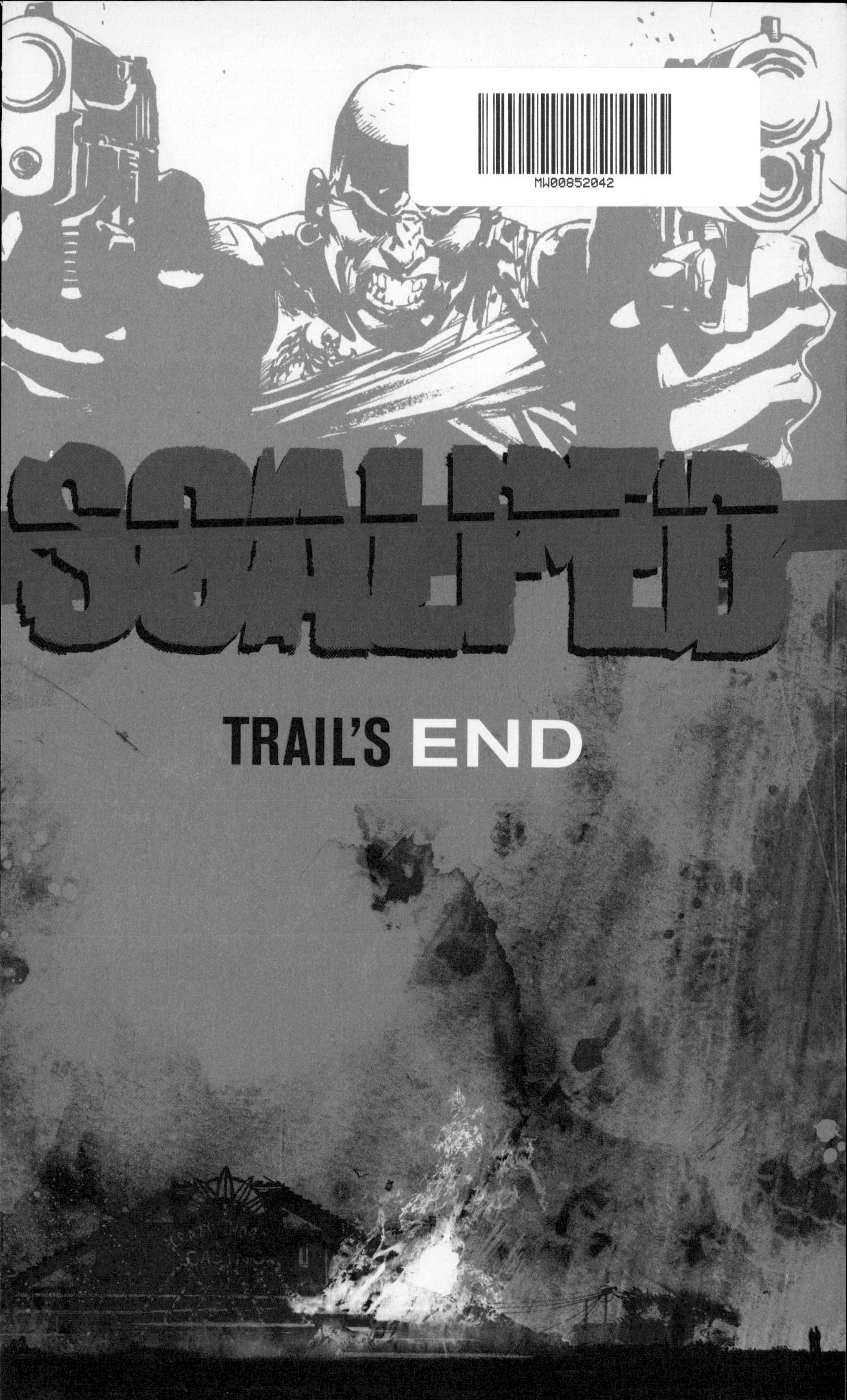
SCALPED
TRAIL'S END

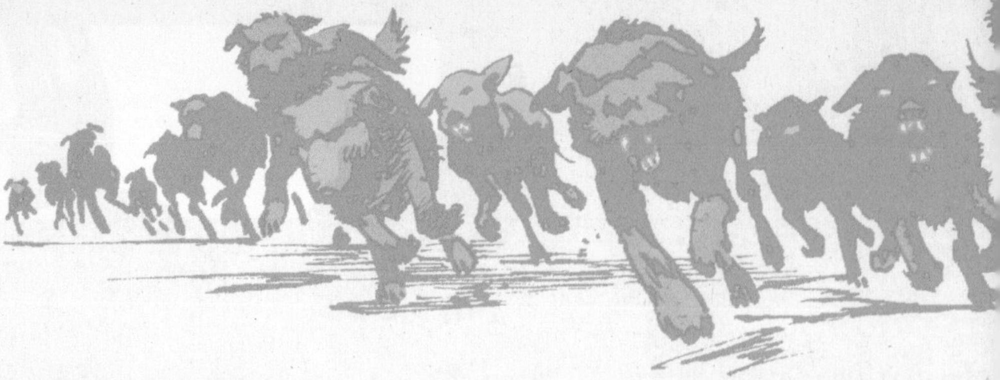

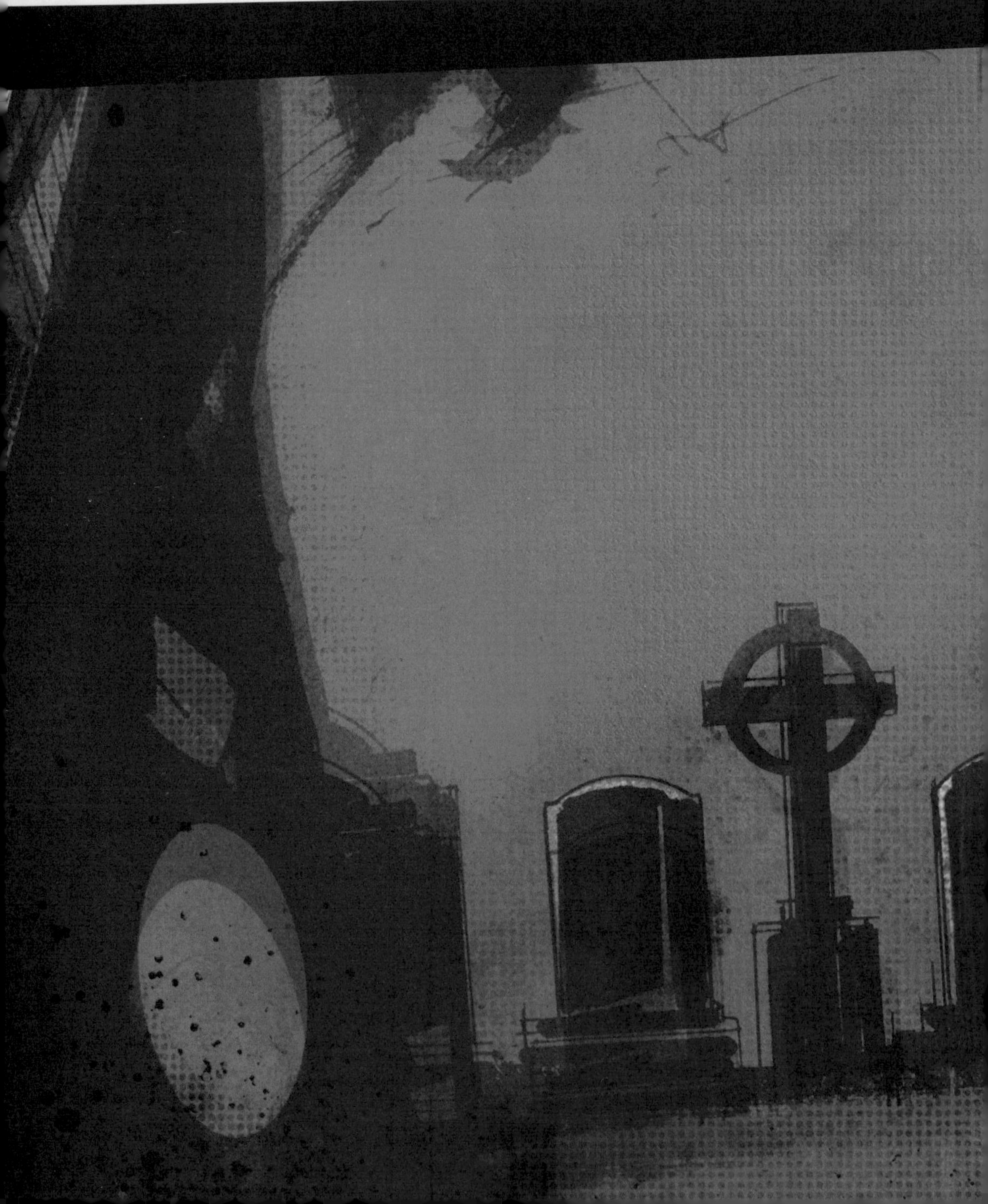

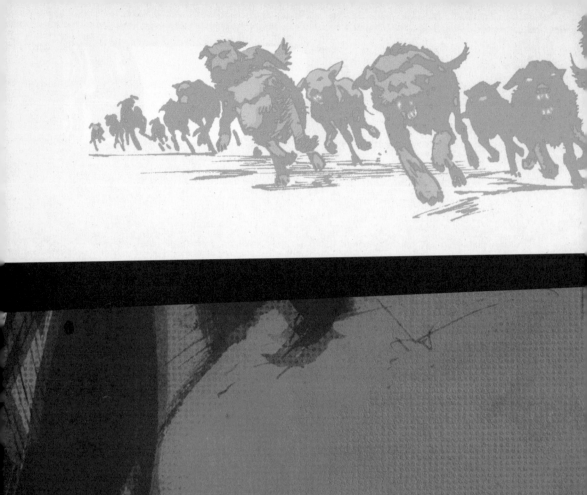

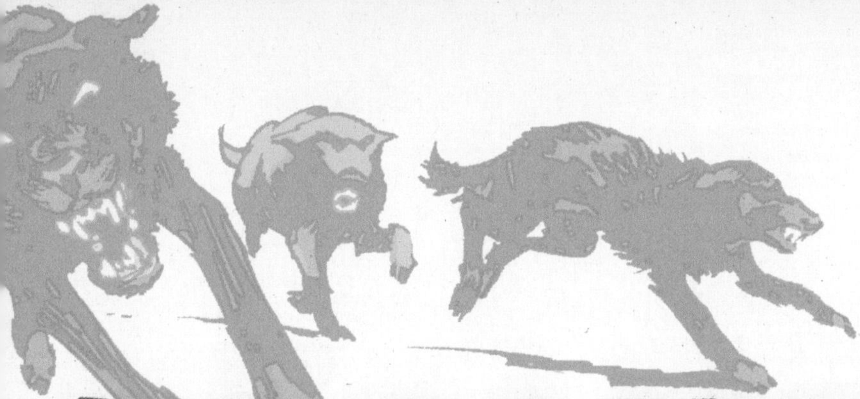

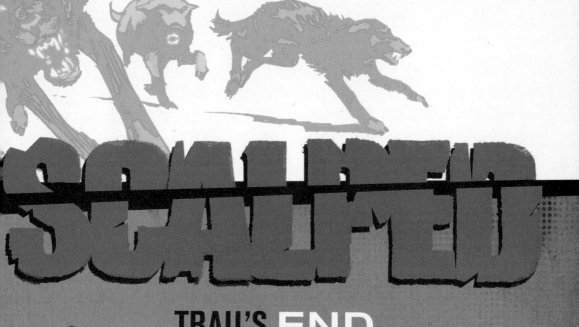

SCALPED

TRAIL'S END

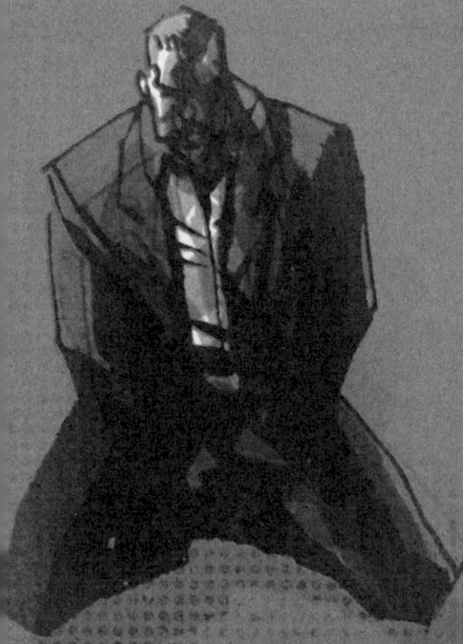

JASON AARON
WRITER

R.M. GUÉRA
ARTIST

GIULIA BRUSCO
COLORIST

SAL CIPRIANO
LETTERER

JOCK
COVER ARTIST

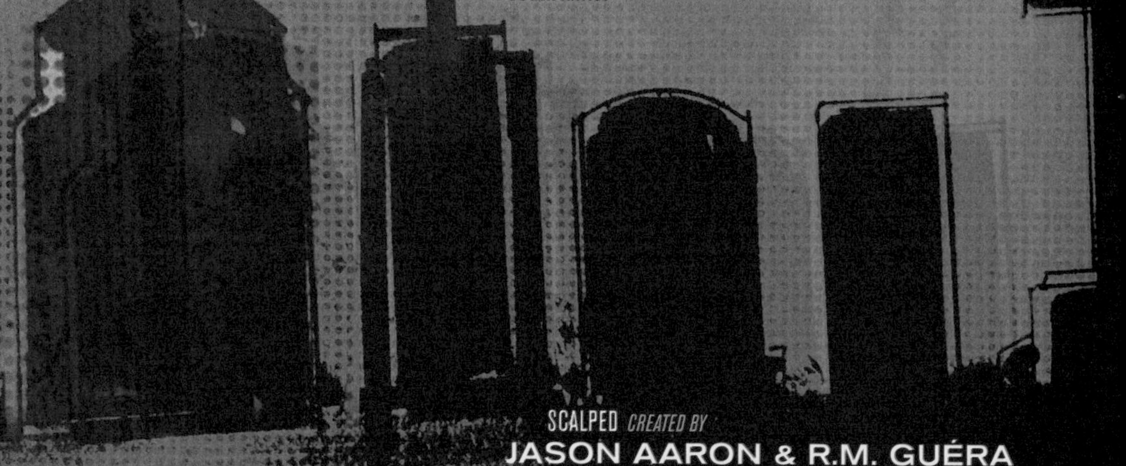

SCALPED *CREATED BY*
JASON AARON & R.M. GUÉRA

SCALPED: TRAIL'S END

Published by DC Comics. Cover, afterword and compilation Copyright © 2012 Jason Aaron and Rajko Milosevic. All Rights Reserved.

Originally published in single magazine form in SCALPED 56-60 Copyright © 2011, 2012 Jason Aaron and Rajko Milosevic. All Rights Reserved. VERTIGO is a trademark of DC Comics. All characters, their distinctive likenesses and related elements featured in this publication are trademarks of DC Comics. The stories, characters and incidents featured in this publication are entirely fictional. DC Comics does not read or accept unsolicited ideas, stories or artwork.

DC Comics, 1700 Broadway, New York, NY 10019, A Warner Bros. Entertainment Company.
Printed in the USA. 9/28/12. First Printing. ISBN: 978-1-4012-3734-9

LIBRARY OF CONGRESS CATALOGING-IN-PUBLICATION DATA

AARON, JASON.
  SCALPED : TRAIL'S END / JASON AARON, R.M. GUÉRA.
    P. CM.
  "ORIGINALLY PUBLISHED IN SINGLE MAGAZINE FORM IN SCALPED 56-60."
  ISBN 978-1-4012-3734-9 (ALK. PAPER)
  1. INDIAN RESERVATIONS—COMIC BOOKS, STRIPS, ETC. 2. GRAPHIC NOVELS. I. GUÉRA,
R. M. II. TITLE. III. TITLE: TRAIL'S END.
  PN6727.A225S36 2012
  741.5'973—DC23
                    2012023760

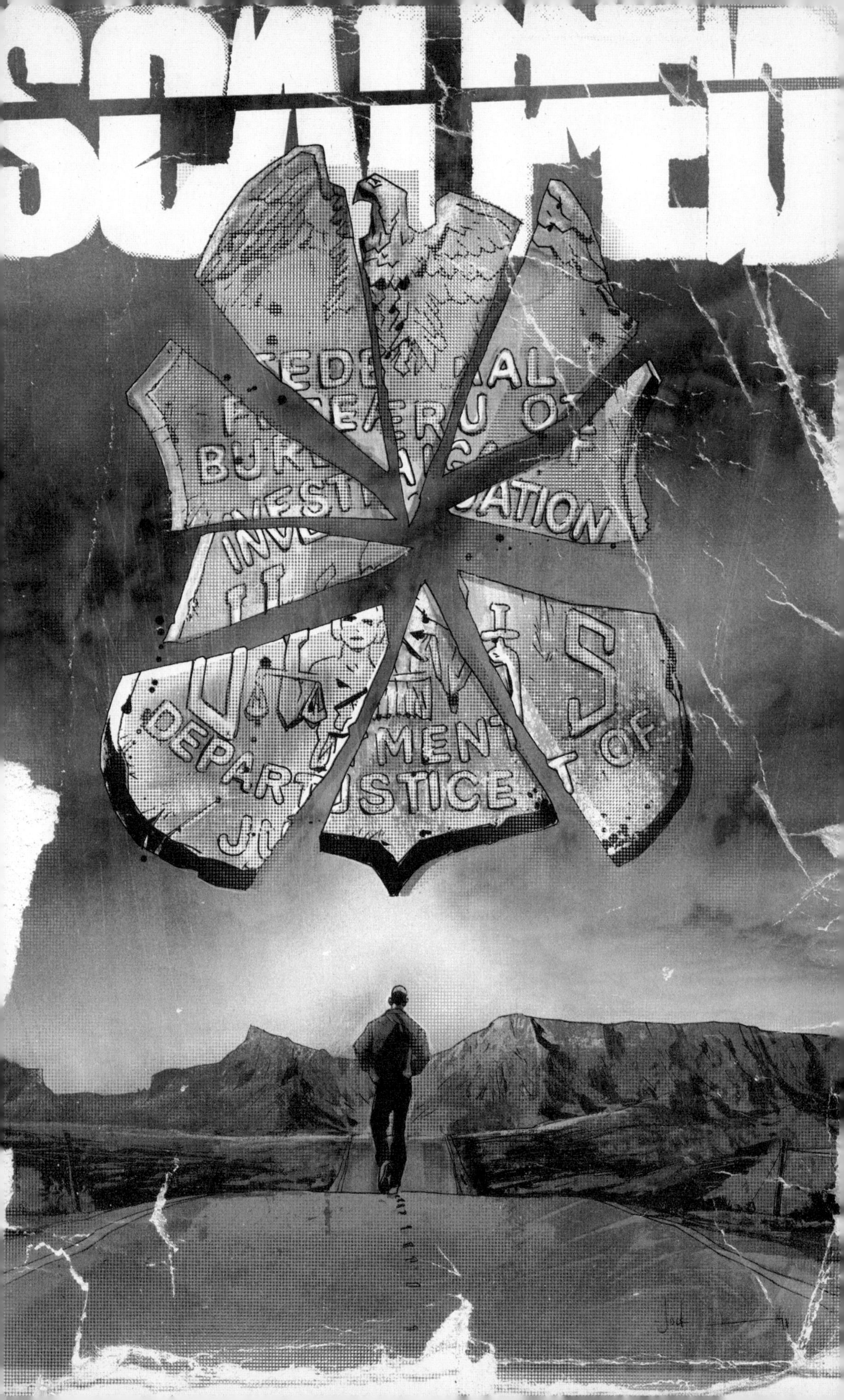

SCALPED
ATION
MENT
JUSTICE

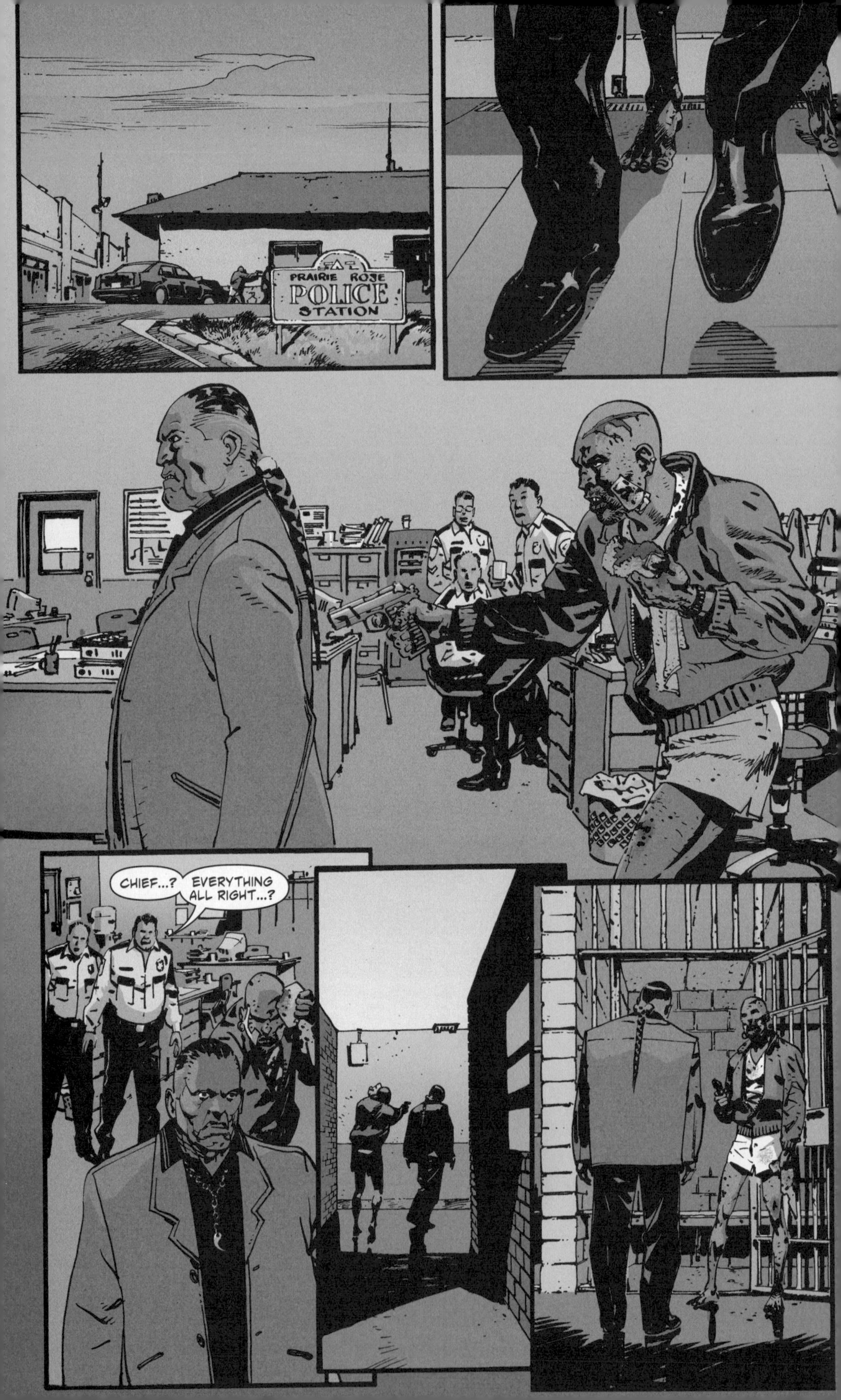
PRAIRIE ROSE
POLICE
STATION
CHIEF...? EVERYTHING ALL RIGHT...?

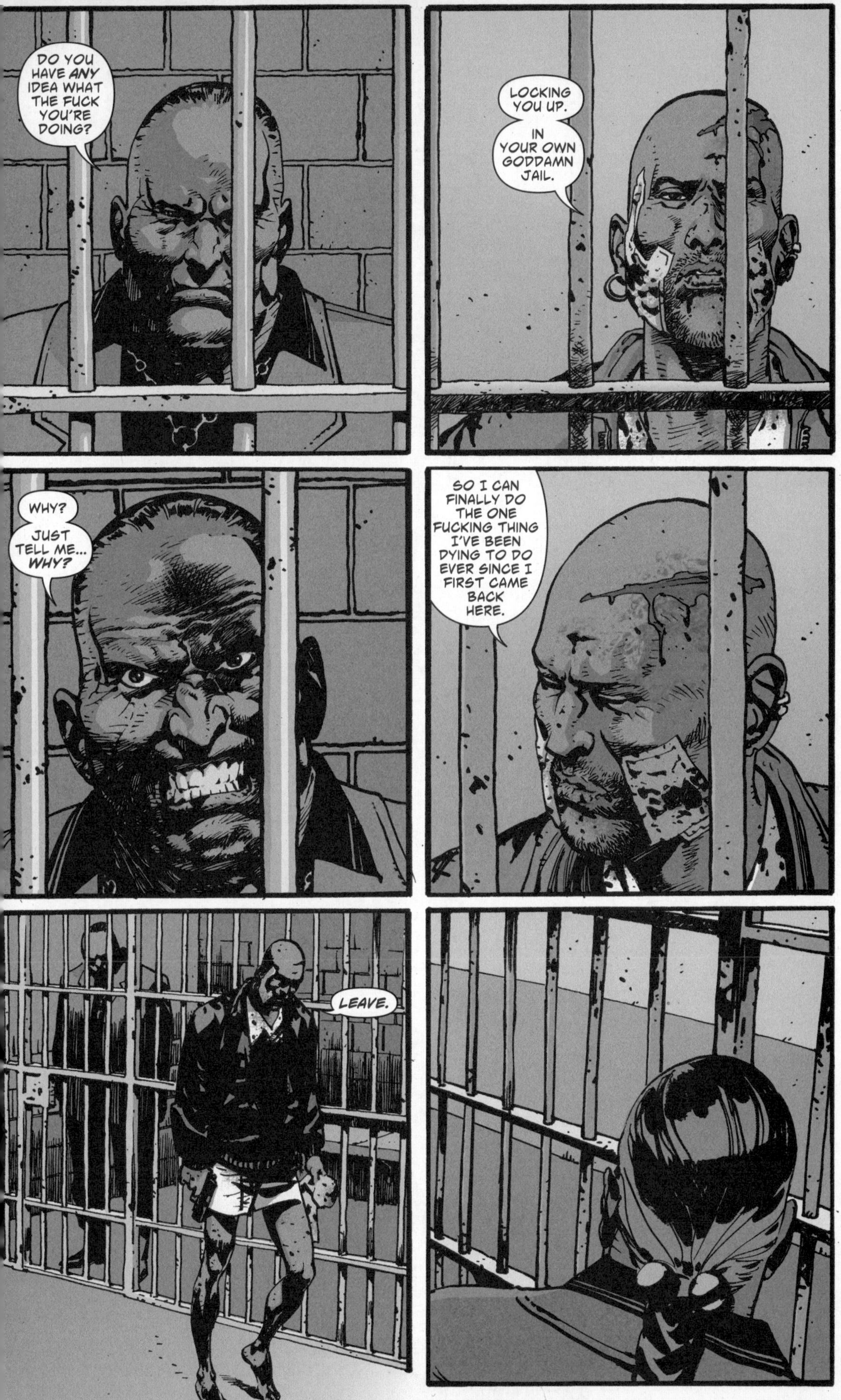
DO YOU HAVE *ANY* IDEA WHAT THE FUCK YOU'RE DOING?
LOCKING YOU UP.
IN YOUR OWN GODDAMN JAIL.
WHY?
JUST TELL ME... *WHY?*
SO I CAN FINALLY DO THE ONE FUCKING THING I'VE BEEN DYING TO DO EVER SINCE I FIRST CAME BACK HERE.
LEAVE.

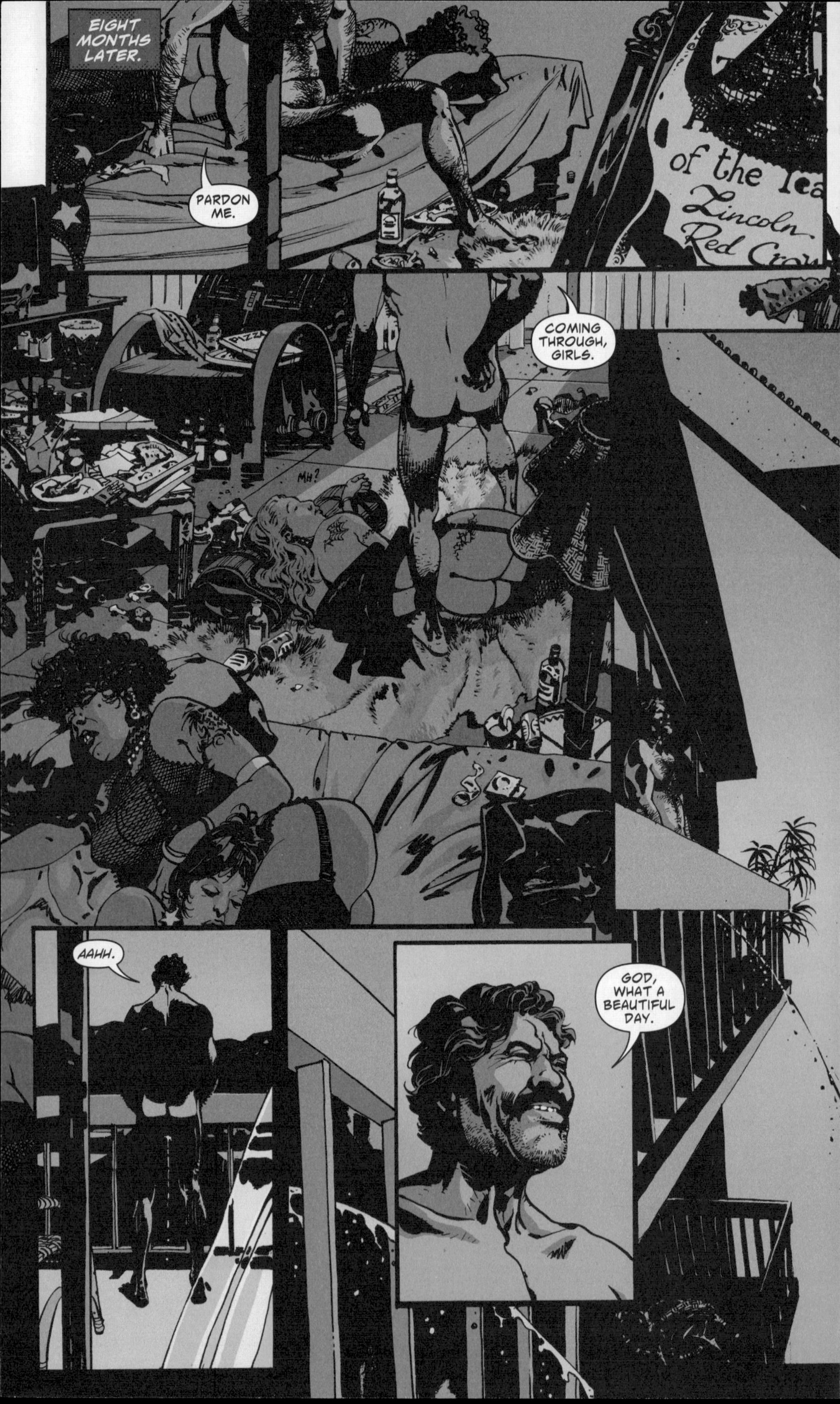
EIGHT MONTHS LATER.
PARDON ME.
of the
Lincoln
Red
COMING THROUGH, GIRLS.
MH?
AAHH.
GOD, WHAT A BEAUTIFUL DAY.

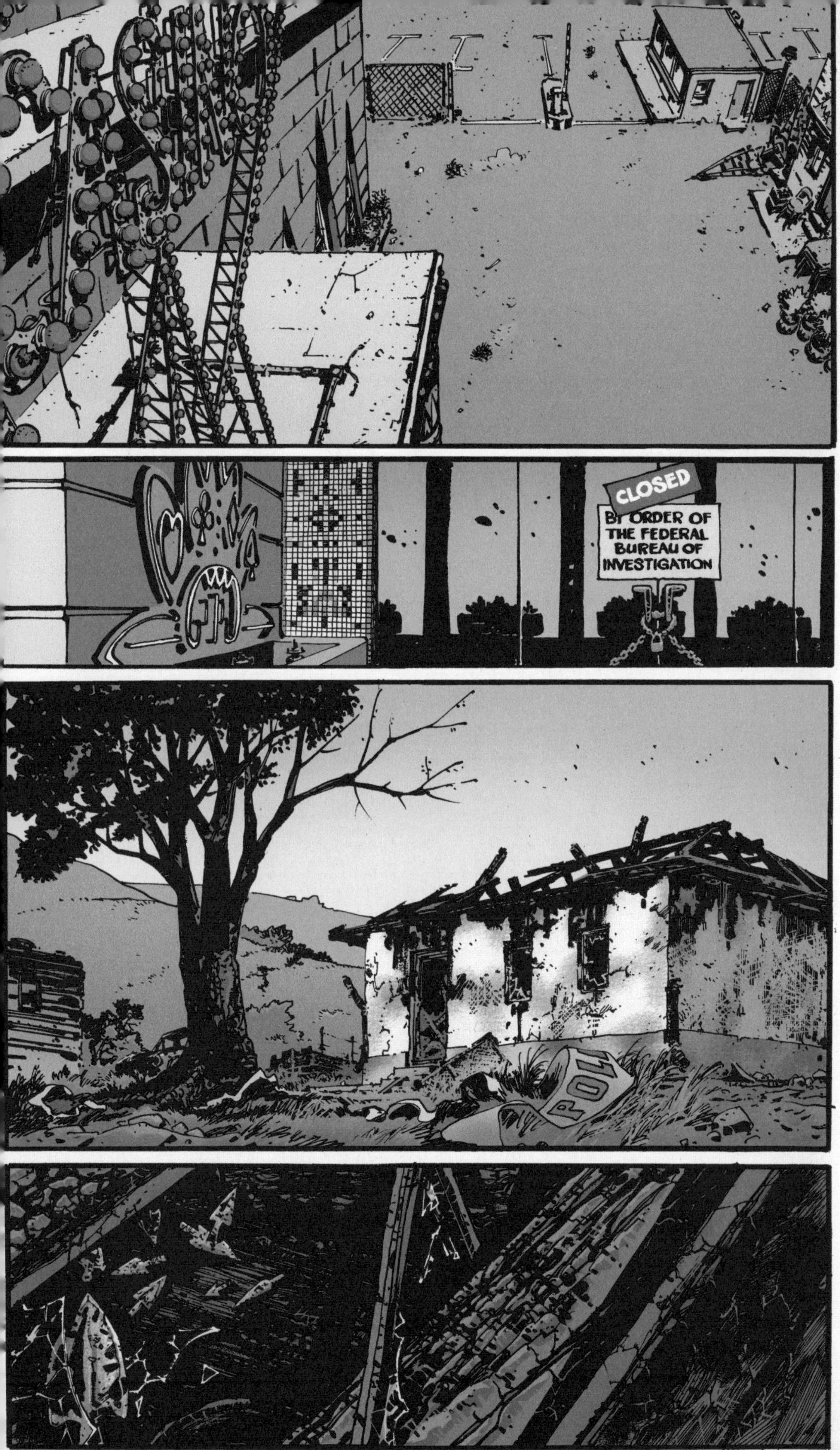
CLOSED
BY ORDER OF
THE FEDERAL
BUREAU OF
INVESTIGATION

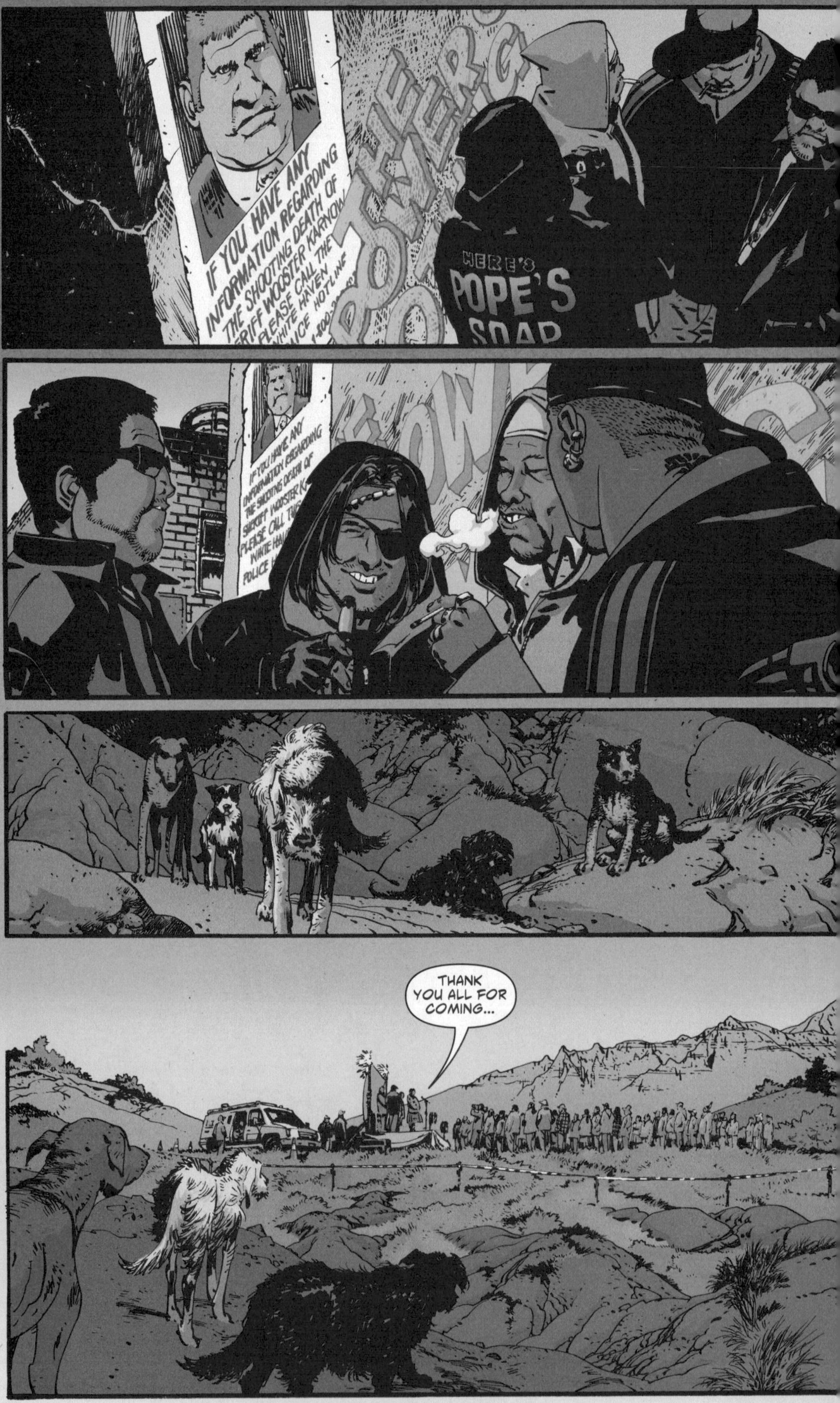
IF YOU HAVE ANY
INFORMATION REGARDING
THE SHOOTING DEATH
RIFF WOOSTER KARNOW
PLEASE CALL THE
WHITE HAVEN
HOTLINE
HERE'S
POPE'S
THANK YOU ALL FOR COMING...

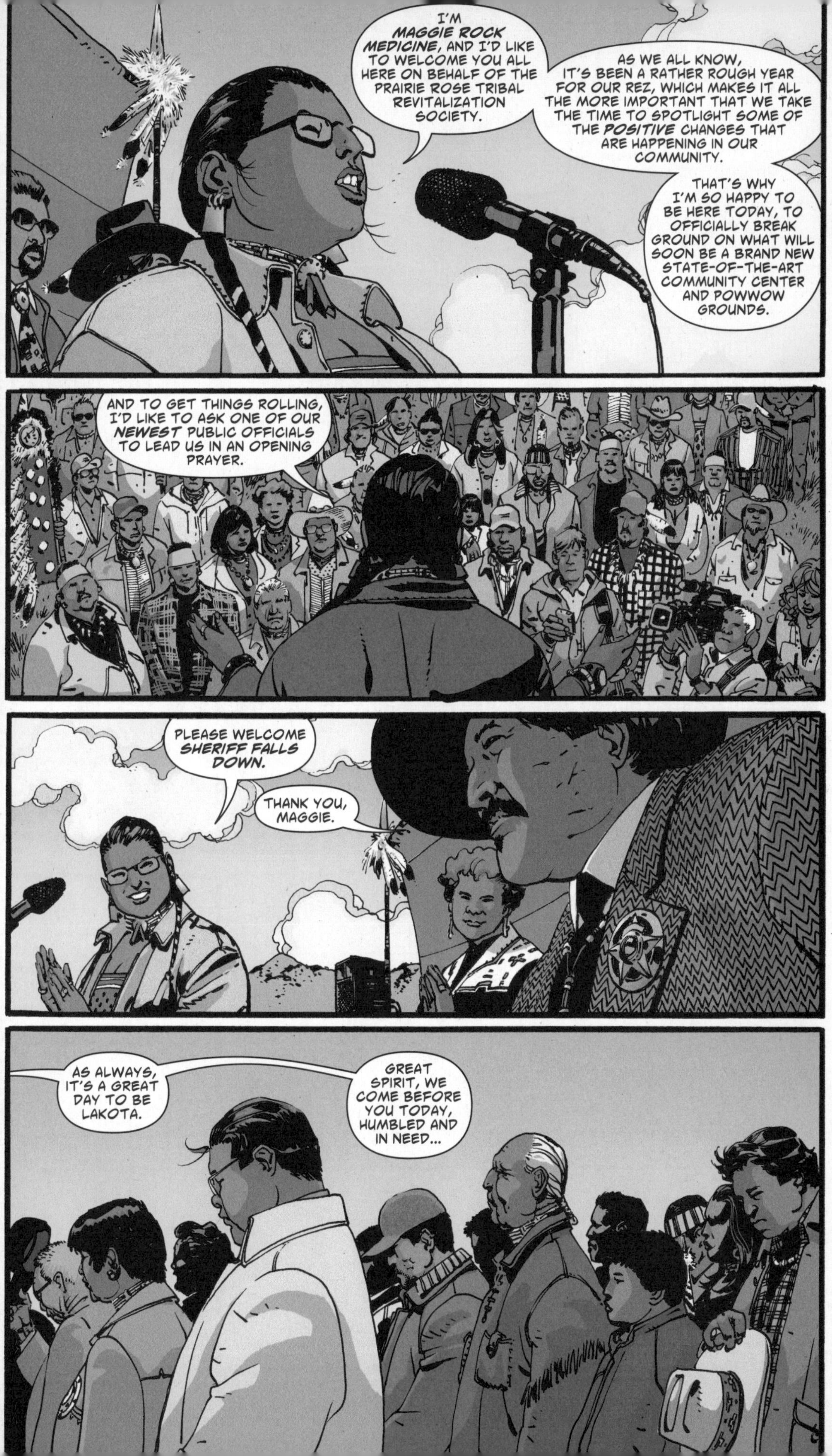
I'M MAGGIE ROCK MEDICINE, AND I'D LIKE TO WELCOME YOU ALL HERE ON BEHALF OF THE PRAIRIE ROSE TRIBAL REVITALIZATION SOCIETY.
AS WE ALL KNOW, IT'S BEEN A RATHER ROUGH YEAR FOR OUR REZ, WHICH MAKES IT ALL THE MORE IMPORTANT THAT WE TAKE THE TIME TO SPOTLIGHT SOME OF THE POSITIVE CHANGES THAT ARE HAPPENING IN OUR COMMUNITY.
THAT'S WHY I'M SO HAPPY TO BE HERE TODAY, TO OFFICIALLY BREAK GROUND ON WHAT WILL SOON BE A BRAND NEW STATE-OF-THE-ART COMMUNITY CENTER AND POWWOW GROUNDS.
AND TO GET THINGS ROLLING, I'D LIKE TO ASK ONE OF OUR NEWEST PUBLIC OFFICIALS TO LEAD US IN AN OPENING PRAYER.
PLEASE WELCOME SHERIFF FALLS DOWN.
THANK YOU, MAGGIE.
AS ALWAYS, IT'S A GREAT DAY TO BE LAKOTA.
GREAT SPIRIT, WE COME BEFORE YOU TODAY, HUMBLED AND IN NEED...

ALL RIGHT, CHIEF, ON YOUR FEET. YOUR LAWYER'S HERE.

HE'LL HAVE TO WAIT.

I'M APPEALING TO A HIGHER COUNSEL.

PENNINGTON COUNTY JAIL

RAPID CITY SOUTH DAKOTA

"SORRY TO HAVE KEPT YOU WAITING."

LET ME GUESS. YOU WERE PRAYING.

I WAS.

THAT'S ALL RIGHT THEN. PRAYING IS GOOD. I HOPE YOU WERE ASKING FOR A MIRACLE.

BECAUSE THAT'S WHAT IT'S GONNA TAKE TO EVER GET YOU OUT OF HERE.

PENNINGTON COUNTY JAIL

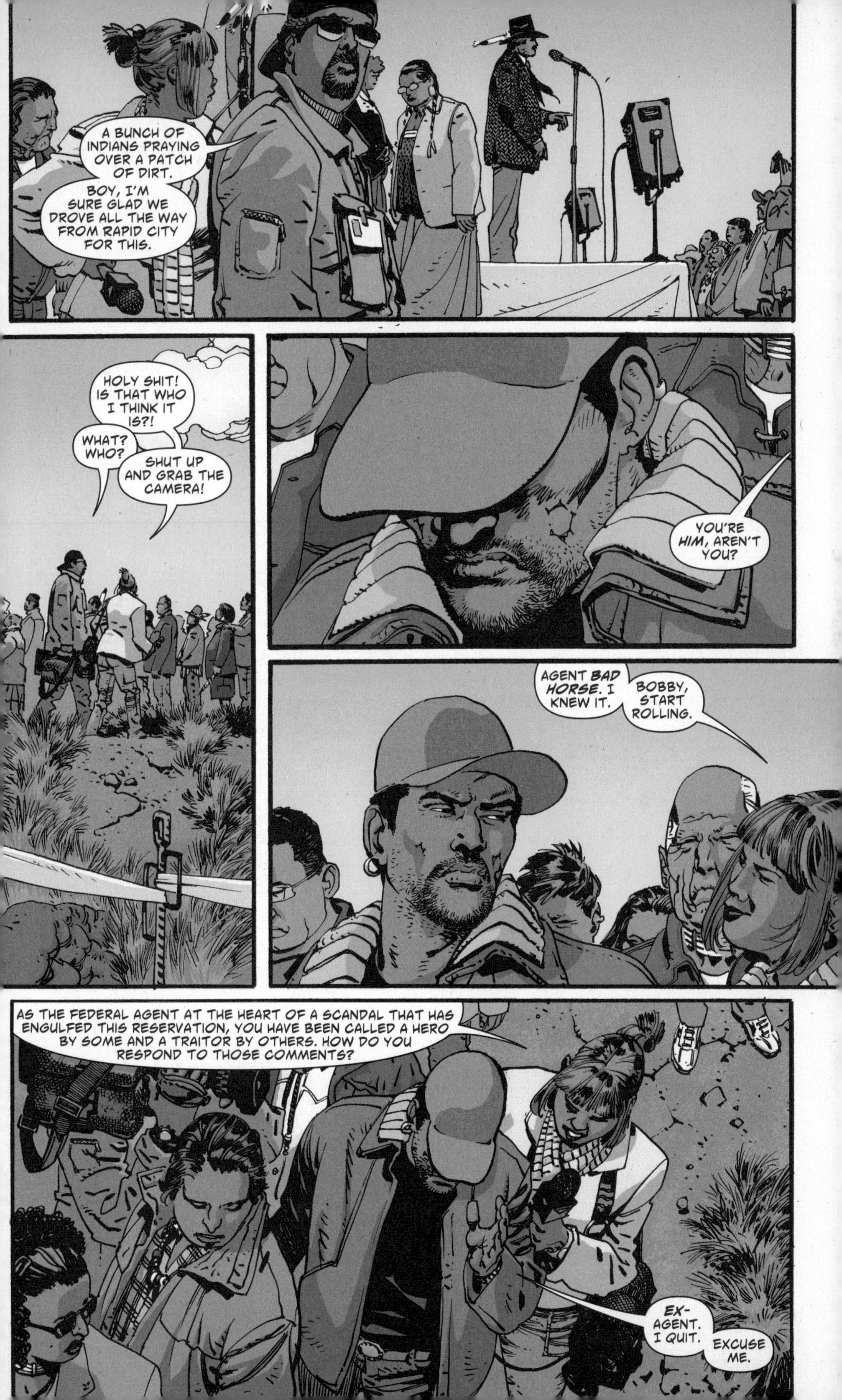

A BUNCH OF INDIANS PRAYING OVER A PATCH OF DIRT.
BOY, I'M SURE GLAD WE DROVE ALL THE WAY FROM RAPID CITY FOR THIS.
HOLY SHIT! IS THAT WHO I THINK IT IS?!
WHAT? WHO?
SHUT UP AND GRAB THE CAMERA!
YOU'RE HIM, AREN'T YOU?
AGENT BAD HORSE. I KNEW IT.
BOBBY, START ROLLING.
AS THE FEDERAL AGENT AT THE HEART OF A SCANDAL THAT HAS ENGULFED THIS RESERVATION, YOU HAVE BEEN CALLED A HERO BY SOME AND A TRAITOR BY OTHERS. HOW DO YOU RESPOND TO THOSE COMMENTS?
EX-AGENT. I QUIT.
EXCUSE ME.

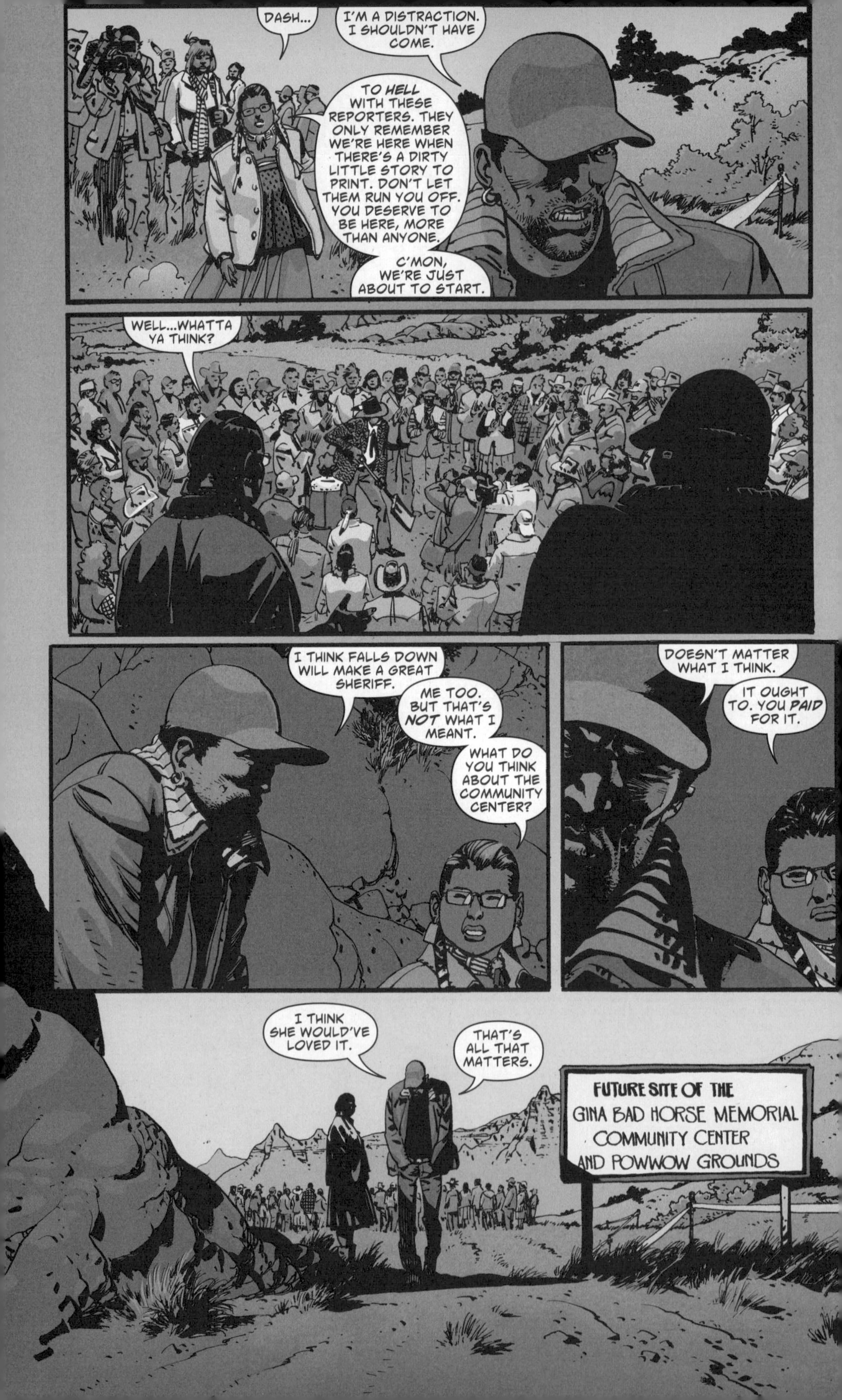
DASH...
I'M A DISTRACTION. I SHOULDN'T HAVE COME.
TO HELL WITH THESE REPORTERS. THEY ONLY REMEMBER WE'RE HERE WHEN THERE'S A DIRTY LITTLE STORY TO PRINT. DON'T LET THEM RUN YOU OFF. YOU DESERVE TO BE HERE, MORE THAN ANYONE.
C'MON, WE'RE JUST ABOUT TO START.
WELL...WHATTA YA THINK?
I THINK FALLS DOWN WILL MAKE A GREAT SHERIFF.
ME TOO. BUT THAT'S NOT WHAT I MEANT.
WHAT DO YOU THINK ABOUT THE COMMUNITY CENTER?
DOESN'T MATTER WHAT I THINK.
IT OUGHT TO. YOU PAID FOR IT.
I THINK SHE WOULD'VE LOVED IT.
THAT'S ALL THAT MATTERS.
FUTURE SITE OF THE
GINA BAD HORSE MEMORIAL
COMMUNITY CENTER
AND POWWOW GROUNDS

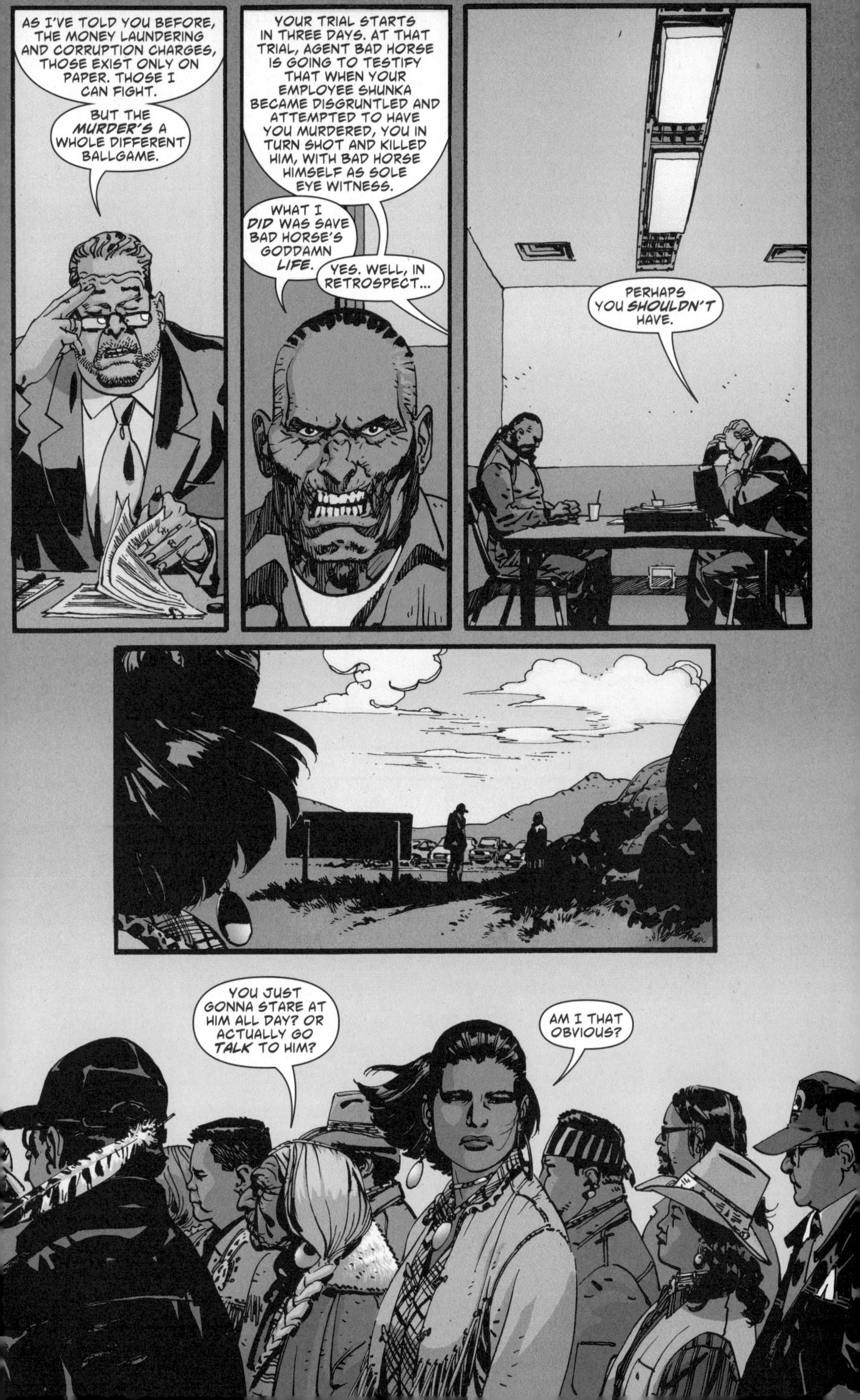
AS I'VE TOLD YOU BEFORE, THE MONEY LAUNDERING AND CORRUPTION CHARGES, THOSE EXIST ONLY ON PAPER. THOSE I CAN FIGHT.
BUT THE MURDER'S A WHOLE DIFFERENT BALLGAME.
YOUR TRIAL STARTS IN THREE DAYS. AT THAT TRIAL, AGENT BAD HORSE IS GOING TO TESTIFY THAT WHEN YOUR EMPLOYEE SHUNKA BECAME DISGRUNTLED AND ATTEMPTED TO HAVE YOU MURDERED, YOU IN TURN SHOT AND KILLED HIM, WITH BAD HORSE HIMSELF AS SOLE EYE WITNESS.
WHAT I DID WAS SAVE BAD HORSE'S GODDAMN LIFE.
YES. WELL, IN RETROSPECT...
PERHAPS YOU SHOULDN'T HAVE.
YOU JUST GONNA STARE AT HIM ALL DAY? OR ACTUALLY GO TALK TO HIM?
AM I THAT OBVIOUS?

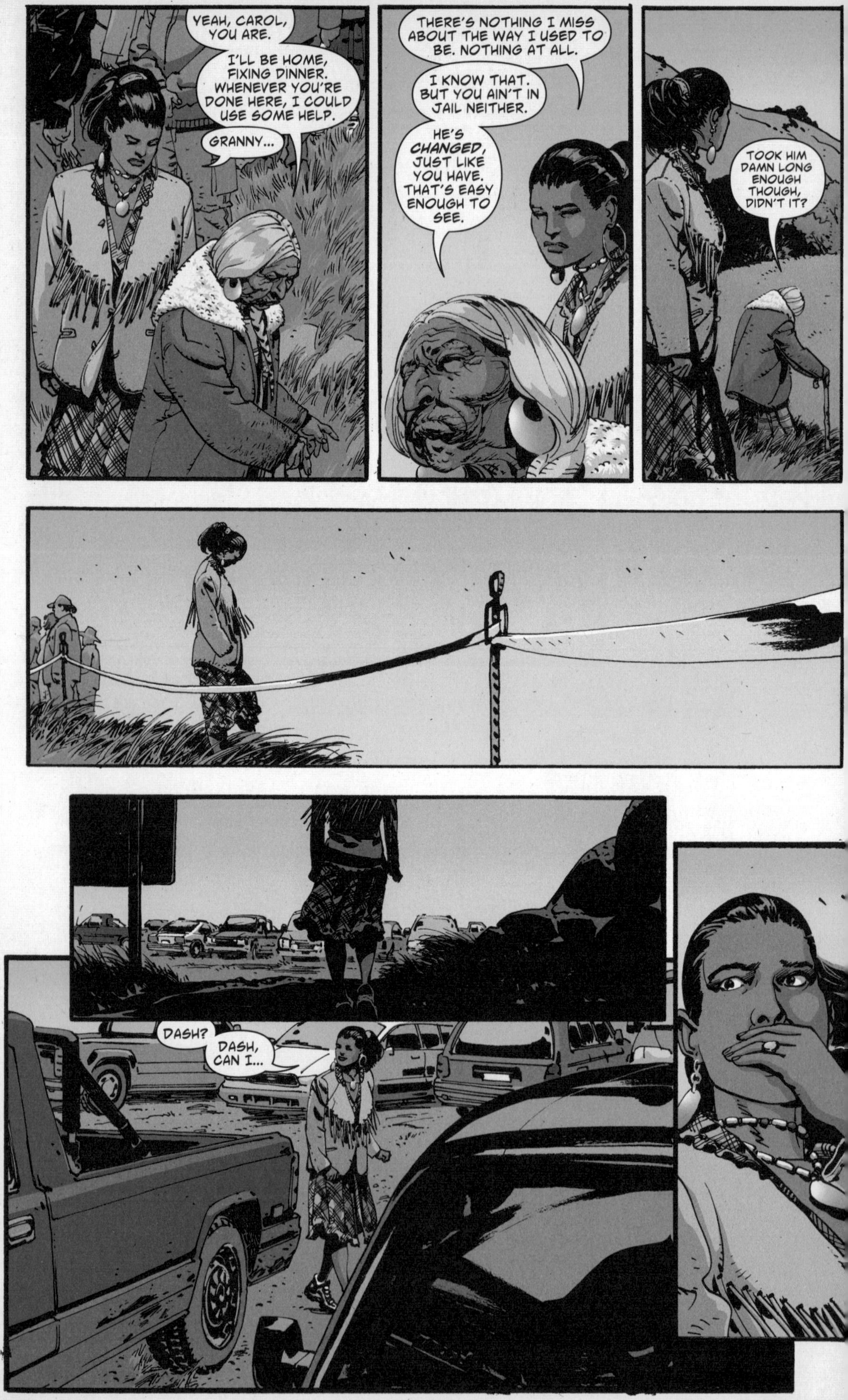
YEAH, CAROL, YOU ARE.
I'LL BE HOME, FIXING DINNER. WHENEVER YOU'RE DONE HERE, I COULD USE SOME HELP.
GRANNY...
THERE'S NOTHING I MISS ABOUT THE WAY I USED TO BE. NOTHING AT ALL.
I KNOW THAT. BUT YOU AIN'T IN JAIL NEITHER.
HE'S *CHANGED*, JUST LIKE YOU HAVE. THAT'S EASY ENOUGH TO SEE.
TOOK HIM DAMN LONG ENOUGH THOUGH, DIDN'T IT?
DASH?
DASH, CAN I...

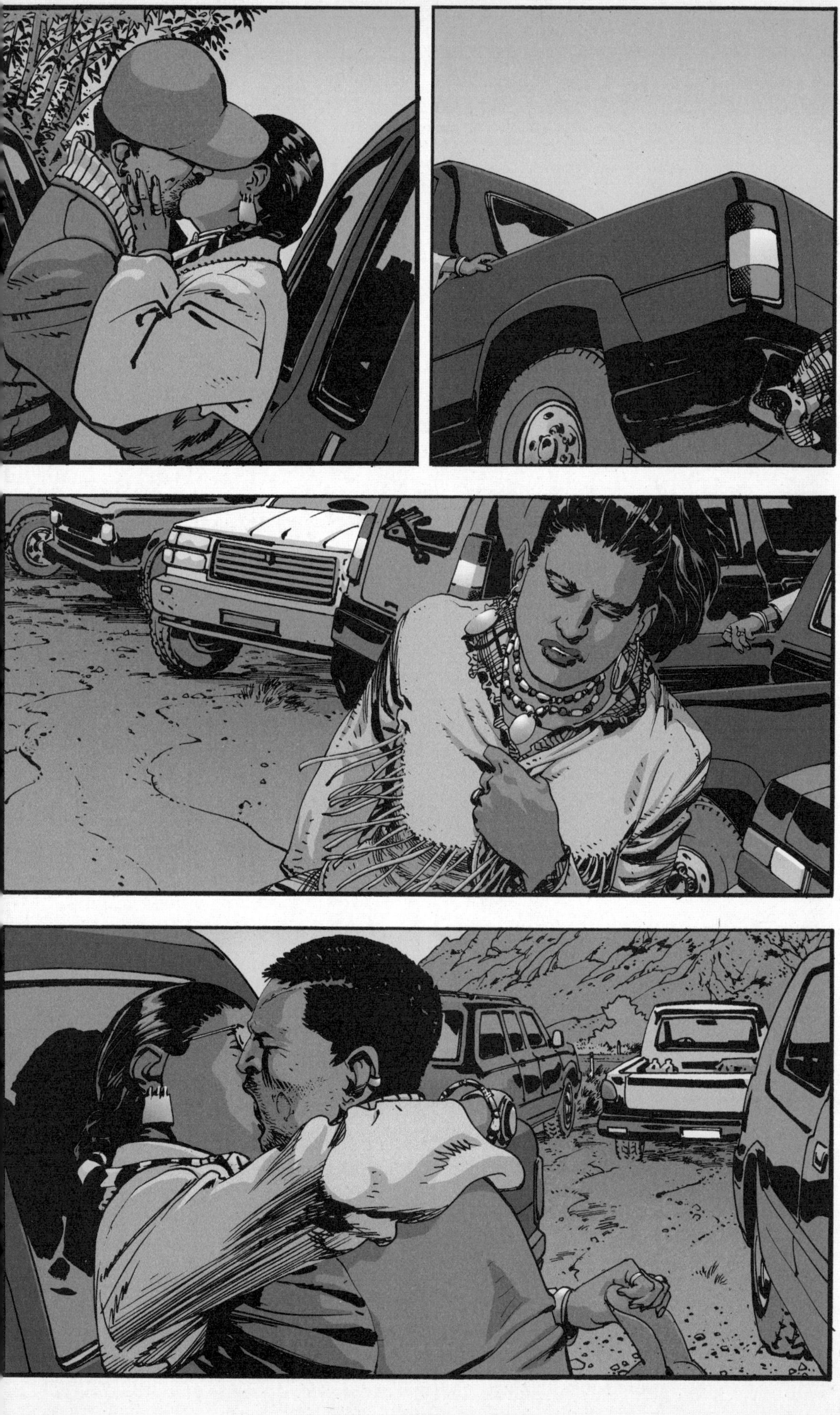

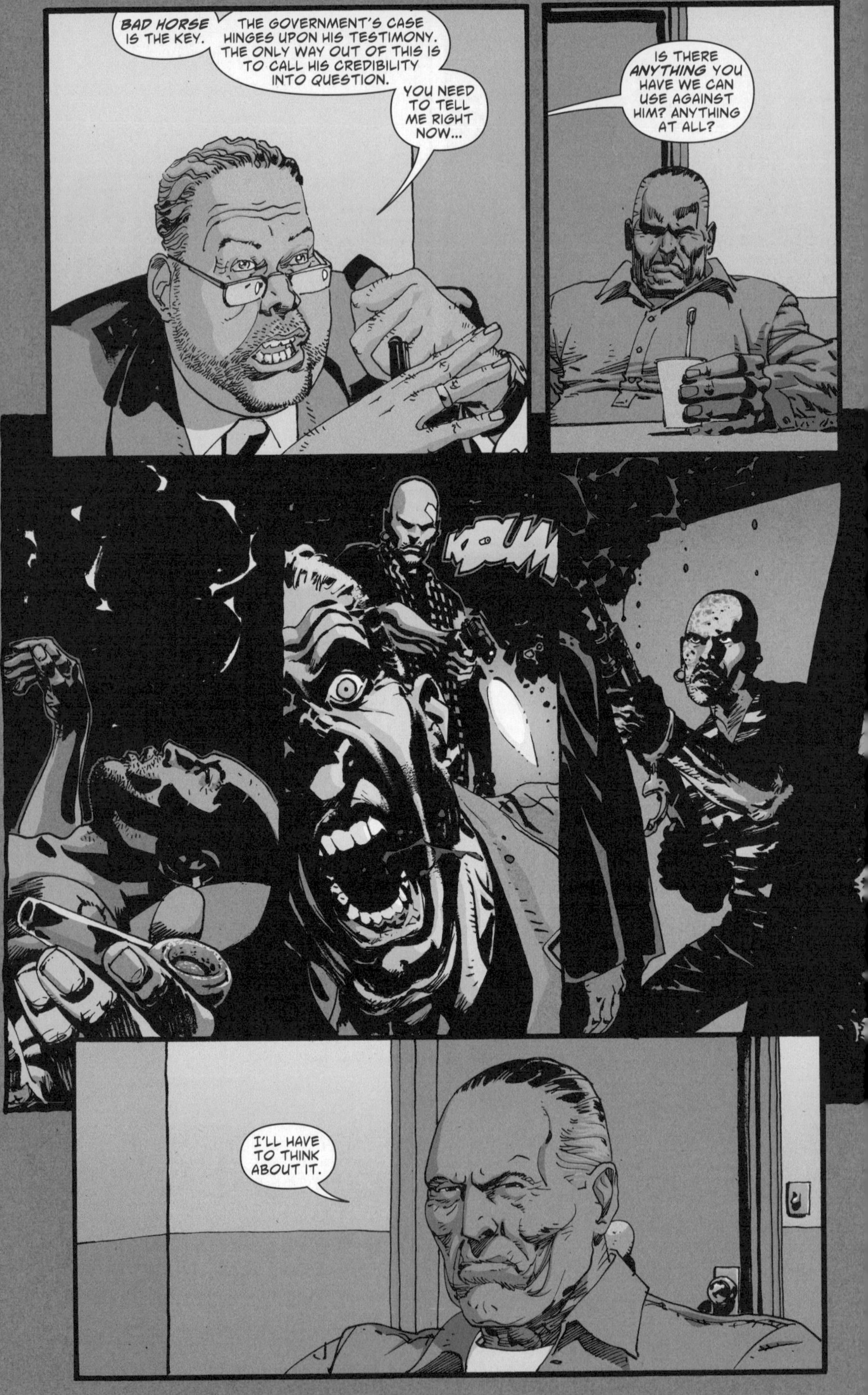
BAD HORSE IS THE KEY.
THE GOVERNMENT'S CASE HINGES UPON HIS TESTIMONY. THE ONLY WAY OUT OF THIS IS TO CALL HIS CREDIBILITY INTO QUESTION.
YOU NEED TO TELL ME RIGHT NOW...
IS THERE ANYTHING YOU HAVE WE CAN USE AGAINST HIM? ANYTHING AT ALL?
KBLAM
I'LL HAVE TO THINK ABOUT IT.

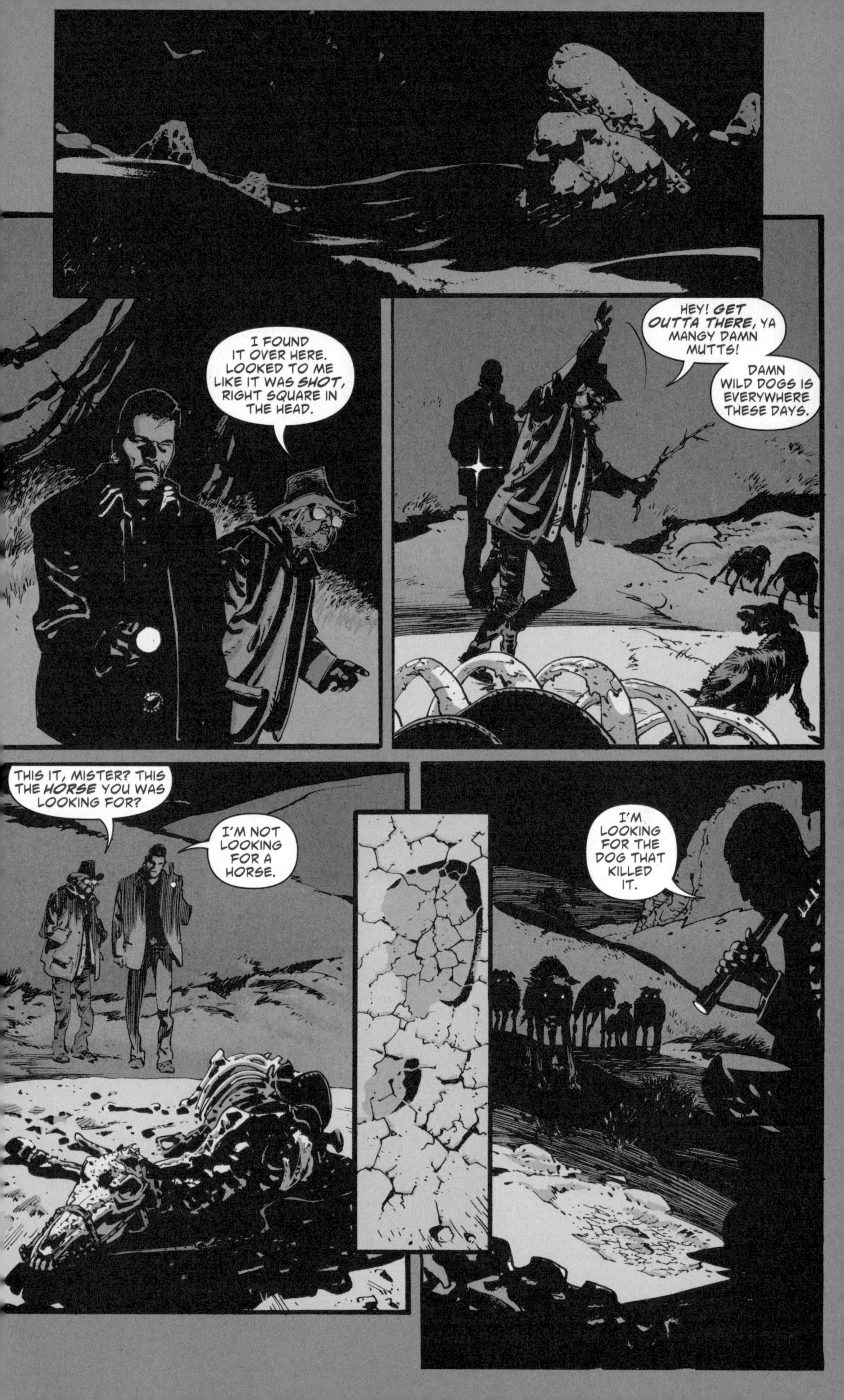
I FOUND IT OVER HERE. LOOKED TO ME LIKE IT WAS SHOT, RIGHT SQUARE IN THE HEAD.
HEY! GET OUTTA THERE, YA MANGY DAMN MUTTS!
DAMN WILD DOGS IS EVERYWHERE THESE DAYS.
THIS IT, MISTER? THIS THE HORSE YOU WAS LOOKING FOR?
I'M NOT LOOKING FOR A HORSE.
I'M LOOKING FOR THE DOG THAT KILLED IT.

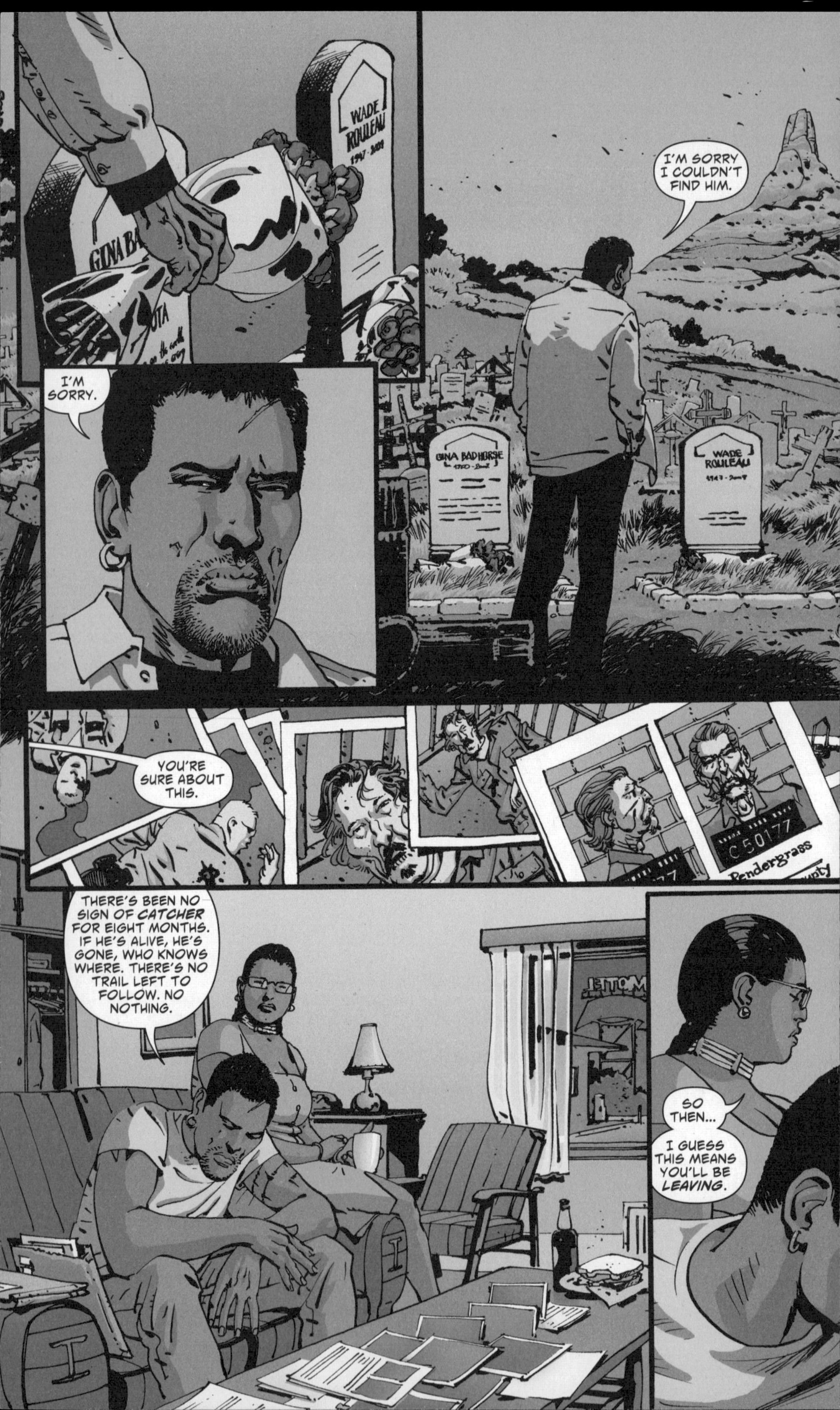
WADE ROULEAU
I'M SORRY I COULDN'T FIND HIM.
I'M SORRY.
GINA BADHORSE
WADE ROULEAU
YOU'RE SURE ABOUT THIS.
C 50177
Pendergrass
THERE'S BEEN NO SIGN OF *CATCHER* FOR EIGHT MONTHS. IF HE'S ALIVE, HE'S GONE, WHO KNOWS WHERE. THERE'S NO TRAIL LEFT TO FOLLOW. NO NOTHING.
SO THEN...
I GUESS THIS MEANS YOU'LL BE *LEAVING*.

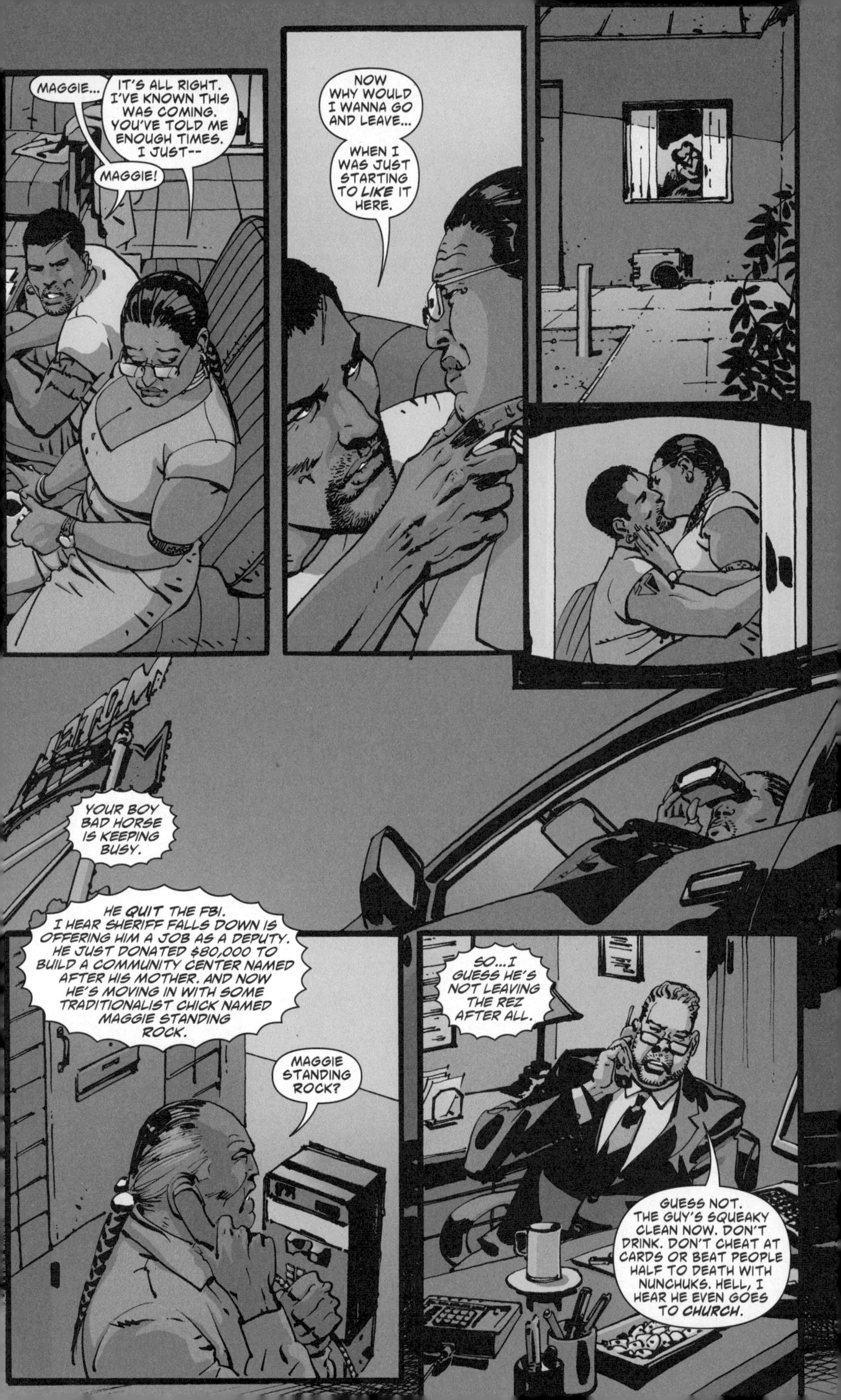
MAGGIE...
IT'S ALL RIGHT. I'VE KNOWN THIS WAS COMING. YOU'VE TOLD ME ENOUGH TIMES. I JUST--
MAGGIE!
NOW WHY WOULD I WANNA GO AND LEAVE...
WHEN I WAS JUST STARTING TO LIKE IT HERE.
YOUR BOY BAD HORSE IS KEEPING BUSY.
HE QUIT THE FBI. I HEAR SHERIFF FALLS DOWN IS OFFERING HIM A JOB AS A DEPUTY. HE JUST DONATED $80,000 TO BUILD A COMMUNITY CENTER NAMED AFTER HIS MOTHER. AND NOW HE'S MOVING IN WITH SOME TRADITIONALIST CHICK NAMED MAGGIE STANDING ROCK.
MAGGIE STANDING ROCK?
SO...I GUESS HE'S NOT LEAVING THE REZ AFTER ALL.
GUESS NOT. THE GUY'S SQUEAKY CLEAN NOW. DON'T DRINK. DON'T CHEAT AT CARDS OR BEAT PEOPLE HALF TO DEATH WITH NUNCHUKS. HELL, I HEAR HE EVEN GOES TO CHURCH.

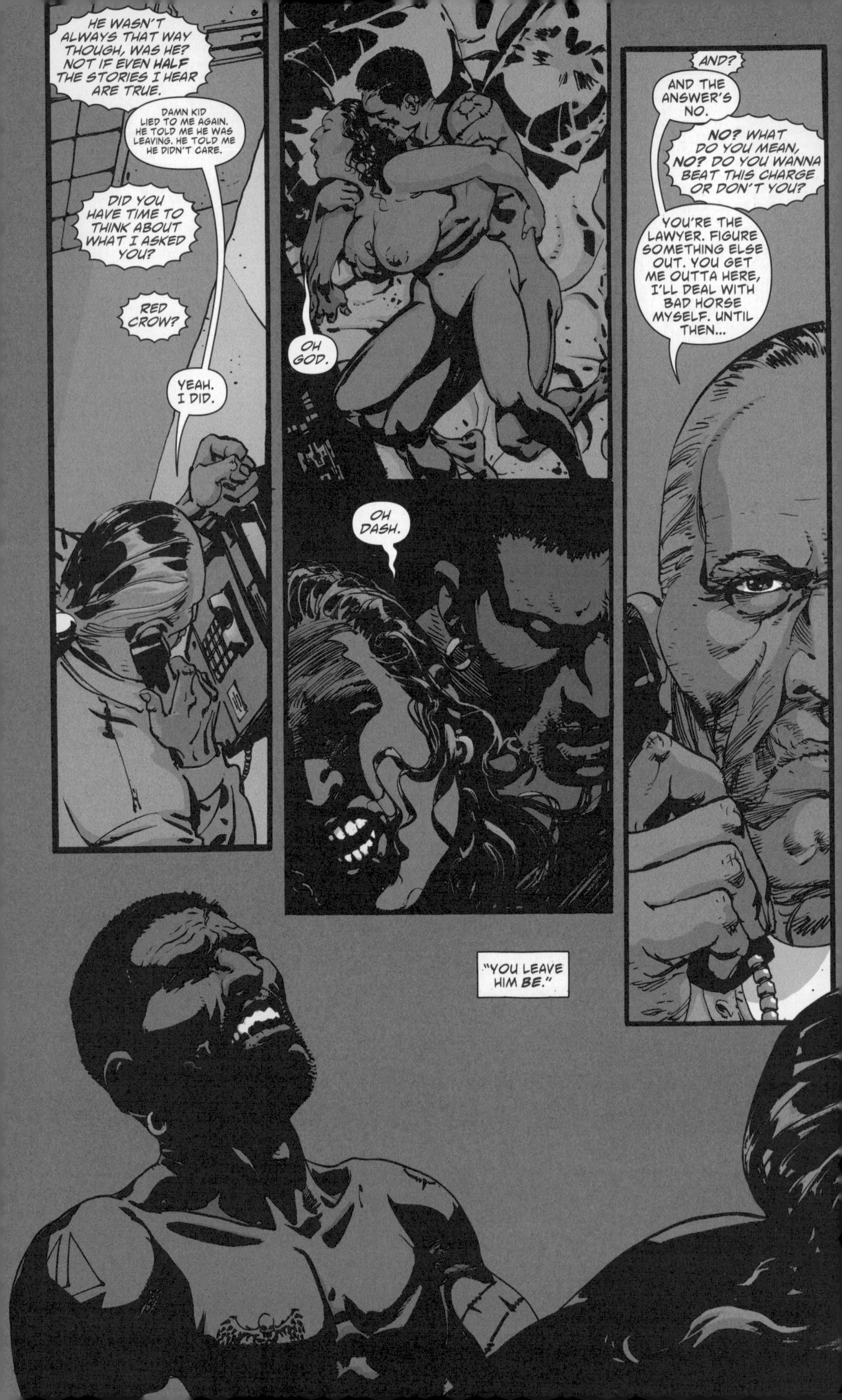
HE WASN'T ALWAYS THAT WAY THOUGH, WAS HE? NOT IF EVEN HALF THE STORIES I HEAR ARE TRUE.
DAMN KID LIED TO ME AGAIN. HE TOLD ME HE WAS LEAVING. HE TOLD ME HE DIDN'T CARE.
DID YOU HAVE TIME TO THINK ABOUT WHAT I ASKED YOU?
RED CROW?
YEAH. I DID.
OH GOD.
OH DASH.
AND?
AND THE ANSWER'S NO.
NO? WHAT DO YOU MEAN, NO? DO YOU WANNA BEAT THIS CHARGE OR DON'T YOU?
YOU'RE THE LAWYER. FIGURE SOMETHING ELSE OUT. YOU GET ME OUTTA HERE, I'LL DEAL WITH BAD HORSE MYSELF. UNTIL THEN...
"YOU LEAVE HIM BE."

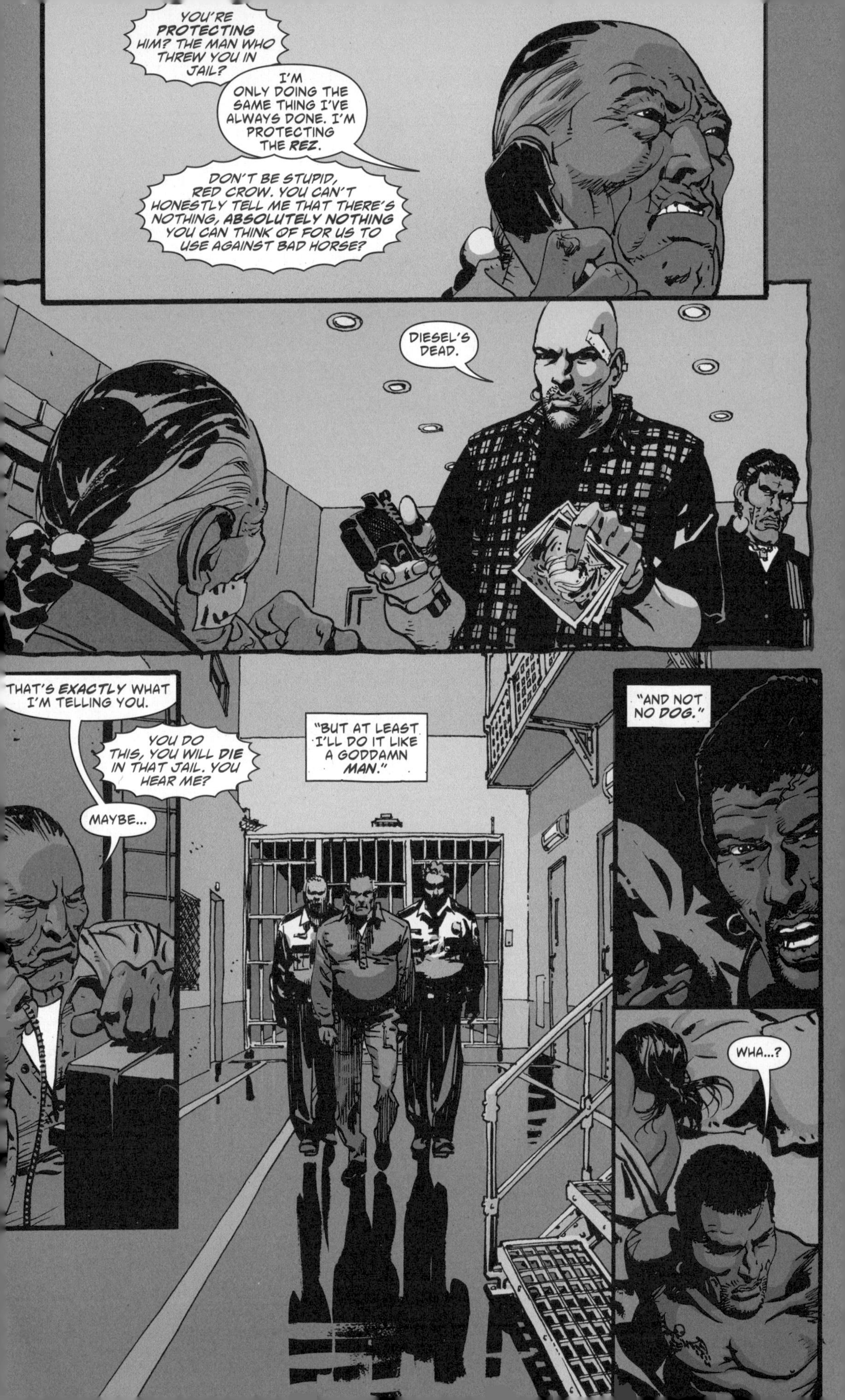
YOU'RE PROTECTING HIM? THE MAN WHO THREW YOU IN JAIL?
I'M ONLY DOING THE SAME THING I'VE ALWAYS DONE. I'M PROTECTING THE REZ.
DON'T BE STUPID, RED CROW. YOU CAN'T HONESTLY TELL ME THAT THERE'S NOTHING, ABSOLUTELY NOTHING YOU CAN THINK OF FOR US TO USE AGAINST BAD HORSE?
DIESEL'S DEAD.
THAT'S EXACTLY WHAT I'M TELLING YOU.
YOU DO THIS, YOU WILL DIE IN THAT JAIL. YOU HEAR ME?
MAYBE...
"BUT AT LEAST I'LL DO IT LIKE A GODDAMN MAN."
"AND NOT NO DOG."
WHA...?

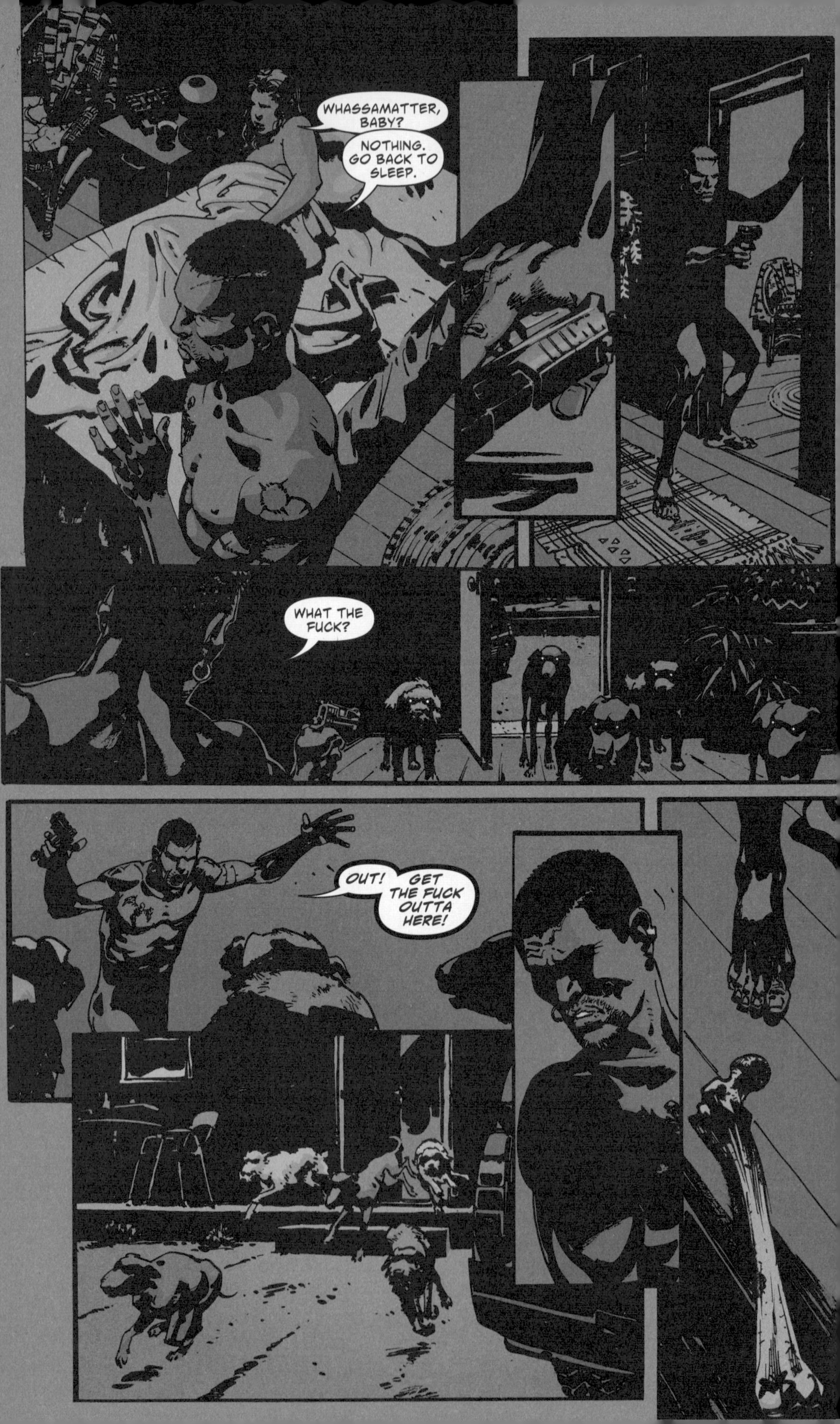
WHASSAMATTER, BABY?
NOTHING. GO BACK TO SLEEP.
WHAT THE FUCK?
OUT!
GET THE FUCK OUTTA HERE!

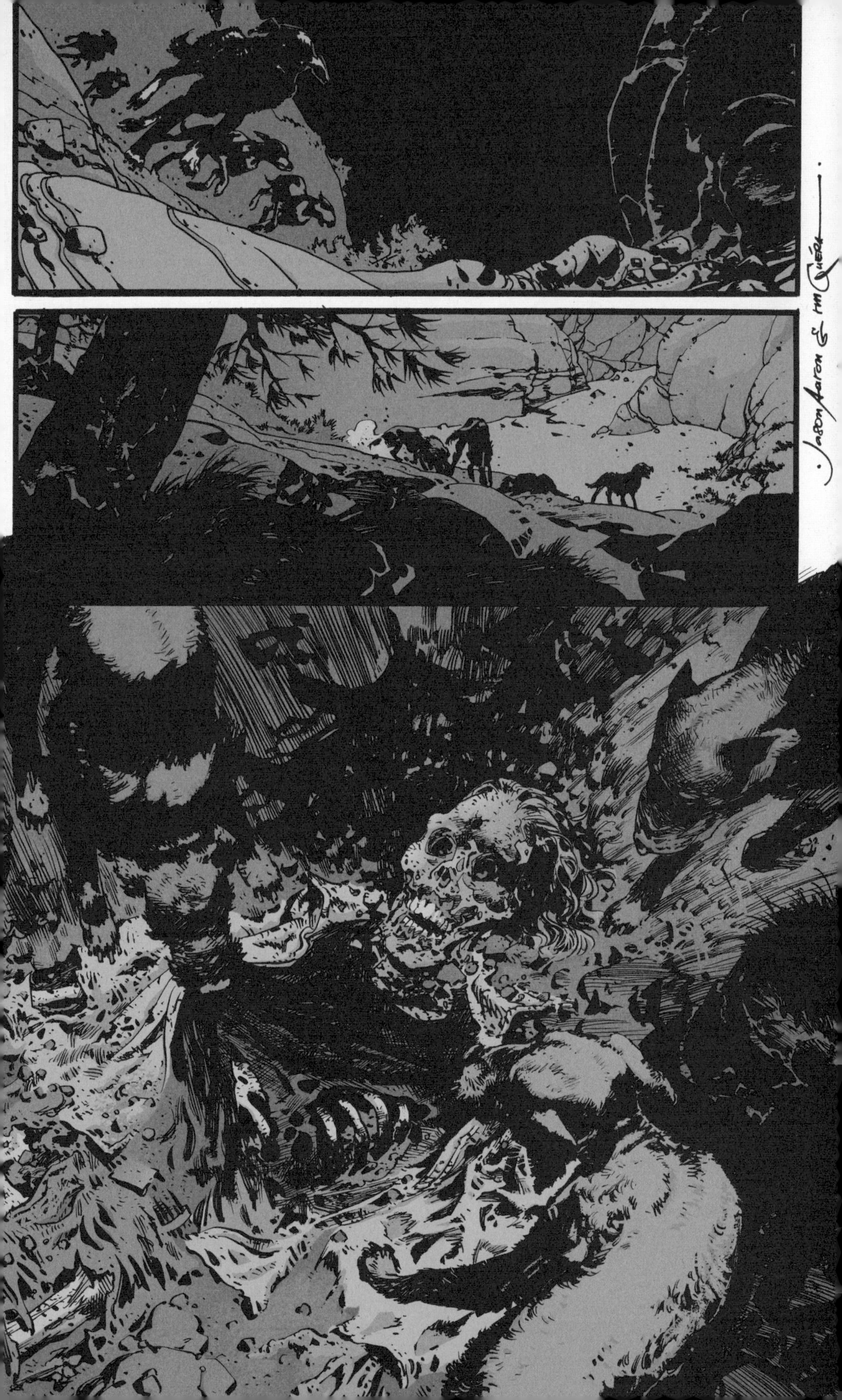
Jason Aaron & RM Guéra

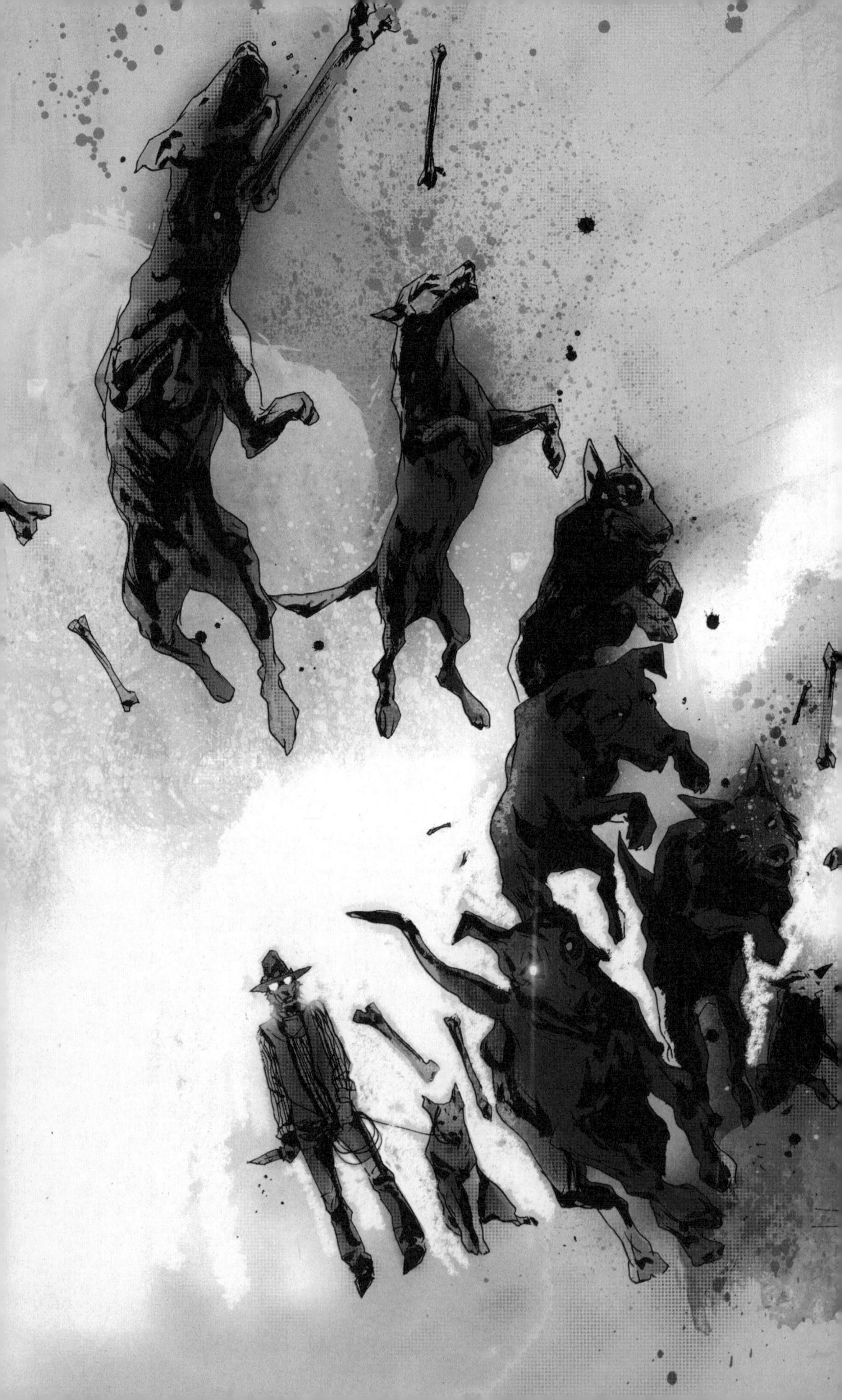

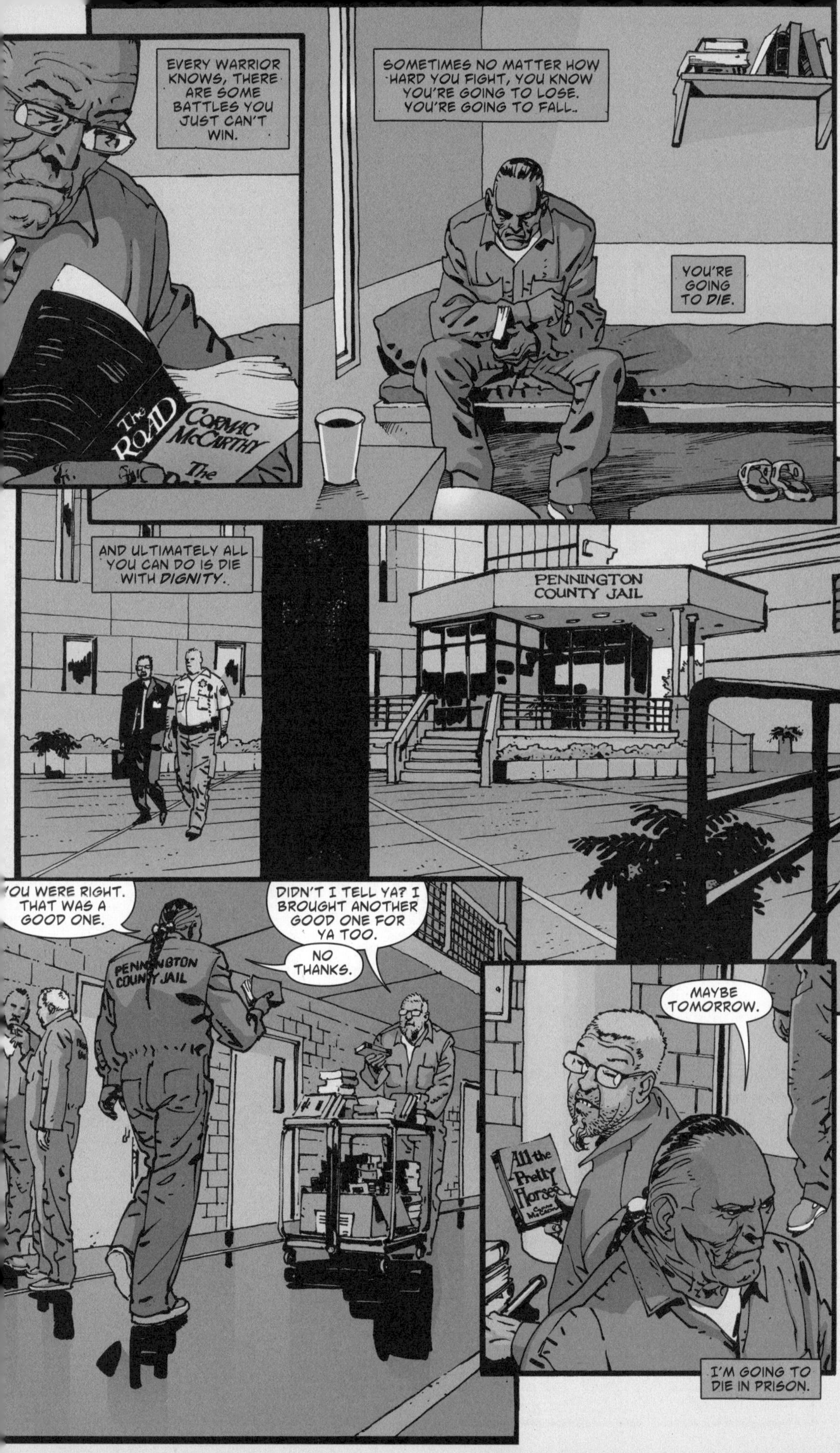
EVERY WARRIOR KNOWS, THERE ARE SOME BATTLES YOU JUST CAN'T WIN.
The ROAD
CORMAC McCARTHY
SOMETIMES NO MATTER HOW HARD YOU FIGHT, YOU KNOW YOU'RE GOING TO LOSE. YOU'RE GOING TO FALL..
YOU'RE GOING TO DIE.
AND ULTIMATELY ALL YOU CAN DO IS DIE WITH DIGNITY.
PENNINGTON COUNTY JAIL
YOU WERE RIGHT. THAT WAS A GOOD ONE.
PENNINGTON COUNTY JAIL
DIDN'T I TELL YA? I BROUGHT ANOTHER GOOD ONE FOR YA TOO.
NO THANKS.
MAYBE TOMORROW.
All the Pretty Horses
I'M GOING TO DIE IN PRISON.

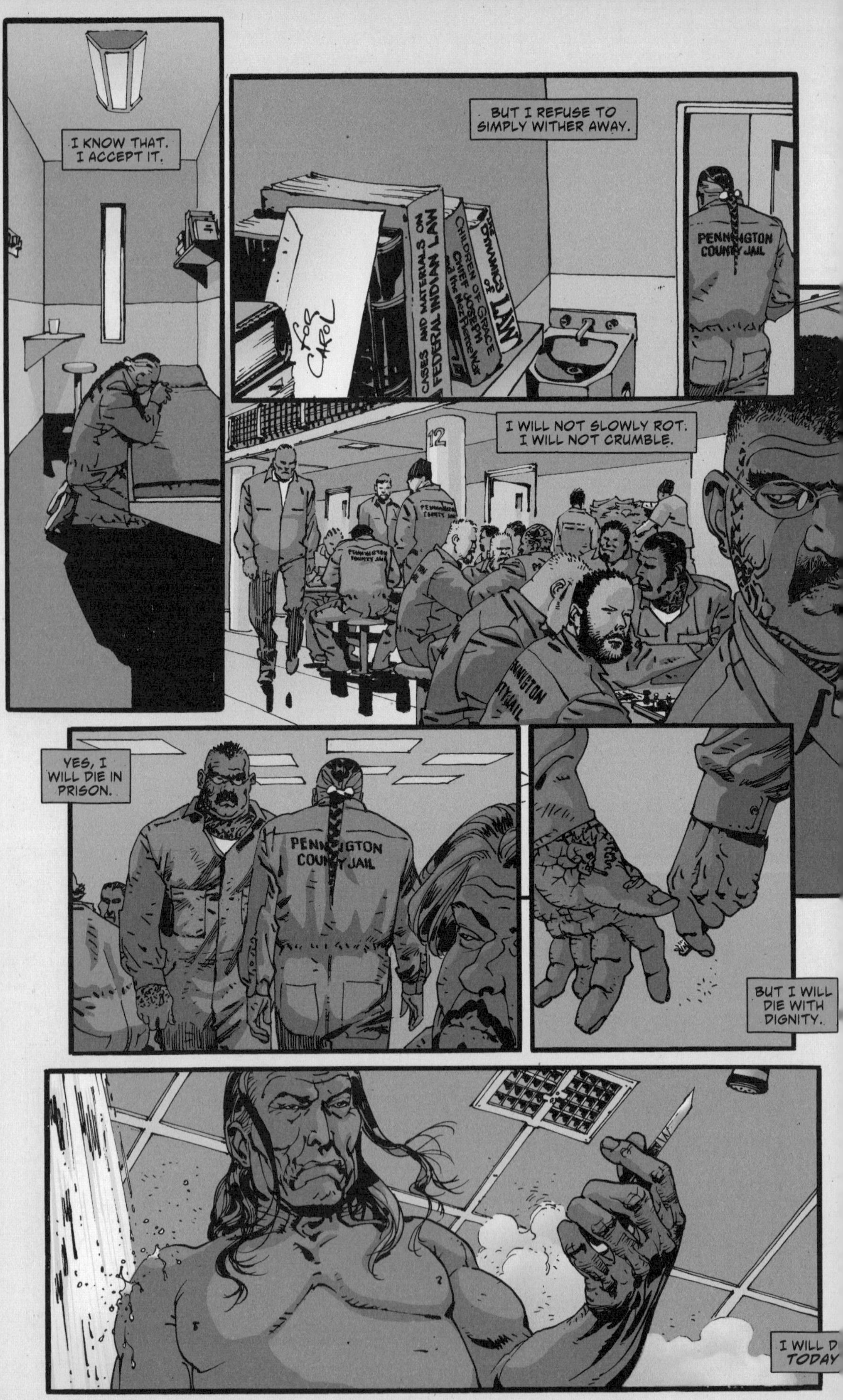
I KNOW THAT. I ACCEPT IT.
BUT I REFUSE TO SIMPLY WITHER AWAY.
FOR CAROL
CASES AND MATERIALS ON FEDERAL INDIAN LAW
CHILDREN OF GRACE CHIEF JOSEPH and the Nez Perce War
THE DYNAMICS OF LAW
PENNINGTON COUNTY JAIL
I WILL NOT SLOWLY ROT. I WILL NOT CRUMBLE.
12
YES, I WILL DIE IN PRISON.
PENNINGTON COUNTY JAIL
BUT I WILL DIE WITH DIGNITY.
TODAY

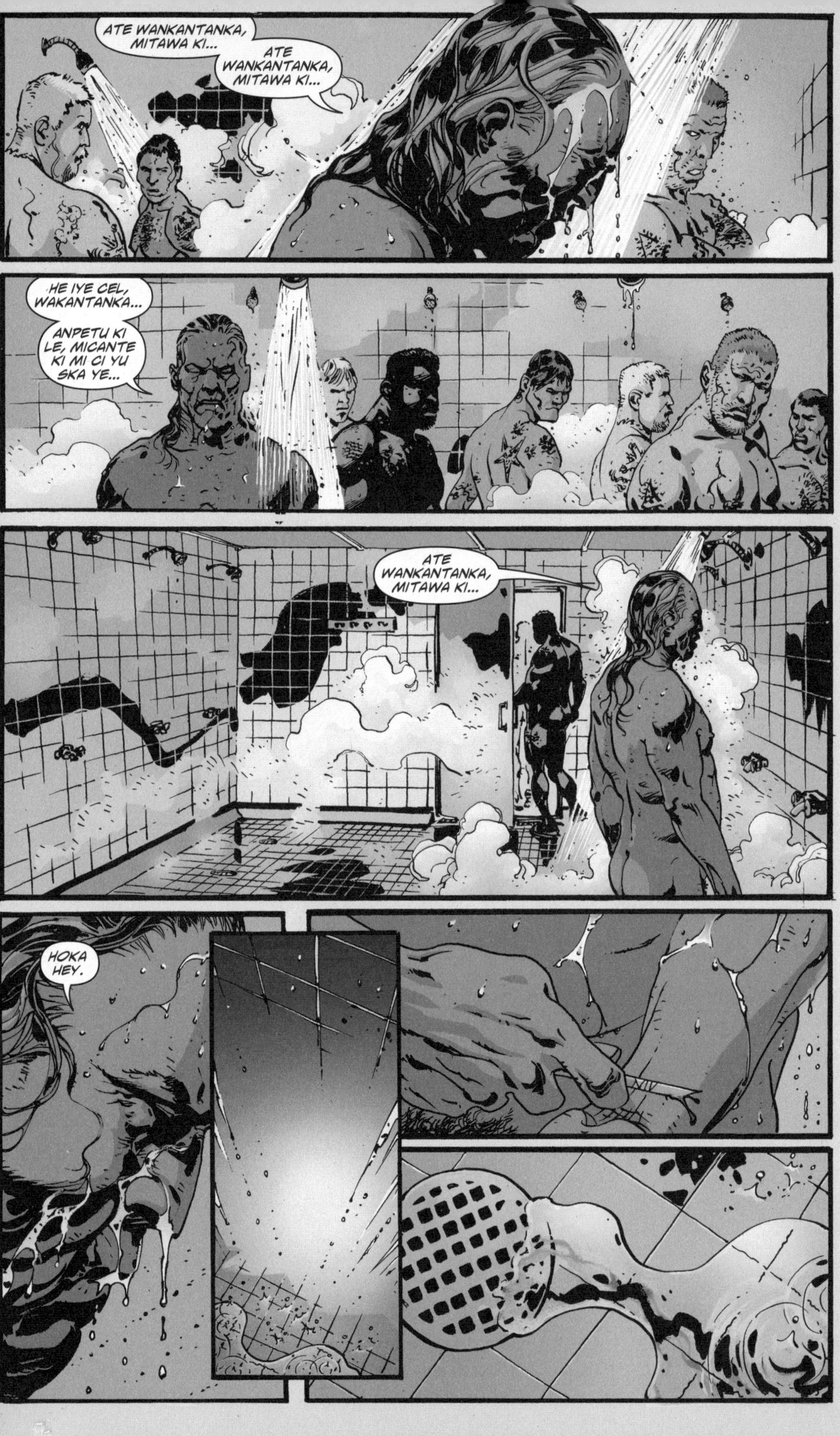
ATE WANKANTANKA, MITAWA KI...
ATE WANKANTANKA, MITAWA KI...
HE IYE CEL, WAKANTANKA...
ANPETU KI LE, MICANTE KI MI CI YU SKA YE...
ATE WANKANTANKA, MITAWA KI...
HOKA HEY.

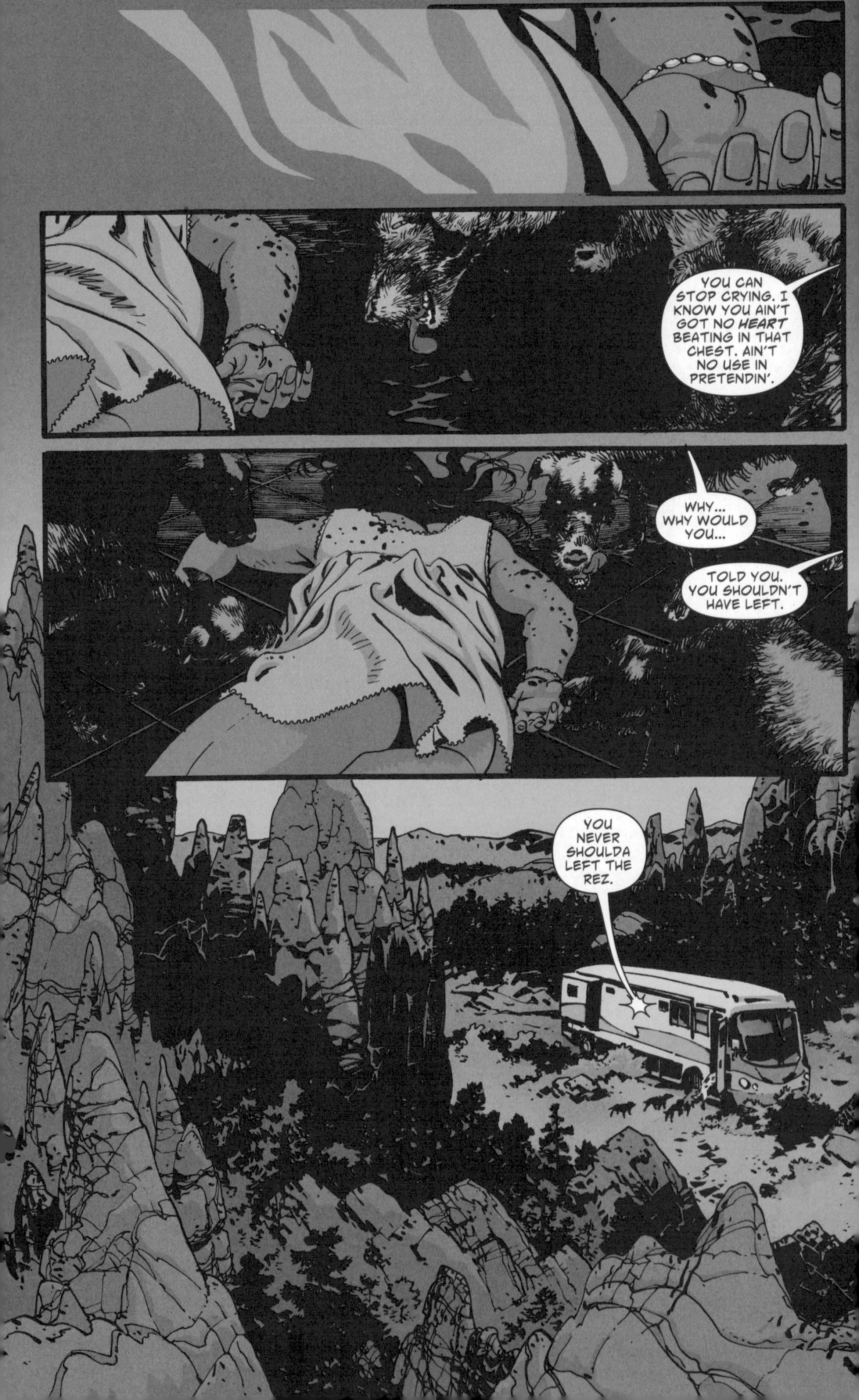
YOU CAN STOP CRYING. I KNOW YOU AIN'T GOT NO *HEART* BEATING IN THAT CHEST. AIN'T NO USE IN PRETENDIN'.
WHY... WHY WOULD YOU...
TOLD YOU. YOU SHOULDN'T HAVE LEFT.
YOU NEVER SHOULDA LEFT THE REZ.

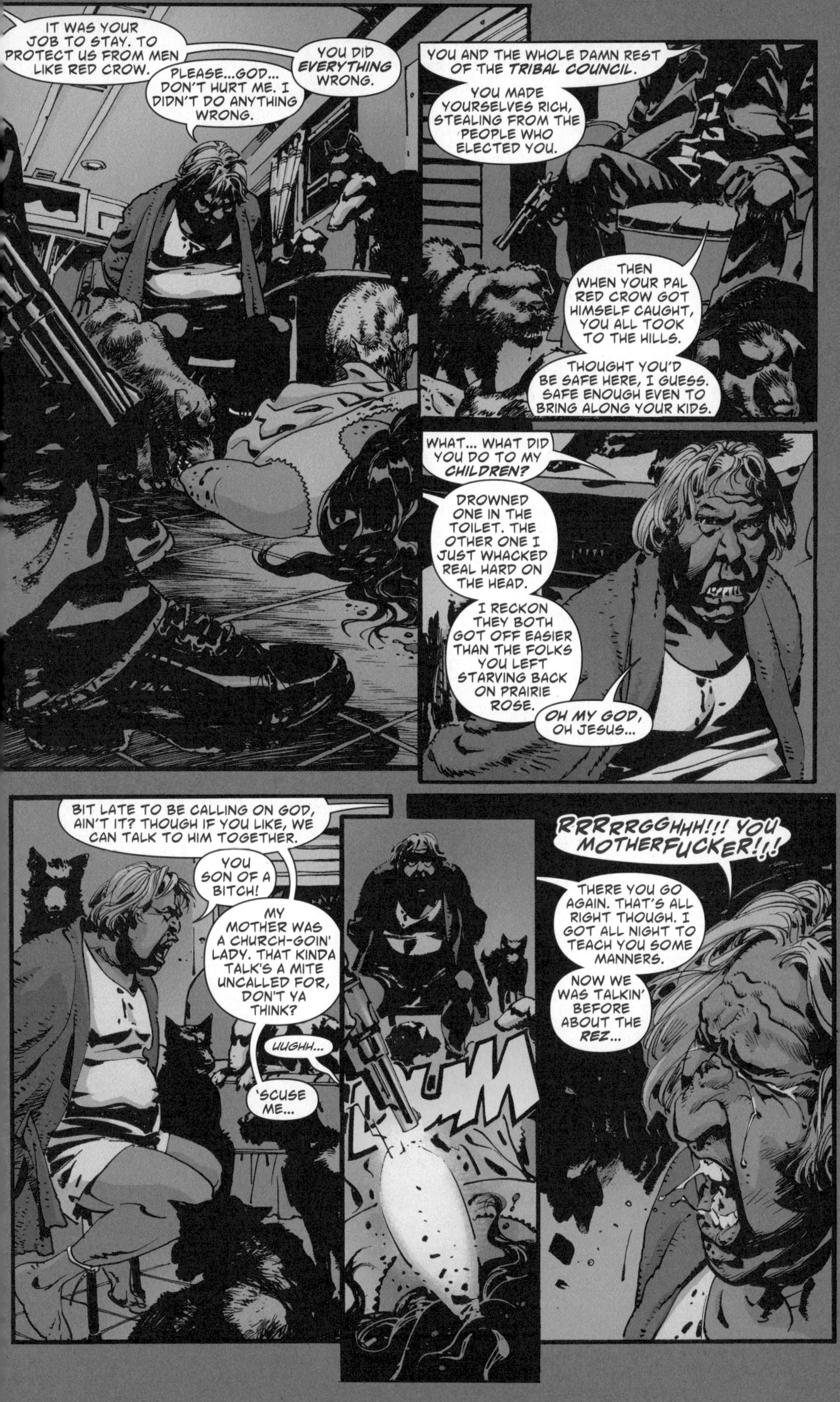

IT WAS YOUR JOB TO STAY. TO PROTECT US FROM MEN LIKE RED CROW.
PLEASE...GOD... DON'T HURT ME. I DIDN'T DO ANYTHING WRONG.
YOU DID *EVERYTHING* WRONG.
YOU AND THE WHOLE DAMN REST OF THE *TRIBAL COUNCIL*.
YOU MADE YOURSELVES RICH, STEALING FROM THE PEOPLE WHO ELECTED YOU.
THEN WHEN YOUR PAL RED CROW GOT HIMSELF CAUGHT, YOU ALL TOOK TO THE HILLS.
THOUGHT YOU'D BE SAFE HERE, I GUESS. SAFE ENOUGH EVEN TO BRING ALONG YOUR KIDS.
WHAT... WHAT DID YOU DO TO MY *CHILDREN?*
DROWNED ONE IN THE TOILET. THE OTHER ONE I JUST WHACKED REAL HARD ON THE HEAD.
I RECKON THEY BOTH GOT OFF EASIER THAN THE FOLKS YOU LEFT STARVING BACK ON PRAIRIE ROSE.
OH MY GOD, OH JESUS...
BIT LATE TO BE CALLING ON GOD, AIN'T IT? THOUGH IF YOU LIKE, WE CAN TALK TO HIM TOGETHER.
YOU SON OF A BITCH!
MY MOTHER WAS A CHURCH-GOIN' LADY. THAT KINDA TALK'S A MITE UNCALLED FOR, DON'T YA THINK?
UUGHH...
'SCUSE ME...
BLAMM
RRRRRGGHHH!!! YOU MOTHERFUCKER!!!
THERE YOU GO AGAIN. THAT'S ALL RIGHT THOUGH. I GOT ALL NIGHT TO TEACH YOU SOME MANNERS.
NOW WE WAS TALKIN' BEFORE ABOUT THE *REZ*...

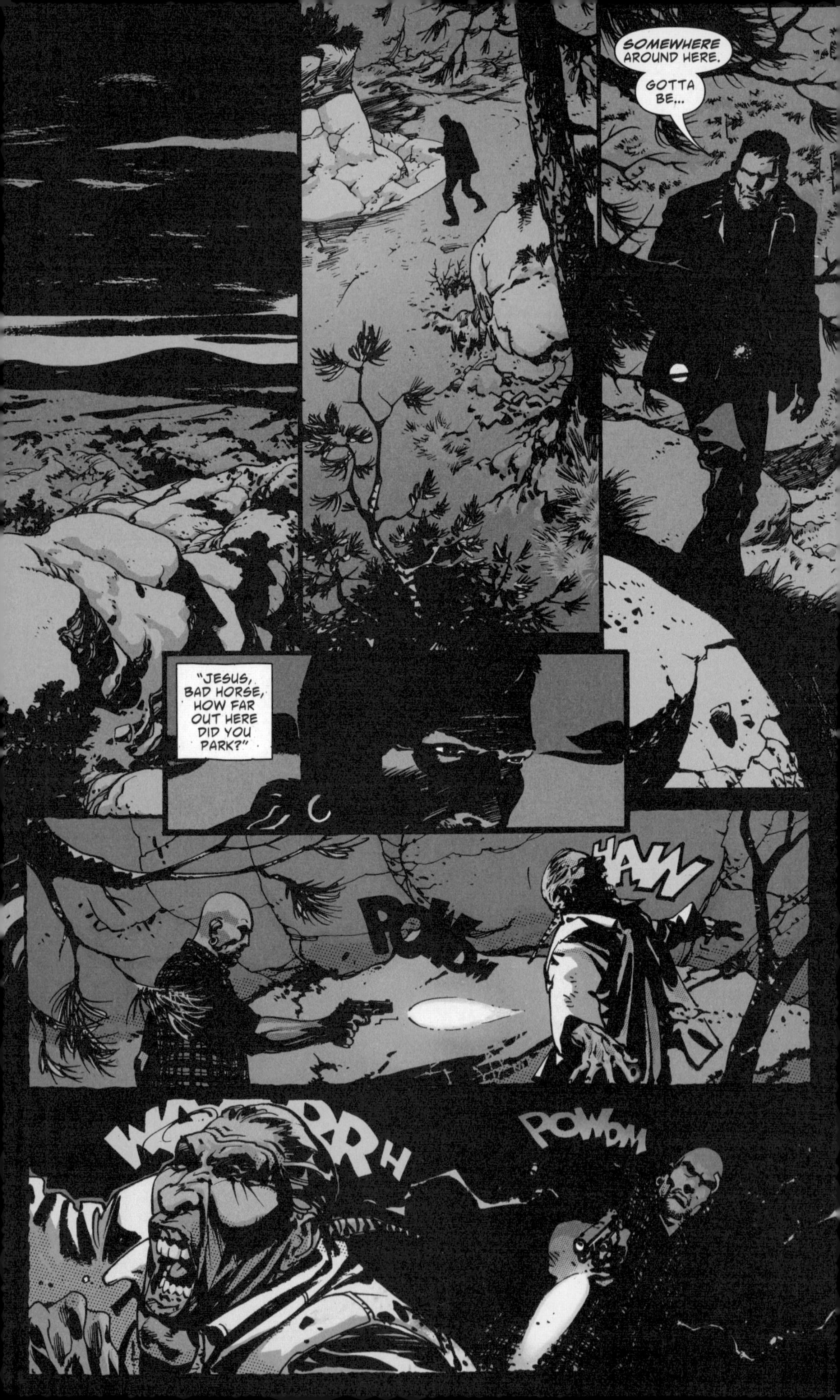
SOMEWHERE AROUND HERE.
GOTTA BE...
"JESUS, BAD HORSE, HOW FAR OUT HERE DID YOU PARK?"
HAW
POWWM

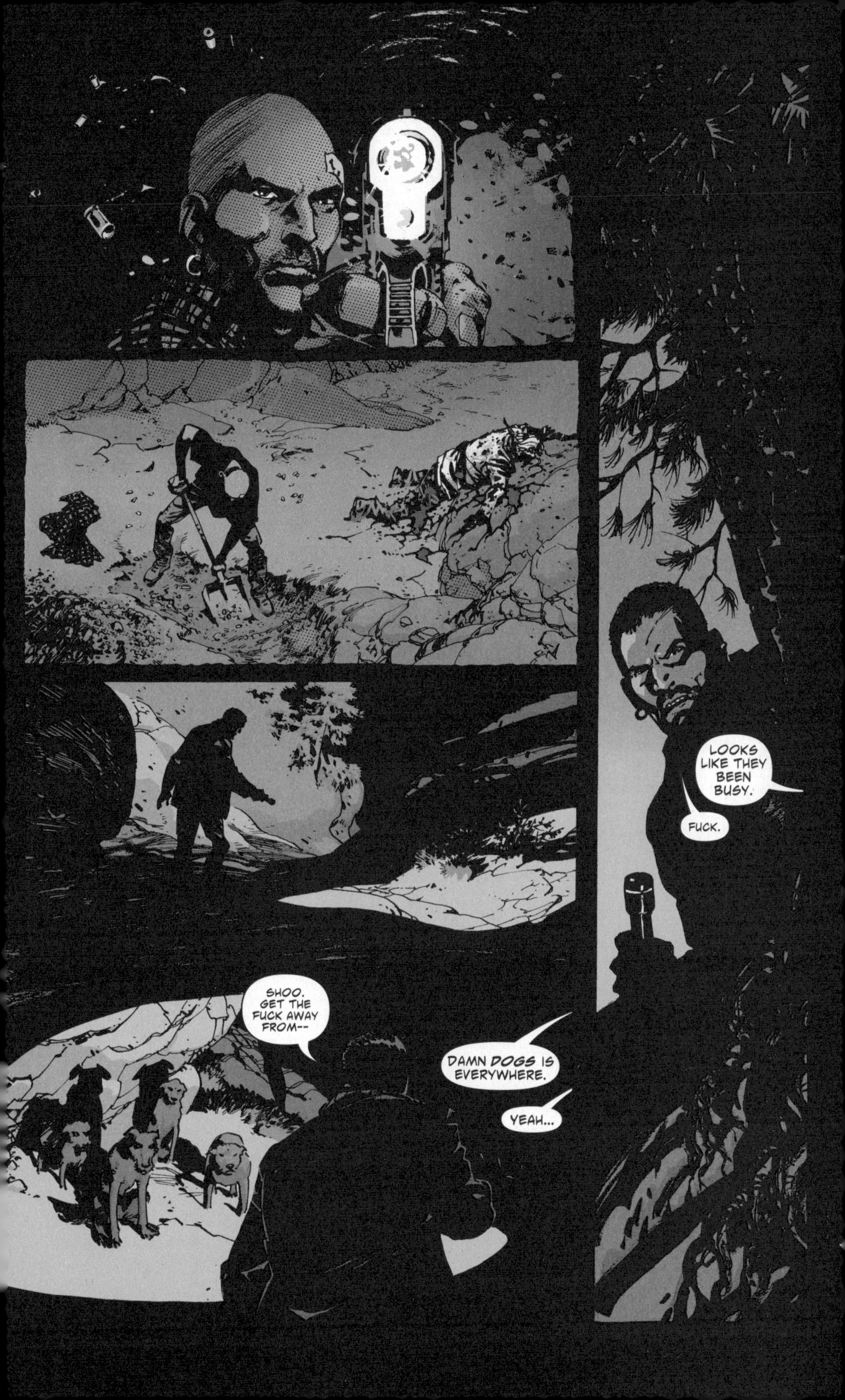
LOOKS LIKE THEY BEEN BUSY.
FUCK.
SHOO. GET THE FUCK AWAY FROM--
DAMN DOGS IS EVERYWHERE.
YEAH...

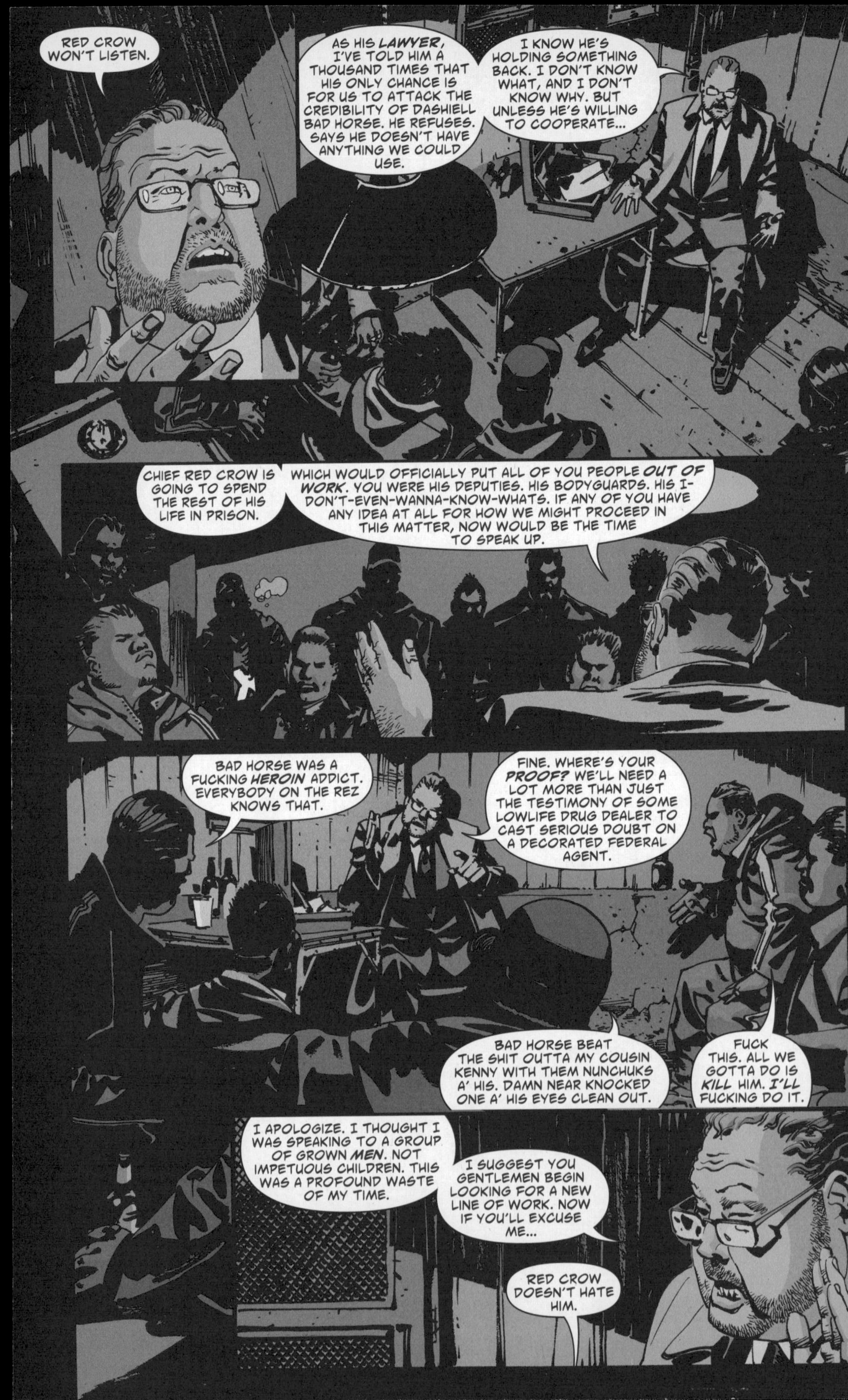
RED CROW WON'T LISTEN.
AS HIS LAWYER, I'VE TOLD HIM A THOUSAND TIMES THAT HIS ONLY CHANCE IS FOR US TO ATTACK THE CREDIBILITY OF DASHIELL BAD HORSE. HE REFUSES. SAYS HE DOESN'T HAVE ANYTHING WE COULD USE.
I KNOW HE'S HOLDING SOMETHING BACK. I DON'T KNOW WHAT, AND I DON'T KNOW WHY. BUT UNLESS HE'S WILLING TO COOPERATE...
CHIEF RED CROW IS GOING TO SPEND THE REST OF HIS LIFE IN PRISON.
WHICH WOULD OFFICIALLY PUT ALL OF YOU PEOPLE OUT OF WORK. YOU WERE HIS DEPUTIES. HIS BODYGUARDS. HIS I-DON'T-EVEN-WANNA-KNOW-WHATS. IF ANY OF YOU HAVE ANY IDEA AT ALL FOR HOW WE MIGHT PROCEED IN THIS MATTER, NOW WOULD BE THE TIME TO SPEAK UP.
BAD HORSE WAS A FUCKING HEROIN ADDICT. EVERYBODY ON THE REZ KNOWS THAT.
FINE. WHERE'S YOUR PROOF? WE'LL NEED A LOT MORE THAN JUST THE TESTIMONY OF SOME LOWLIFE DRUG DEALER TO CAST SERIOUS DOUBT ON A DECORATED FEDERAL AGENT.
BAD HORSE BEAT THE SHIT OUTTA MY COUSIN KENNY WITH THEM NUNCHUKS A' HIS. DAMN NEAR KNOCKED ONE A' HIS EYES CLEAN OUT.
FUCK THIS. ALL WE GOTTA DO IS KILL HIM. I'LL FUCKING DO IT.
I APOLOGIZE. I THOUGHT I WAS SPEAKING TO A GROUP OF GROWN MEN. NOT IMPETUOUS CHILDREN. THIS WAS A PROFOUND WASTE OF MY TIME.
I SUGGEST YOU GENTLEMEN BEGIN LOOKING FOR A NEW LINE OF WORK. NOW IF YOU'LL EXCUSE ME...
RED CROW DOESN'T HATE HIM.

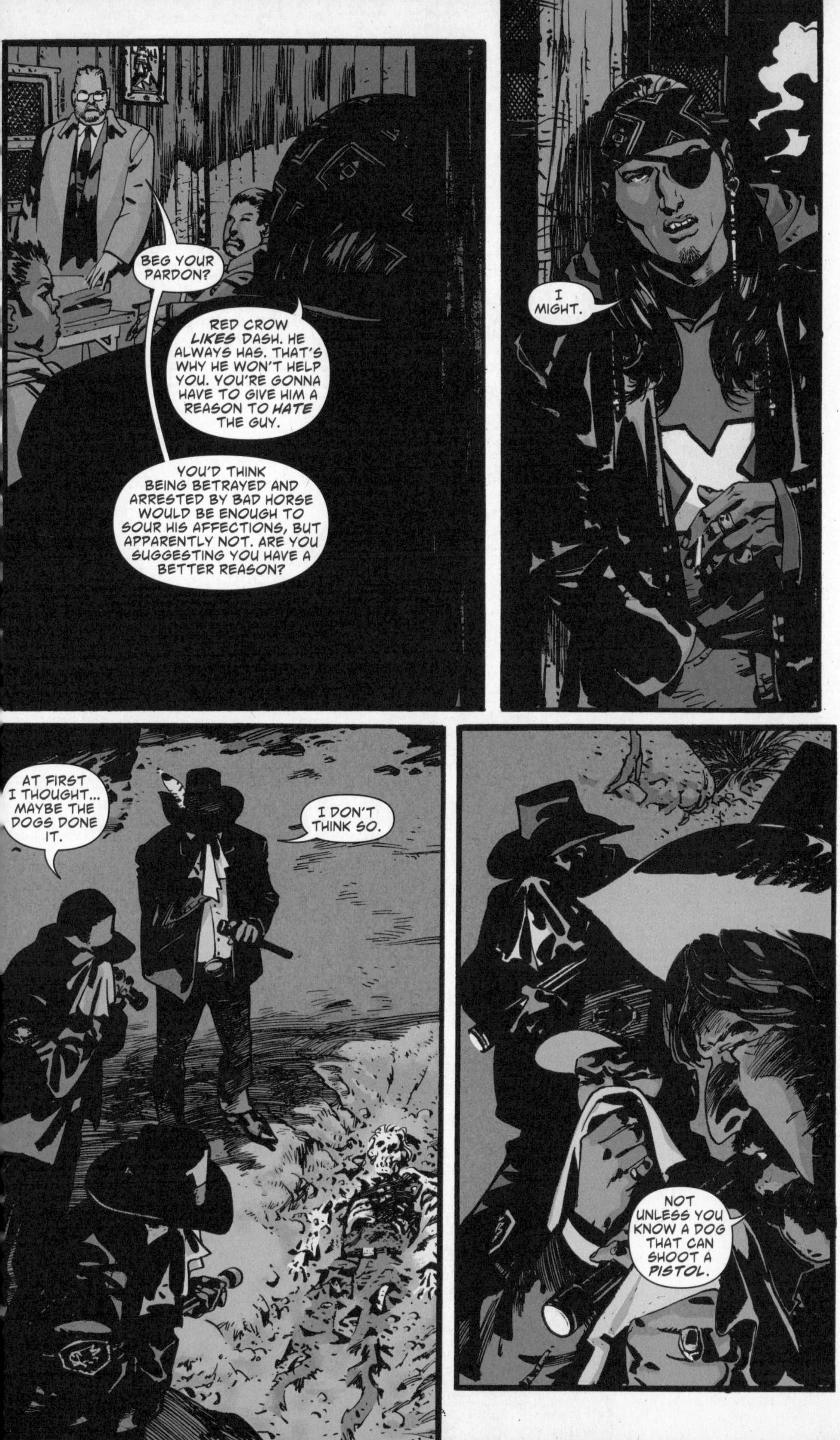
BEG YOUR PARDON?
RED CROW LIKES DASH. HE ALWAYS HAS. THAT'S WHY HE WON'T HELP YOU. YOU'RE GONNA HAVE TO GIVE HIM A REASON TO HATE THE GUY.
YOU'D THINK BEING BETRAYED AND ARRESTED BY BAD HORSE WOULD BE ENOUGH TO SOUR HIS AFFECTIONS, BUT APPARENTLY NOT. ARE YOU SUGGESTING YOU HAVE A BETTER REASON?
I MIGHT.
AT FIRST I THOUGHT... MAYBE THE DOGS DONE IT.
I DON'T THINK SO.
NOT UNLESS YOU KNOW A DOG THAT CAN SHOOT A PISTOL.

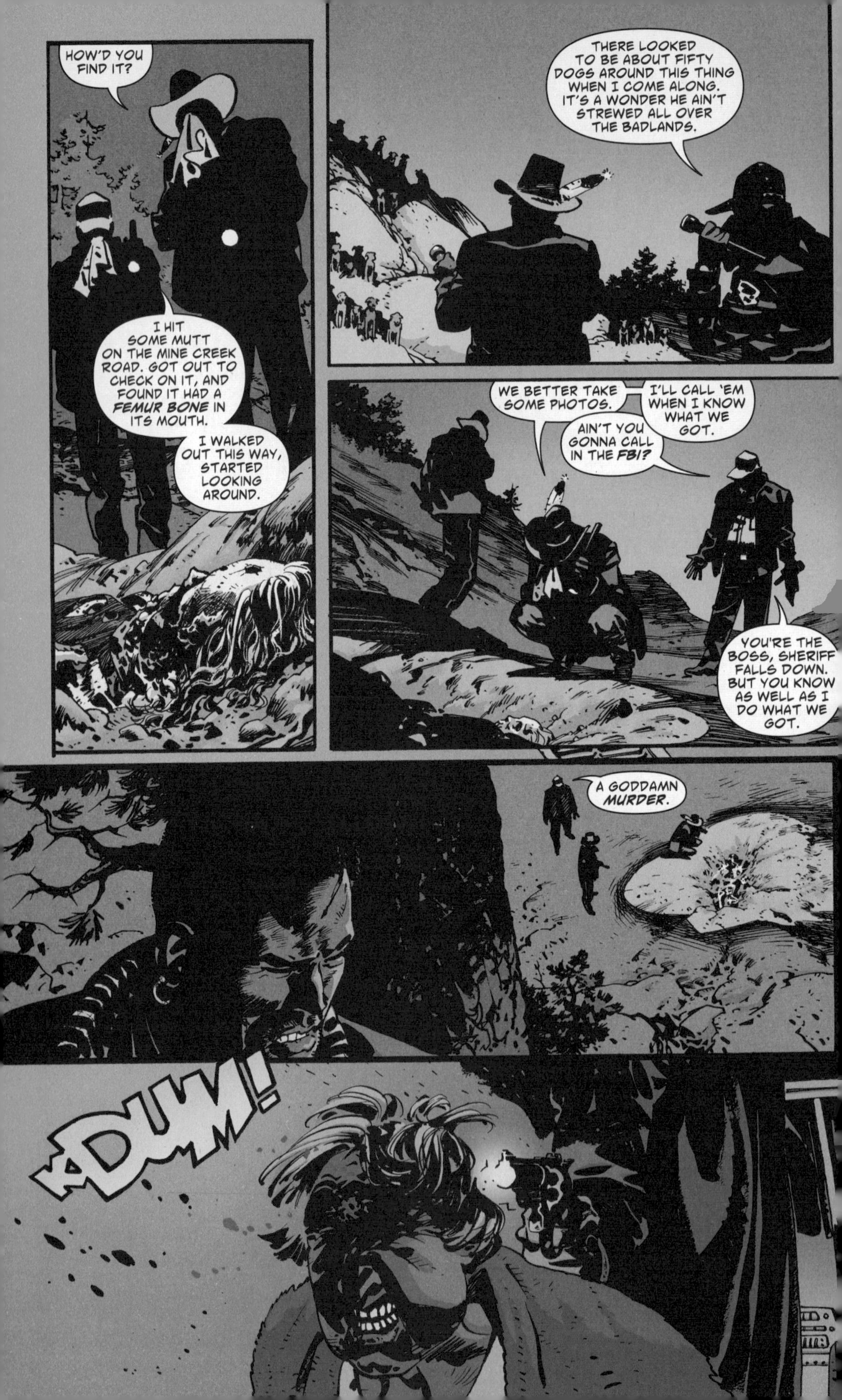

HOW'D YOU FIND IT?
I HIT SOME MUTT ON THE MINE CREEK ROAD. GOT OUT TO CHECK ON IT, AND FOUND IT HAD A *FEMUR BONE* IN ITS MOUTH.
I WALKED OUT THIS WAY, STARTED LOOKING AROUND.
THERE LOOKED TO BE ABOUT FIFTY DOGS AROUND THIS THING WHEN I COME ALONG. IT'S A WONDER HE AIN'T STREWED ALL OVER THE BADLANDS.
WE BETTER TAKE SOME PHOTOS.
AIN'T YOU GONNA CALL IN THE *FBI?*
I'LL CALL 'EM WHEN I KNOW WHAT WE GOT.
YOU'RE THE BOSS, SHERIFF FALLS DOWN. BUT YOU KNOW AS WELL AS I DO WHAT WE GOT.
A GODDAMN *MURDER*.
KDUM!

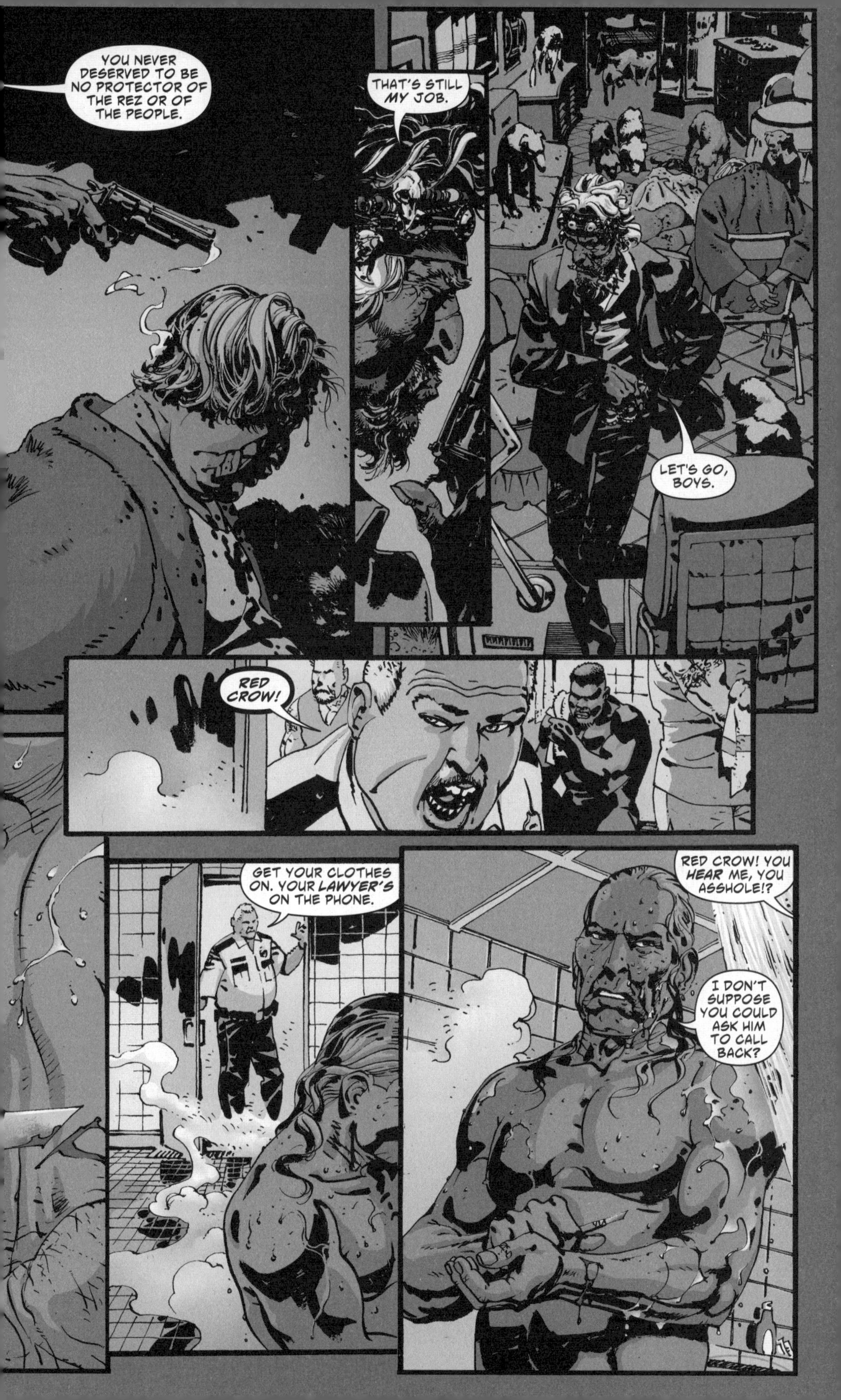
YOU NEVER DESERVED TO BE NO PROTECTOR OF THE REZ OR OF THE PEOPLE.
THAT'S STILL MY JOB.
LET'S GO, BOYS.
RED CROW!
GET YOUR CLOTHES ON. YOUR LAWYER'S ON THE PHONE.
RED CROW! YOU HEAR ME, YOU ASSHOLE!?
I DON'T SUPPOSE YOU COULD ASK HIM TO CALL BACK?

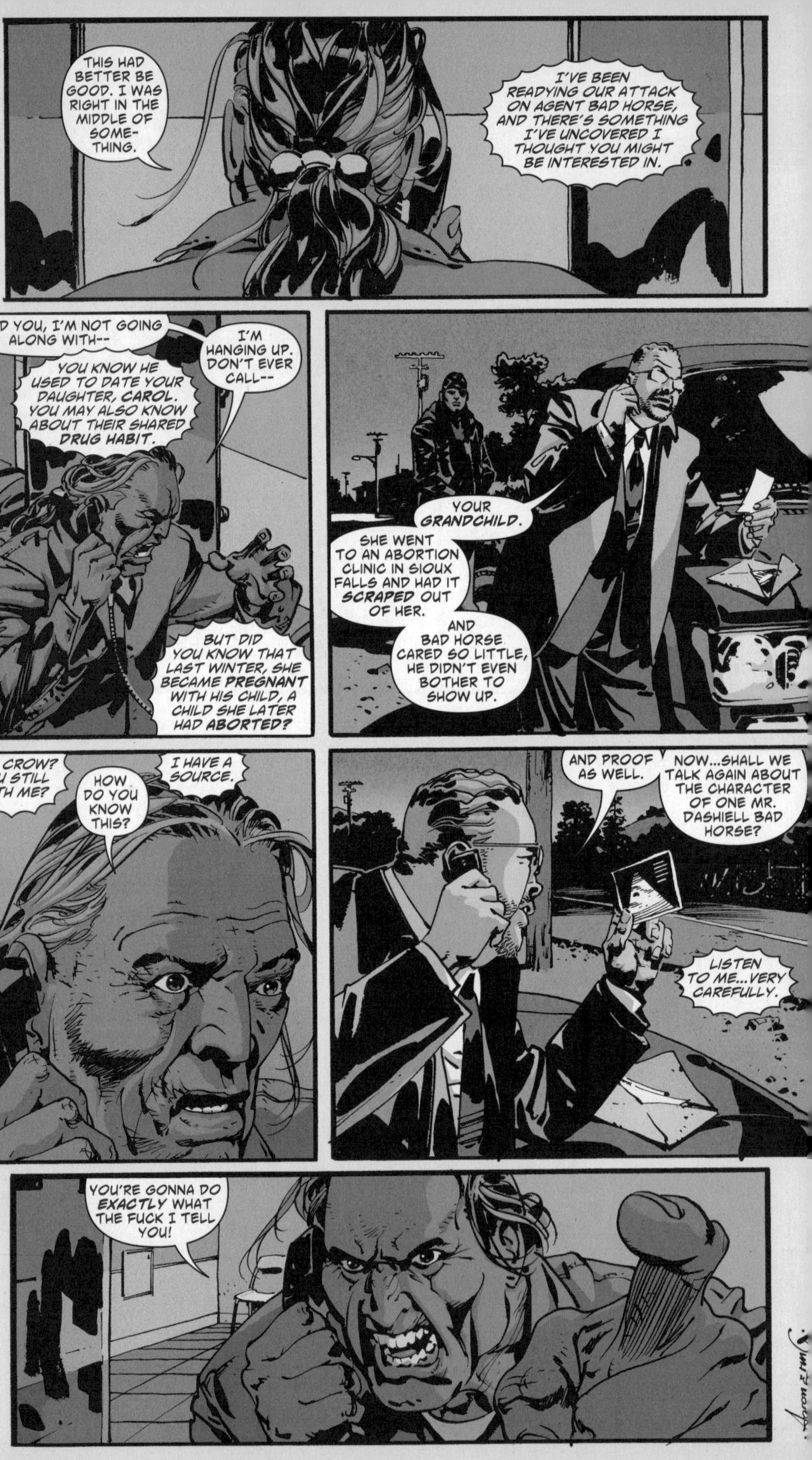
THIS HAD BETTER BE GOOD. I WAS RIGHT IN THE MIDDLE OF SOME-THING.
I'VE BEEN READYING OUR ATTACK ON AGENT BAD HORSE, AND THERE'S SOMETHING I'VE UNCOVERED I THOUGHT YOU MIGHT BE INTERESTED IN.
I TOLD YOU, I'M NOT GOING ALONG WITH--
YOU KNOW HE USED TO DATE YOUR DAUGHTER, CAROL. YOU MAY ALSO KNOW ABOUT THEIR SHARED DRUG HABIT.
I'M HANGING UP. DON'T EVER CALL--
BUT DID YOU KNOW THAT LAST WINTER, SHE BECAME PREGNANT WITH HIS CHILD, A CHILD SHE LATER HAD ABORTED?
YOUR GRANDCHILD.
SHE WENT TO AN ABORTION CLINIC IN SIOUX FALLS AND HAD IT SCRAPED OUT OF HER.
AND BAD HORSE CARED SO LITTLE, HE DIDN'T EVEN BOTHER TO SHOW UP.
RED CROW? YOU STILL WITH ME?
HOW DO YOU KNOW THIS?
I HAVE A SOURCE.
AND PROOF AS WELL.
NOW...SHALL WE TALK AGAIN ABOUT THE CHARACTER OF ONE MR. DASHIELL BAD HORSE?
LISTEN TO ME...VERY CAREFULLY.
YOU'RE GONNA DO EXACTLY WHAT THE FUCK I TELL YOU!

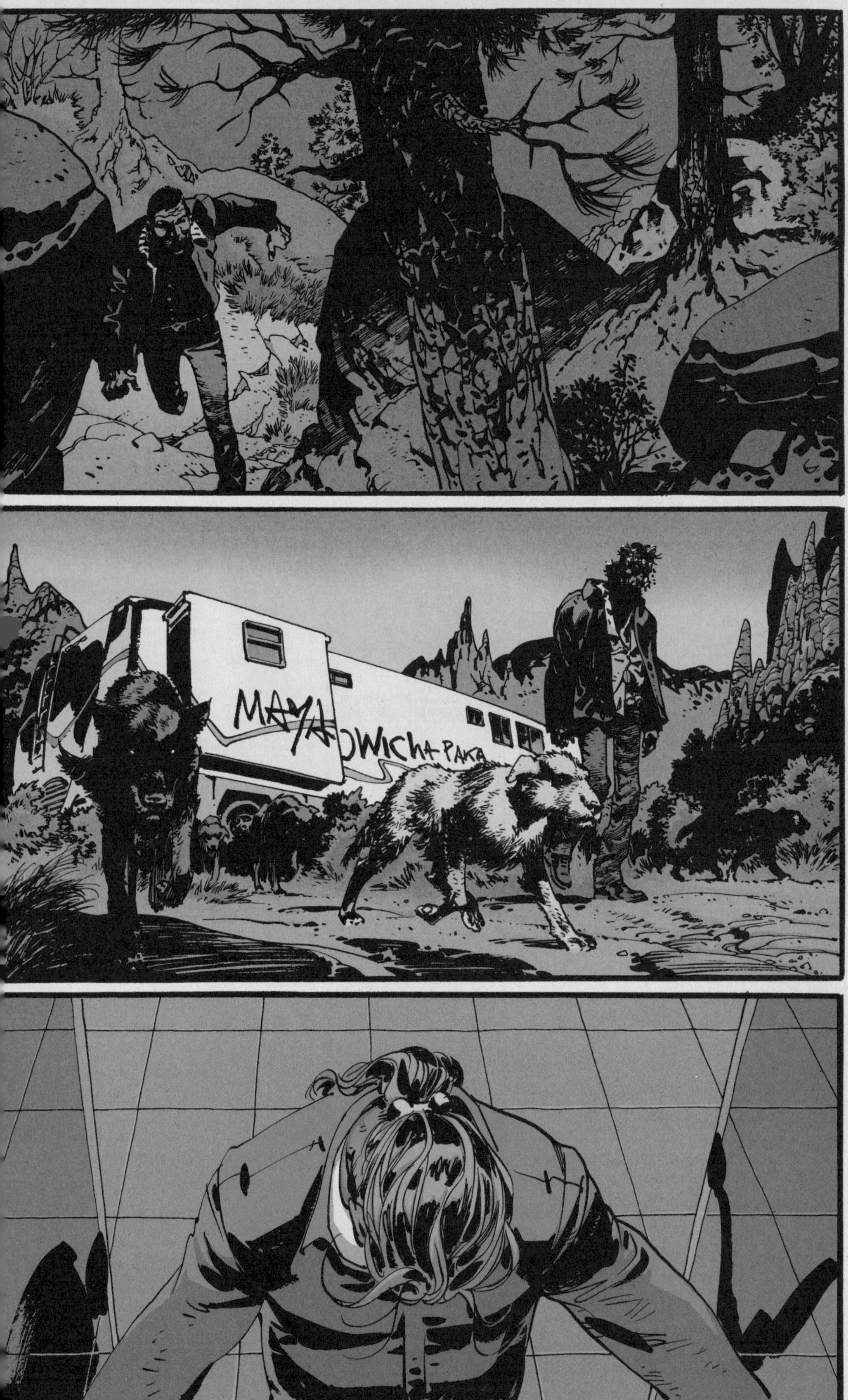
MAMA
OWICHA PAKA

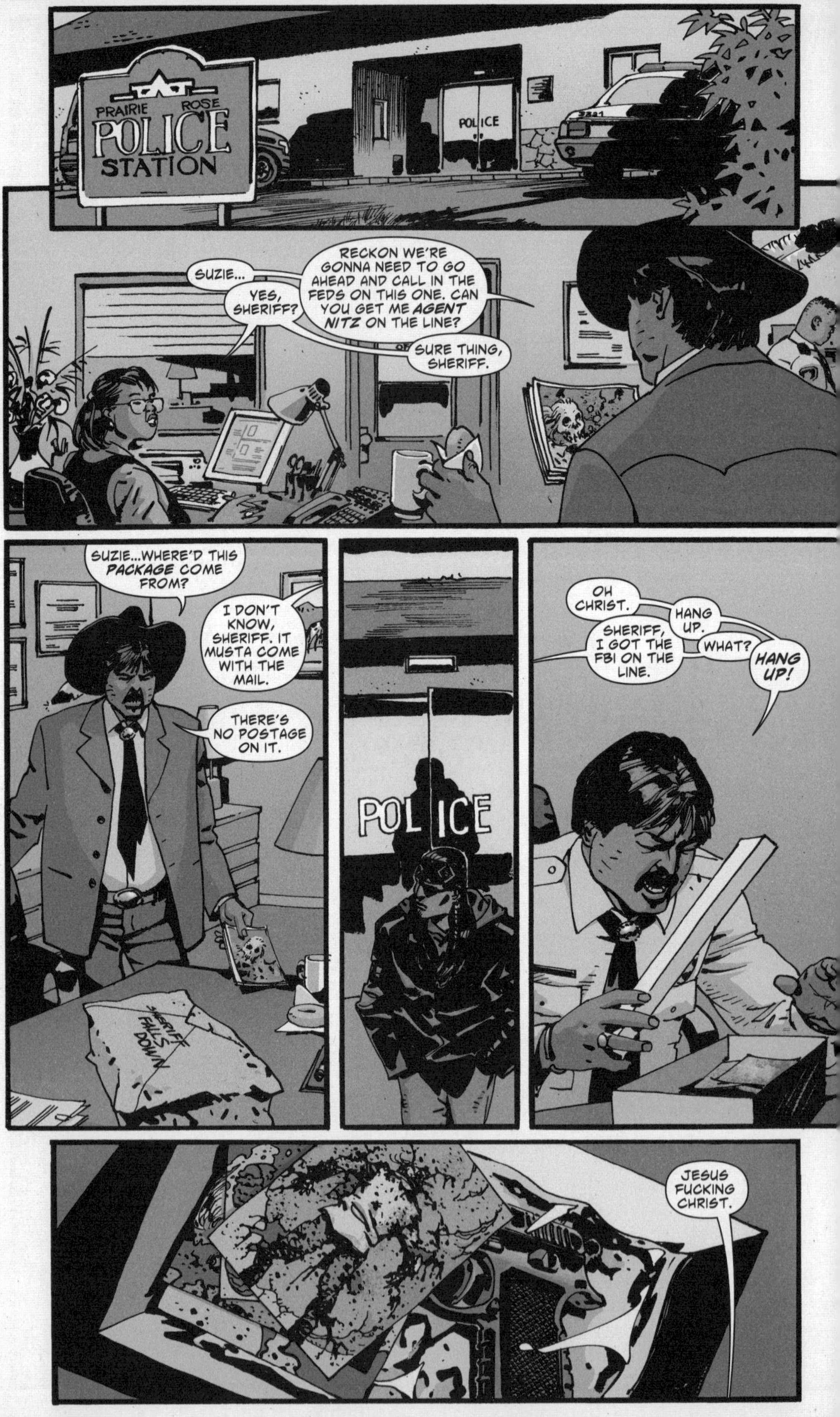
PRAIRIE ROSE
POLICE
STATION
POLICE
SUZIE...
YES, SHERIFF?
RECKON WE'RE GONNA NEED TO GO AHEAD AND CALL IN THE FEDS ON THIS ONE. CAN YOU GET ME AGENT NITZ ON THE LINE?
SURE THING, SHERIFF.
SUZIE...WHERE'D THIS PACKAGE COME FROM?
I DON'T KNOW, SHERIFF. IT MUSTA COME WITH THE MAIL.
THERE'S NO POSTAGE ON IT.
SHERIFF FALLS DOWN
POLICE
OH CHRIST.
SHERIFF, I GOT THE FBI ON THE LINE.
HANG UP.
WHAT?
HANG UP!
JESUS FUCKING CHRIST.

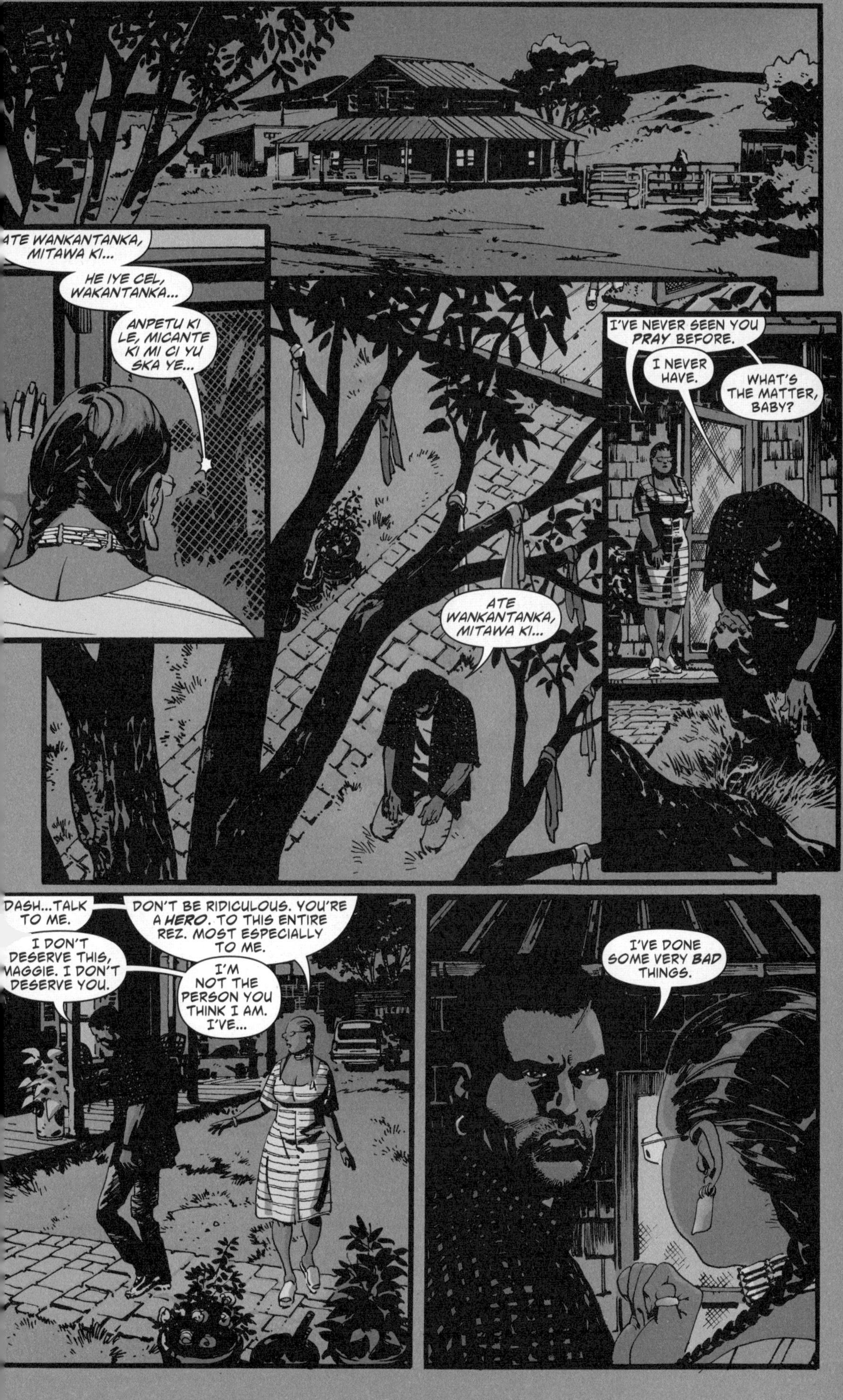

ATE WANKANTANKA, MITAWA KI...
HE IYE CEL, WAKANTANKA...
ANPETU KI LE, MICANTE KI MI CI YU SKA YE...
ATE WANKANTANKA, MITAWA KI...
I'VE NEVER SEEN YOU PRAY BEFORE.
I NEVER HAVE.
WHAT'S THE MATTER, BABY?
DASH...TALK TO ME.
I DON'T DESERVE THIS, MAGGIE. I DON'T DESERVE YOU.
DON'T BE RIDICULOUS. YOU'RE A HERO. TO THIS ENTIRE REZ. MOST ESPECIALLY TO ME.
I'M NOT THE PERSON YOU THINK I AM. I'VE...
I'VE DONE SOME VERY BAD THINGS.

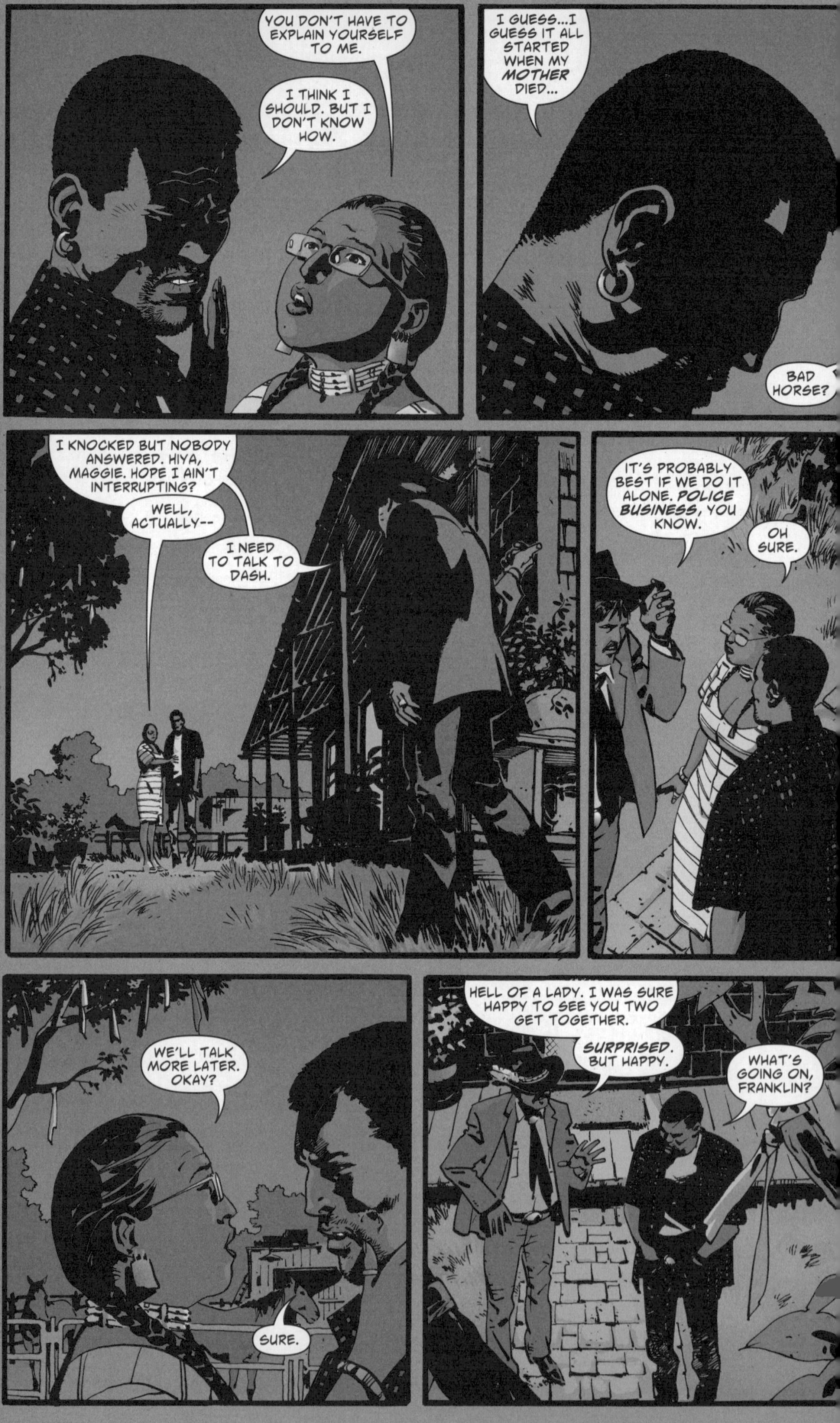
YOU DON'T HAVE TO EXPLAIN YOURSELF TO ME.
I THINK I SHOULD. BUT I DON'T KNOW HOW.
I GUESS...I GUESS IT ALL STARTED WHEN MY MOTHER DIED...
BAD HORSE?
I KNOCKED BUT NOBODY ANSWERED. HIYA, MAGGIE. HOPE I AIN'T INTERRUPTING?
WELL, ACTUALLY--
I NEED TO TALK TO DASH.
IT'S PROBABLY BEST IF WE DO IT ALONE. POLICE BUSINESS, YOU KNOW.
OH SURE.
WE'LL TALK MORE LATER. OKAY?
SURE.
HELL OF A LADY. I WAS SURE HAPPY TO SEE YOU TWO GET TOGETHER.
SURPRISED. BUT HAPPY.
WHAT'S GOING ON, FRANKLIN?

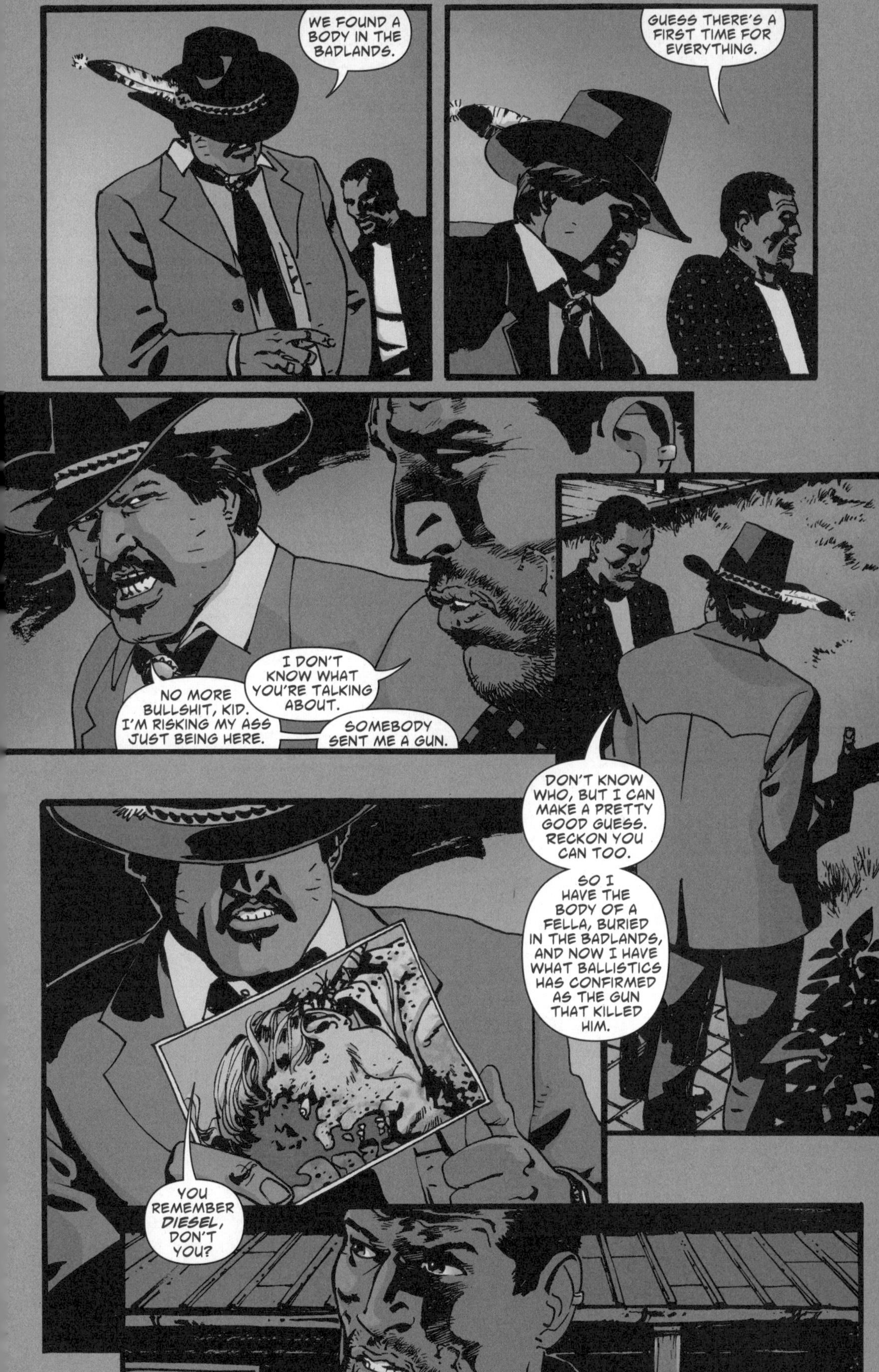

WE FOUND A BODY IN THE BADLANDS.
GUESS THERE'S A FIRST TIME FOR EVERYTHING.
NO MORE BULLSHIT, KID. I'M RISKING MY ASS JUST BEING HERE.
I DON'T KNOW WHAT YOU'RE TALKING ABOUT.
SOMEBODY SENT ME A GUN.
DON'T KNOW WHO, BUT I CAN MAKE A PRETTY GOOD GUESS. RECKON YOU CAN TOO.
SO I HAVE THE BODY OF A FELLA, BURIED IN THE BADLANDS, AND NOW I HAVE WHAT BALLISTICS HAS CONFIRMED AS THE GUN THAT KILLED HIM.
YOU REMEMBER DIESEL, DON'T YOU?

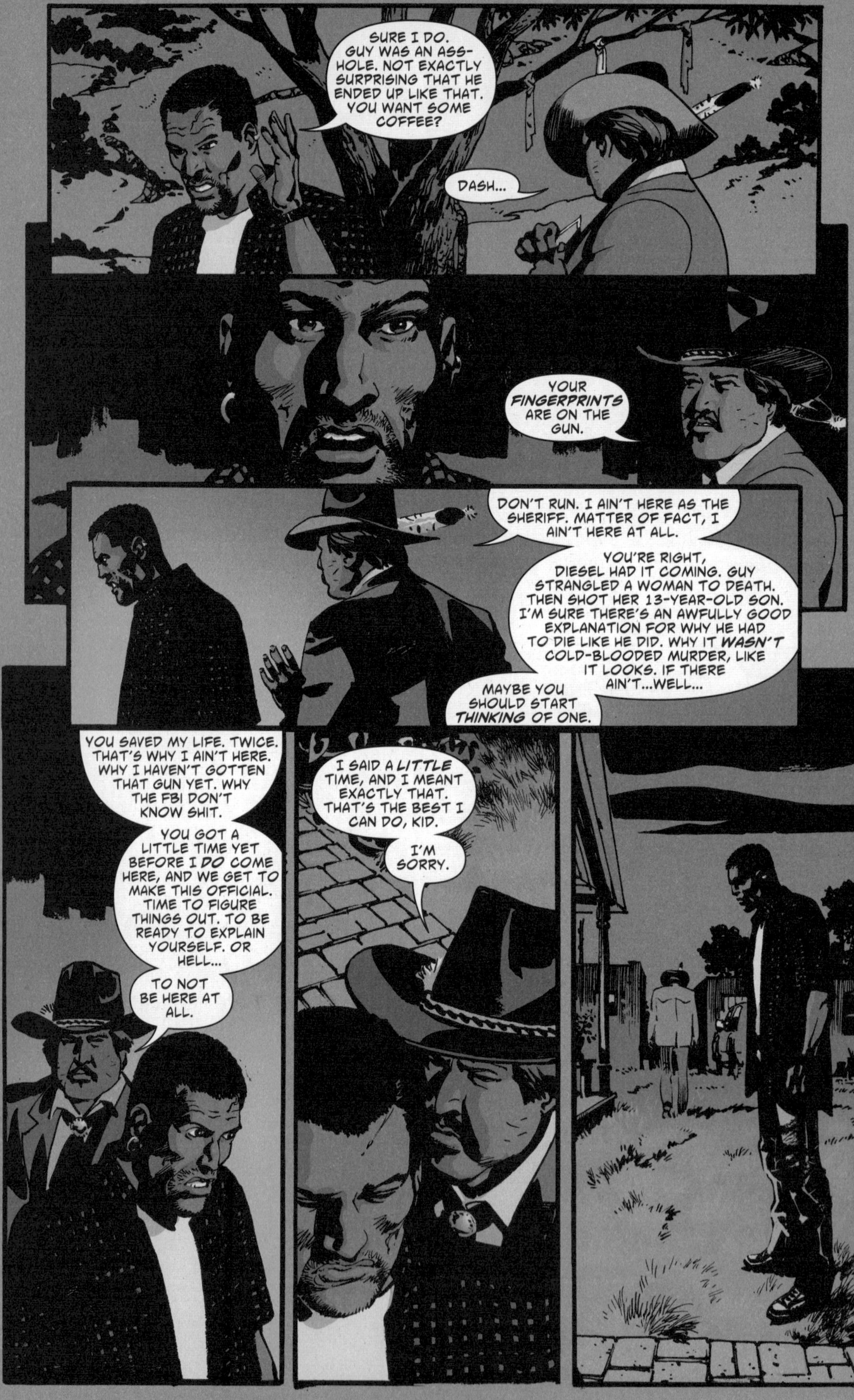

SURE I DO. GUY WAS AN ASS-HOLE. NOT EXACTLY SURPRISING THAT HE ENDED UP LIKE THAT. YOU WANT SOME COFFEE?
DASH...
YOUR FINGERPRINTS ARE ON THE GUN.
DON'T RUN. I AIN'T HERE AS THE SHERIFF. MATTER OF FACT, I AIN'T HERE AT ALL.
YOU'RE RIGHT, DIESEL HAD IT COMING. GUY STRANGLED A WOMAN TO DEATH. THEN SHOT HER 13-YEAR-OLD SON. I'M SURE THERE'S AN AWFULLY GOOD EXPLANATION FOR WHY HE HAD TO DIE LIKE HE DID. WHY IT WASN'T COLD-BLOODED MURDER, LIKE IT LOOKS. IF THERE AIN'T...WELL...
MAYBE YOU SHOULD START THINKING OF ONE.
YOU SAVED MY LIFE. TWICE. THAT'S WHY I AIN'T HERE. WHY I HAVEN'T GOTTEN THAT GUN YET. WHY THE FBI DON'T KNOW SHIT.
YOU GOT A LITTLE TIME YET BEFORE I DO COME HERE, AND WE GET TO MAKE THIS OFFICIAL. TIME TO FIGURE THINGS OUT. TO BE READY TO EXPLAIN YOURSELF. OR HELL...
TO NOT BE HERE AT ALL.
I SAID A LITTLE TIME, AND I MEANT EXACTLY THAT. THAT'S THE BEST I CAN DO, KID.
I'M SORRY.

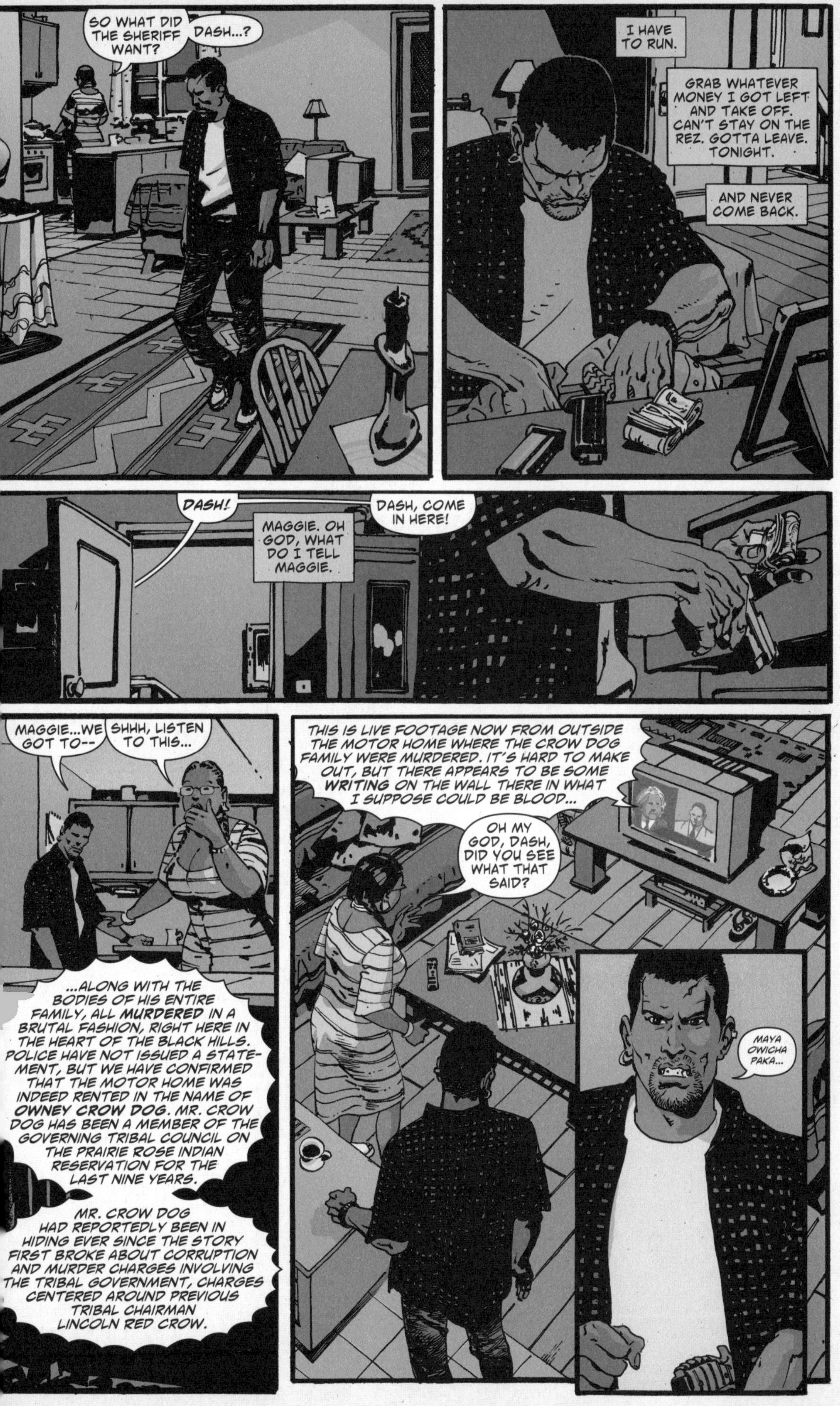
SO WHAT DID THE SHERIFF WANT?
DASH...?
I HAVE TO RUN.
GRAB WHATEVER MONEY I GOT LEFT AND TAKE OFF. CAN'T STAY ON THE REZ. GOTTA LEAVE. TONIGHT.
AND NEVER COME BACK.
DASH!
MAGGIE. OH GOD, WHAT DO I TELL MAGGIE.
DASH, COME IN HERE!
MAGGIE...WE GOT TO--
SHHH, LISTEN TO THIS...
...ALONG WITH THE BODIES OF HIS ENTIRE FAMILY, ALL MURDERED IN A BRUTAL FASHION, RIGHT HERE IN THE HEART OF THE BLACK HILLS. POLICE HAVE NOT ISSUED A STATEMENT, BUT WE HAVE CONFIRMED THAT THE MOTOR HOME WAS INDEED RENTED IN THE NAME OF OWNEY CROW DOG. MR. CROW DOG HAS BEEN A MEMBER OF THE GOVERNING TRIBAL COUNCIL ON THE PRAIRIE ROSE INDIAN RESERVATION FOR THE LAST NINE YEARS.
MR. CROW DOG HAD REPORTEDLY BEEN IN HIDING EVER SINCE THE STORY FIRST BROKE ABOUT CORRUPTION AND MURDER CHARGES INVOLVING THE TRIBAL GOVERNMENT, CHARGES CENTERED AROUND PREVIOUS TRIBAL CHAIRMAN LINCOLN RED CROW.
THIS IS LIVE FOOTAGE NOW FROM OUTSIDE THE MOTOR HOME WHERE THE CROW DOG FAMILY WERE MURDERED. IT'S HARD TO MAKE OUT, BUT THERE APPEARS TO BE SOME WRITING ON THE WALL THERE IN WHAT I SUPPOSE COULD BE BLOOD...
OH MY GOD, DASH, DID YOU SEE WHAT THAT SAID?
MAYA OWICHA PAKA...

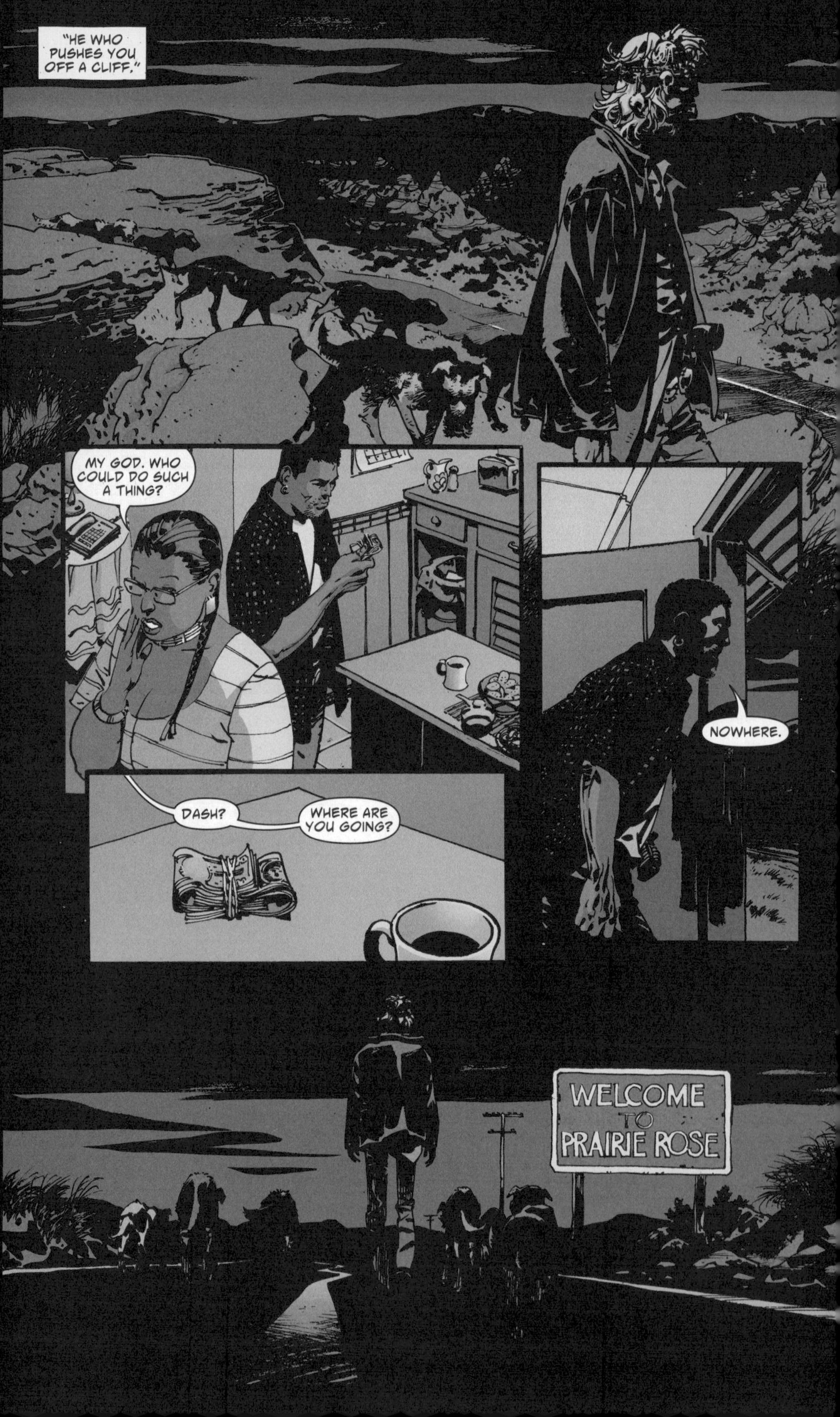
"HE WHO PUSHES YOU OFF A CLIFF."
MY GOD. WHO COULD DO SUCH A THING?
DASH?
WHERE ARE YOU GOING?
NOWHERE.
WELCOME TO PRAIRIE ROSE

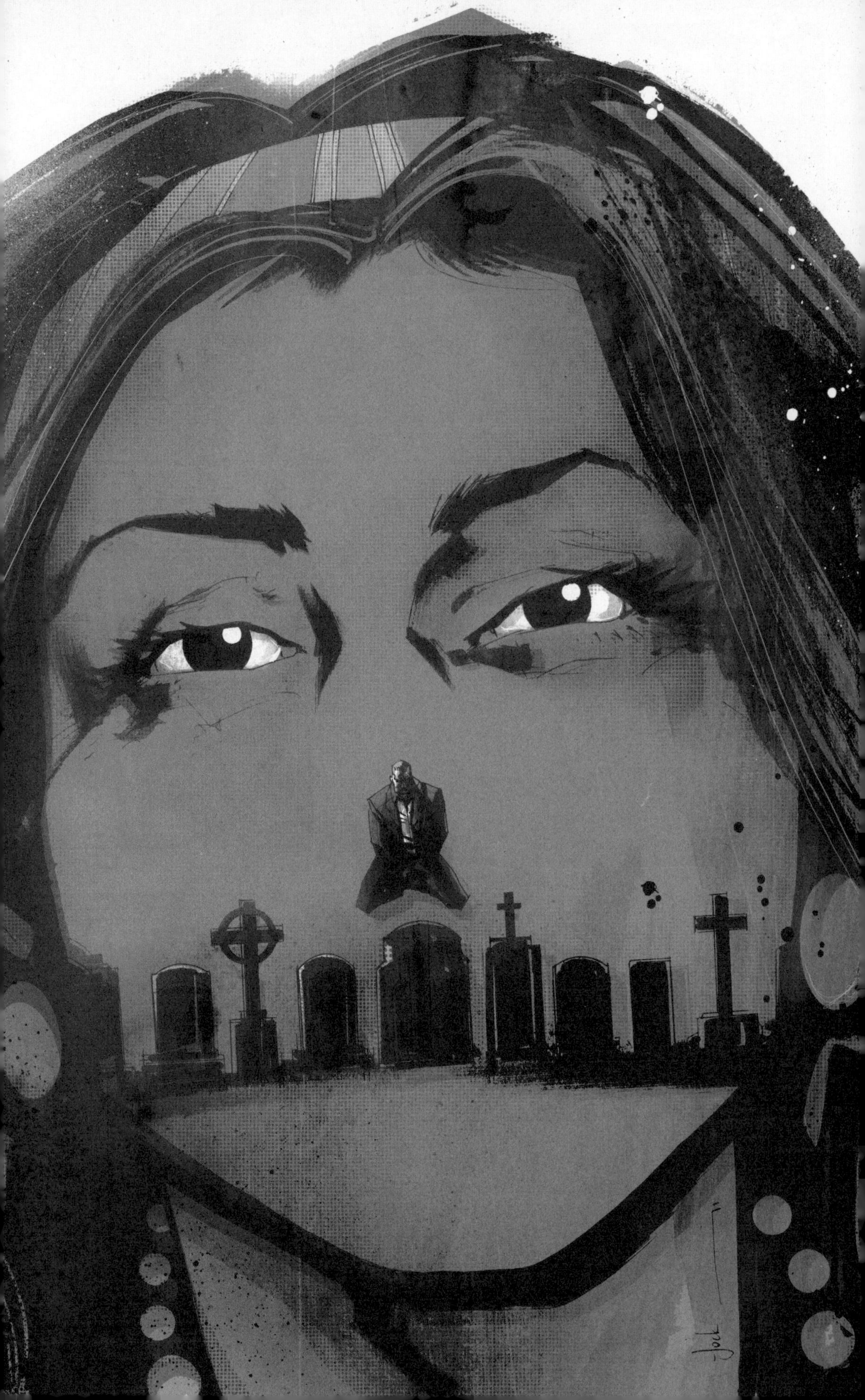

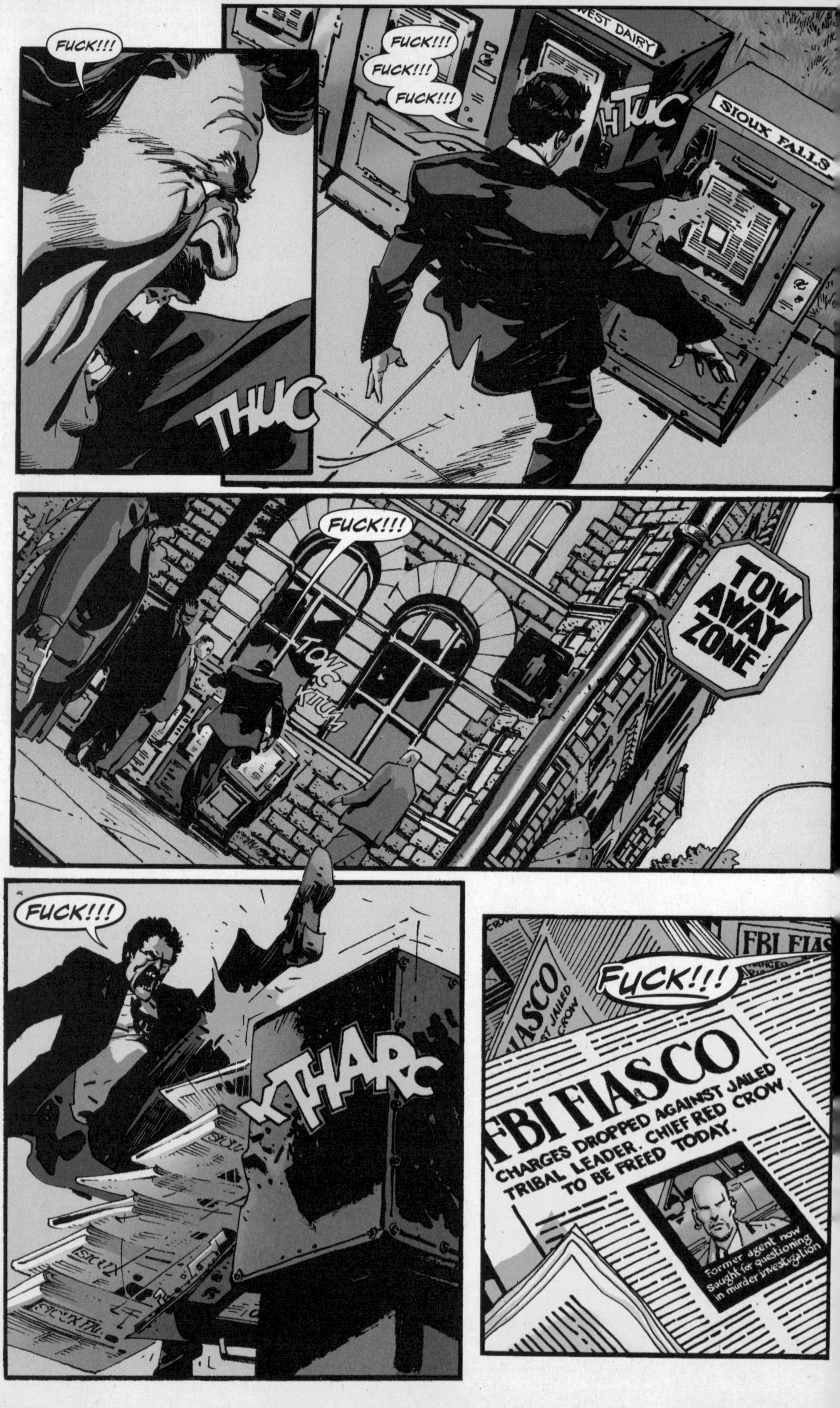
FUCK!!!
THUC
FUCK!!!
FUCK!!!
FUCK!!!
WEST DAIRY
HTUC
SIOUX FALLS
FUCK!!!
TOW AWAY ZONE
FUCK!!!
THARC
FUCK!!!
FBI FIASCO
CHARGES DROPPED AGAINST JAILED TRIBAL LEADER. CHIEF RED CROW TO BE FREED TODAY.
Former agent now sought for questioning in murder investigation

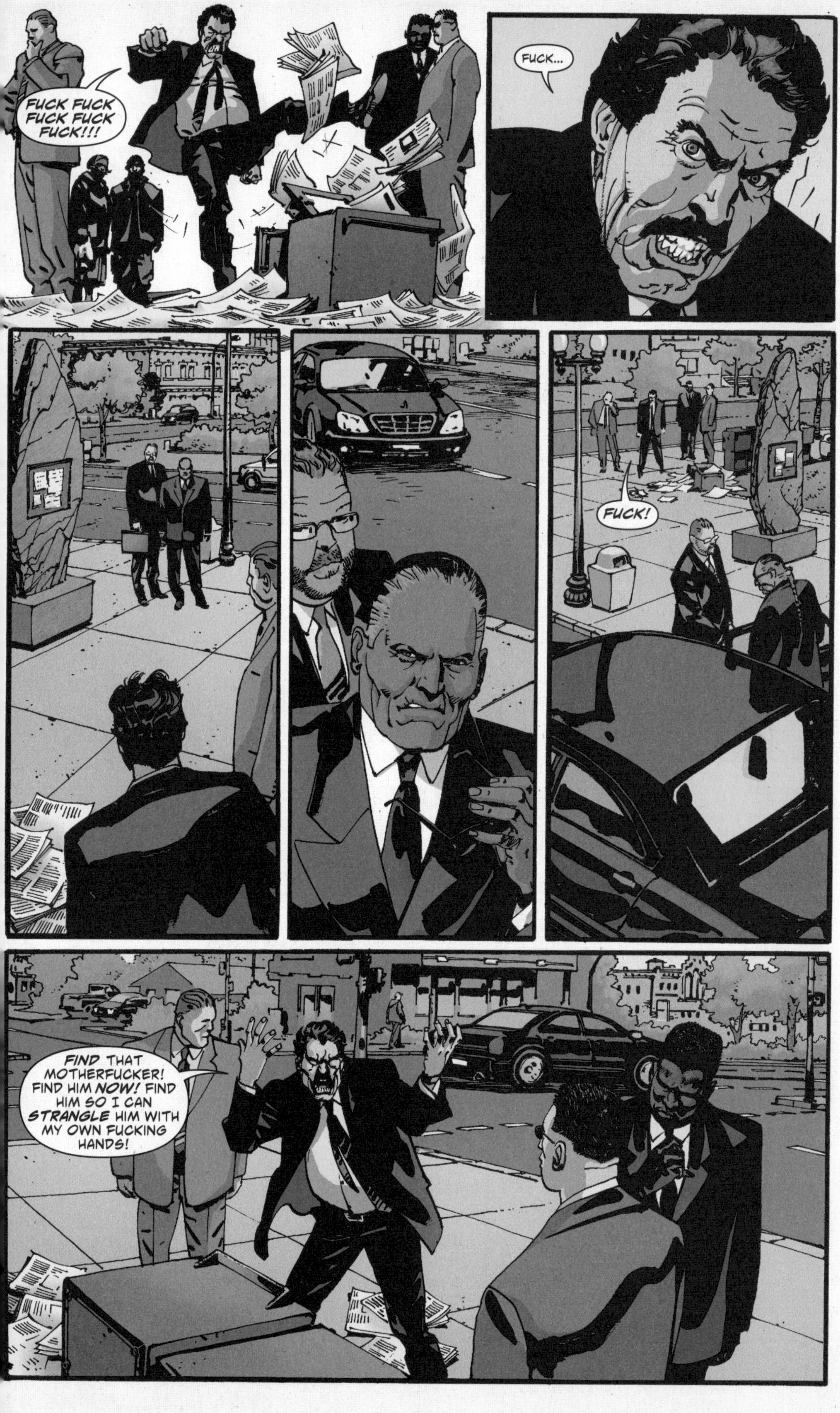
FUCK FUCK FUCK FUCK FUCK!!!
FUCK...
FUCK!
FIND THAT MOTHERFUCKER! FIND HIM NOW! FIND HIM SO I CAN STRANGLE HIM WITH MY OWN FUCKING HANDS!

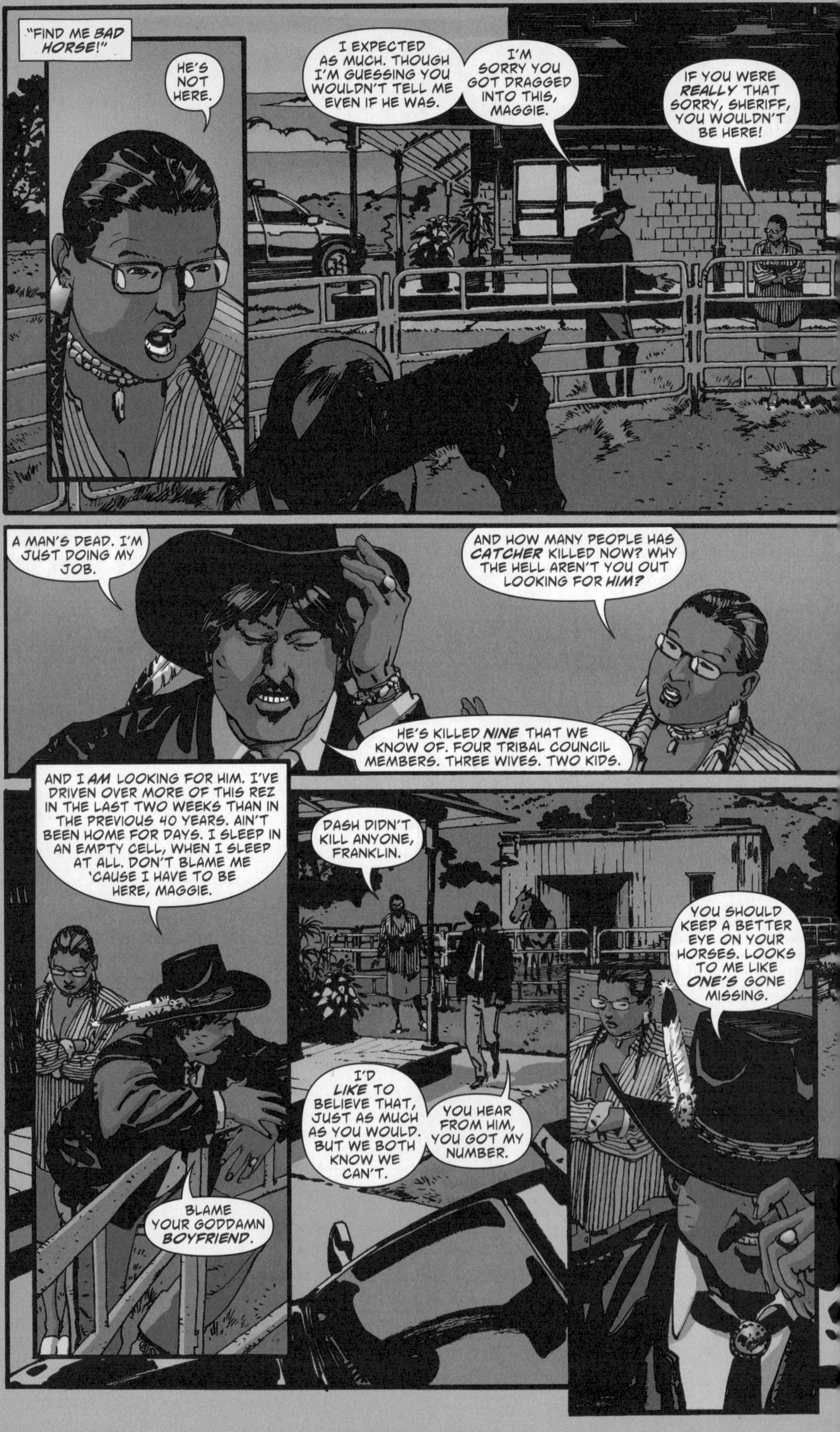
"FIND ME BAD HORSE!"
HE'S NOT HERE.
I EXPECTED AS MUCH. THOUGH I'M GUESSING YOU WOULDN'T TELL ME EVEN IF HE WAS.
I'M SORRY YOU GOT DRAGGED INTO THIS, MAGGIE.
IF YOU WERE REALLY THAT SORRY, SHERIFF, YOU WOULDN'T BE HERE!
A MAN'S DEAD. I'M JUST DOING MY JOB.
AND HOW MANY PEOPLE HAS CATCHER KILLED NOW? WHY THE HELL AREN'T YOU OUT LOOKING FOR HIM?
HE'S KILLED NINE THAT WE KNOW OF. FOUR TRIBAL COUNCIL MEMBERS. THREE WIVES. TWO KIDS.
AND I AM LOOKING FOR HIM. I'VE DRIVEN OVER MORE OF THIS REZ IN THE LAST TWO WEEKS THAN IN THE PREVIOUS 40 YEARS. AIN'T BEEN HOME FOR DAYS. I SLEEP IN AN EMPTY CELL, WHEN I SLEEP AT ALL. DON'T BLAME ME 'CAUSE I HAVE TO BE HERE, MAGGIE.
BLAME YOUR GODDAMN BOYFRIEND.
DASH DIDN'T KILL ANYONE, FRANKLIN.
I'D LIKE TO BELIEVE THAT, JUST AS MUCH AS YOU WOULD. BUT WE BOTH KNOW WE CAN'T.
YOU HEAR FROM HIM, YOU GOT MY NUMBER.
YOU SHOULD KEEP A BETTER EYE ON YOUR HORSES. LOOKS TO ME LIKE ONE'S GONE MISSING.

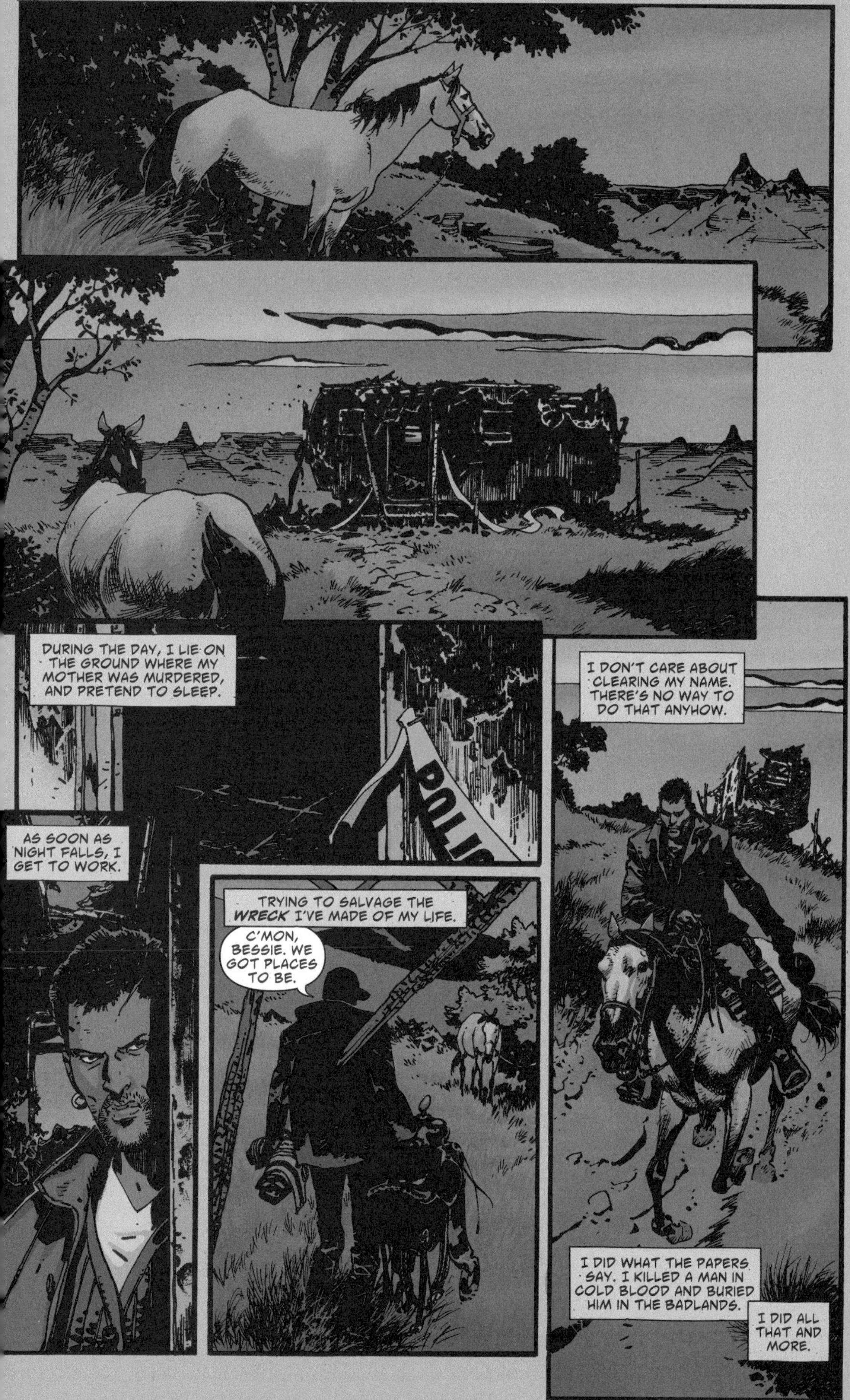

DURING THE DAY, I LIE ON THE GROUND WHERE MY MOTHER WAS MURDERED, AND PRETEND TO SLEEP.
POLI
AS SOON AS NIGHT FALLS, I GET TO WORK.
TRYING TO SALVAGE THE *WRECK* I'VE MADE OF MY LIFE.
C'MON, BESSIE. WE GOT PLACES TO BE.
I DON'T CARE ABOUT CLEARING MY NAME. THERE'S NO WAY TO DO THAT ANYHOW.
I DID WHAT THE PAPERS SAY. I KILLED A MAN IN COLD BLOOD AND BURIED HIM IN THE BADLANDS.
I DID ALL THAT AND MORE.

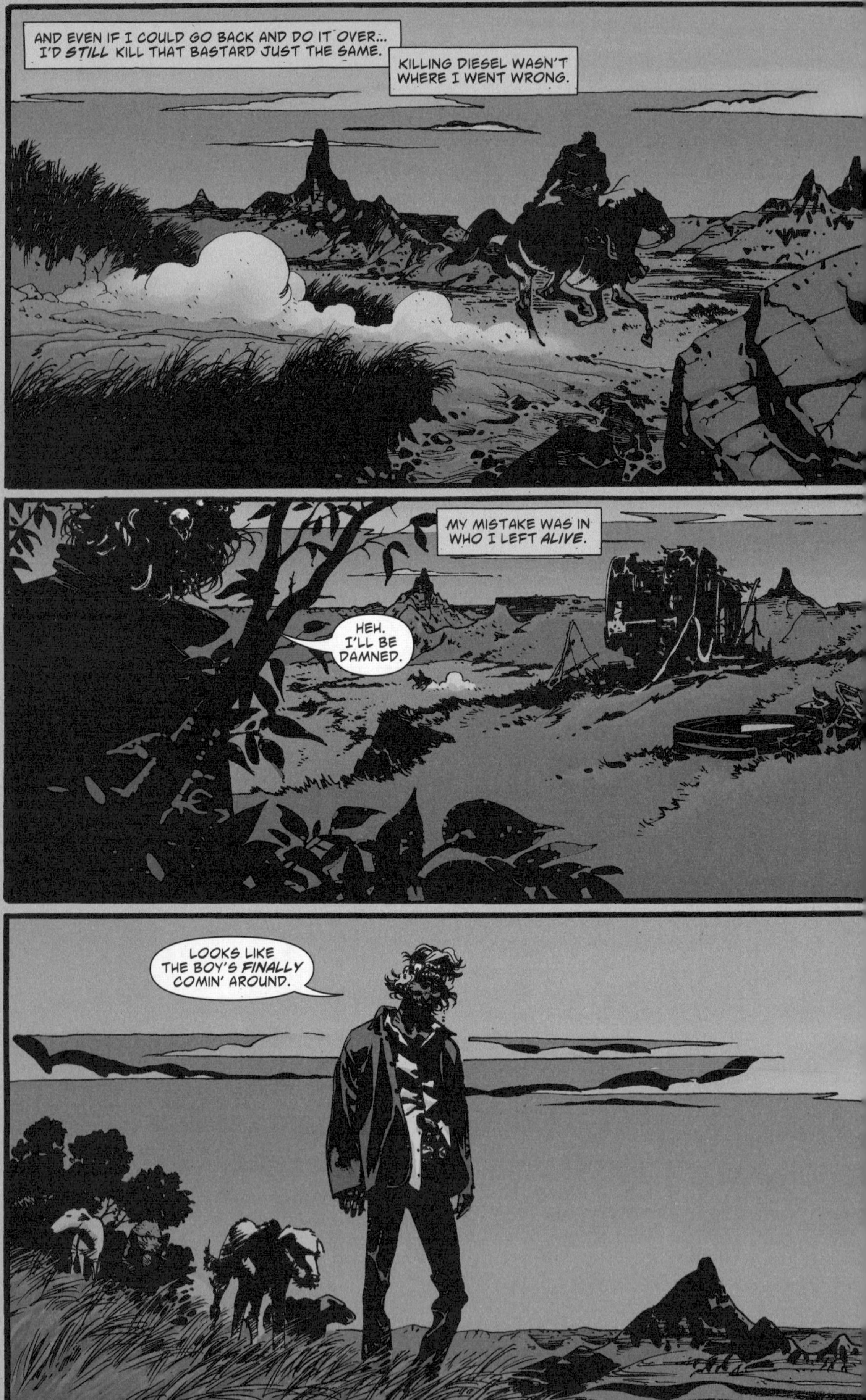
AND EVEN IF I COULD GO BACK AND DO IT OVER... I'D STILL KILL THAT BASTARD JUST THE SAME.
KILLING DIESEL WASN'T WHERE I WENT WRONG.
MY MISTAKE WAS IN WHO I LEFT ALIVE.
HEH. I'LL BE DAMNED.
LOOKS LIKE THE BOY'S FINALLY COMIN' AROUND.

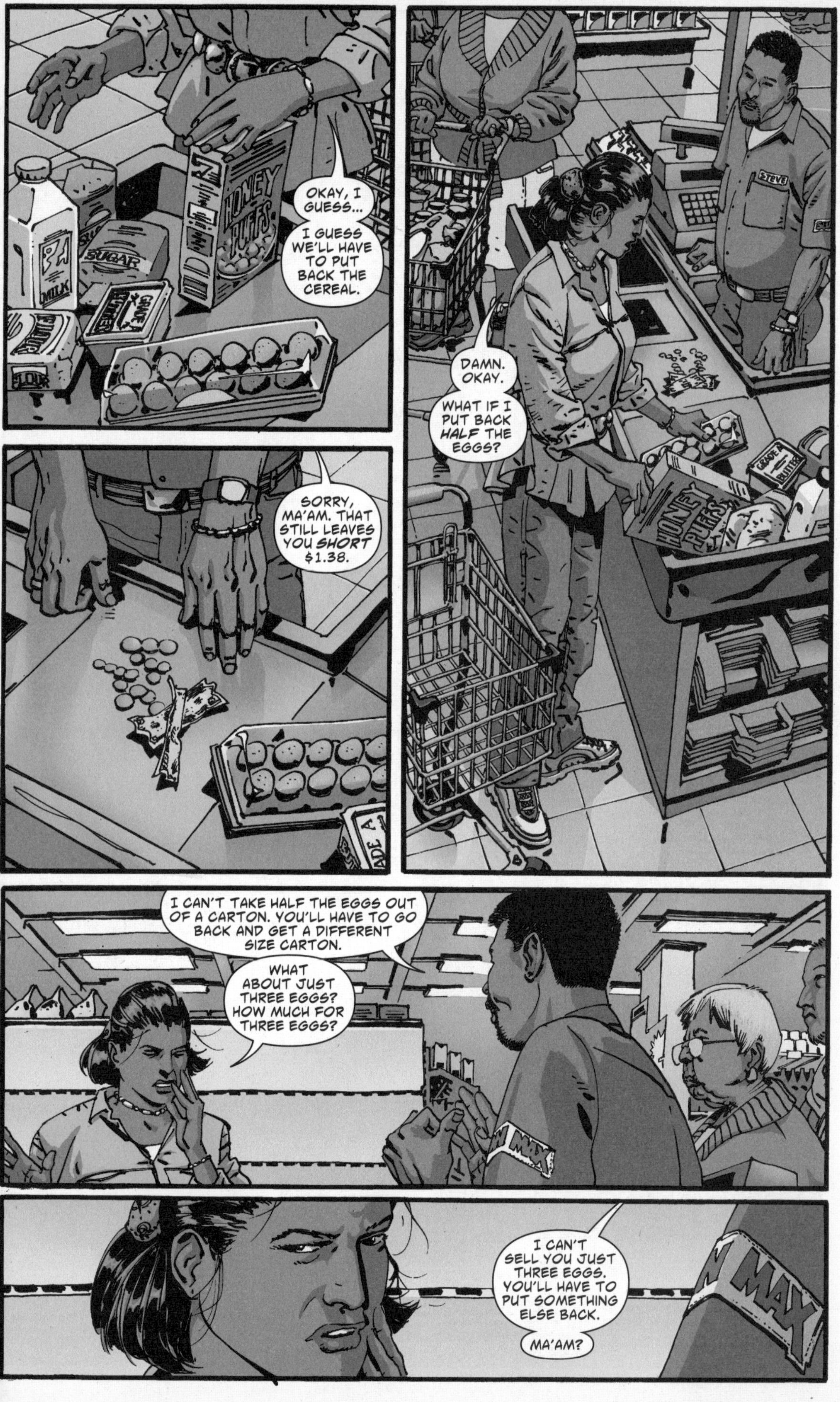
OKAY, I GUESS...
I GUESS WE'LL HAVE TO PUT BACK THE CEREAL.
HONEY PUFFS
SUGAR
MILK
FLOUR
DAMN. OKAY.
WHAT IF I PUT BACK *HALF* THE EGGS?
STEVE
SORRY, MA'AM. THAT STILL LEAVES YOU *SHORT* $1.38.
I CAN'T TAKE HALF THE EGGS OUT OF A CARTON. YOU'LL HAVE TO GO BACK AND GET A DIFFERENT SIZE CARTON.
WHAT ABOUT JUST THREE EGGS? HOW MUCH FOR THREE EGGS?
I CAN'T SELL YOU JUST THREE EGGS. YOU'LL HAVE TO PUT SOMETHING ELSE BACK.
MA'AM?
MAX

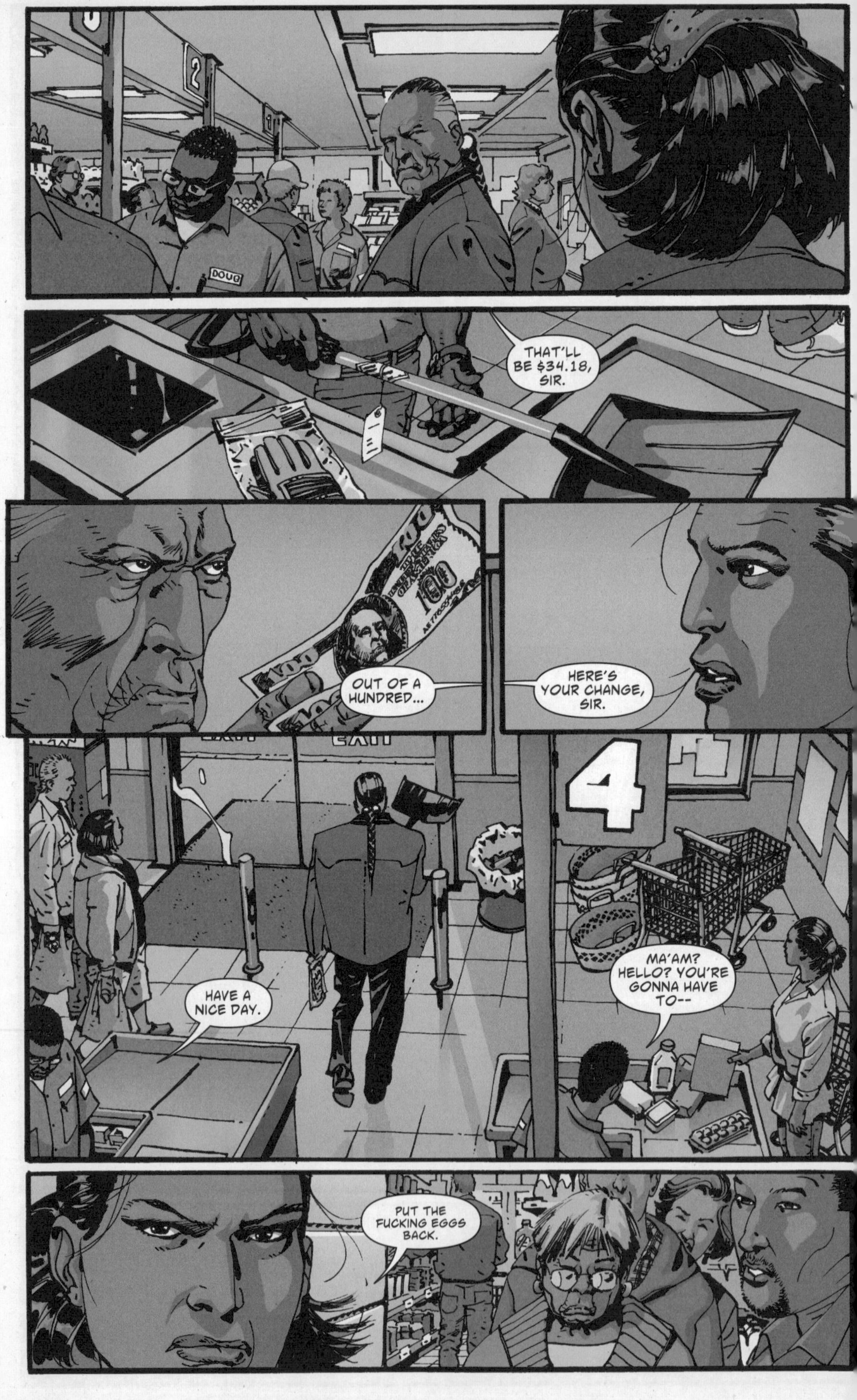
DOUG
THAT'LL BE $34.18, SIR.
OUT OF A HUNDRED...
HERE'S YOUR CHANGE, SIR.
EXIT
EXIT
4
HAVE A NICE DAY.
MA'AM? HELLO? YOU'RE GONNA HAVE TO--
PUT THE FUCKING EGGS BACK.

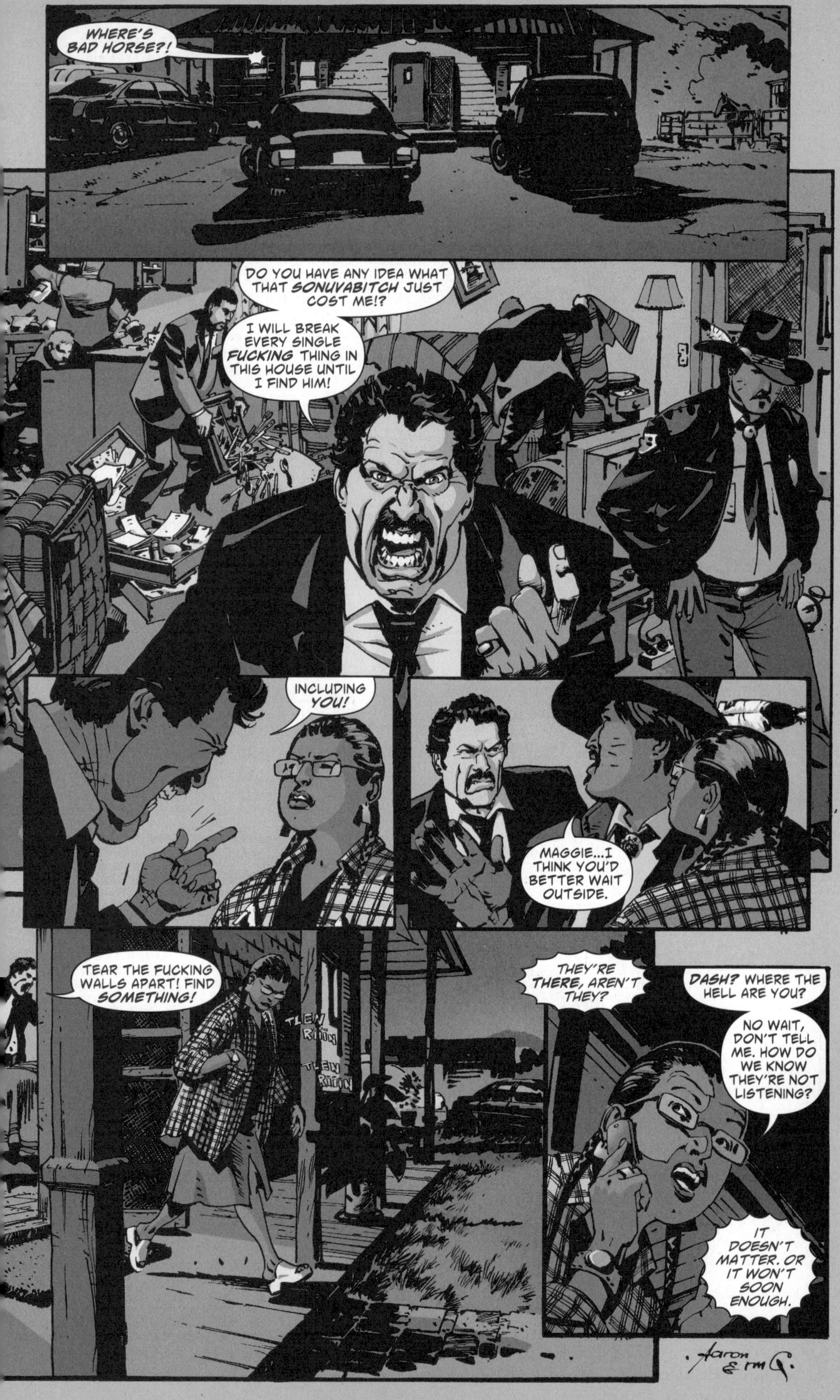
WHERE'S BAD HORSE?!
DO YOU HAVE ANY IDEA WHAT THAT *SONUVABITCH* JUST COST ME!?
I WILL BREAK EVERY SINGLE *FUCKING* THING IN THIS HOUSE UNTIL I FIND HIM!
INCLUDING *YOU!*
MAGGIE...I THINK YOU'D BETTER WAIT OUTSIDE.
TEAR THE FUCKING WALLS APART! FIND *SOMETHING!*
TLEEN RIIIN
TLEEN RIIIN
THEY'RE *THERE,* AREN'T THEY?
DASH? WHERE THE HELL ARE YOU?
NO WAIT, DON'T TELL ME. HOW DO WE KNOW THEY'RE NOT LISTENING?
IT DOESN'T MATTER. OR IT WON'T SOON ENOUGH.
Aaron & RM G.

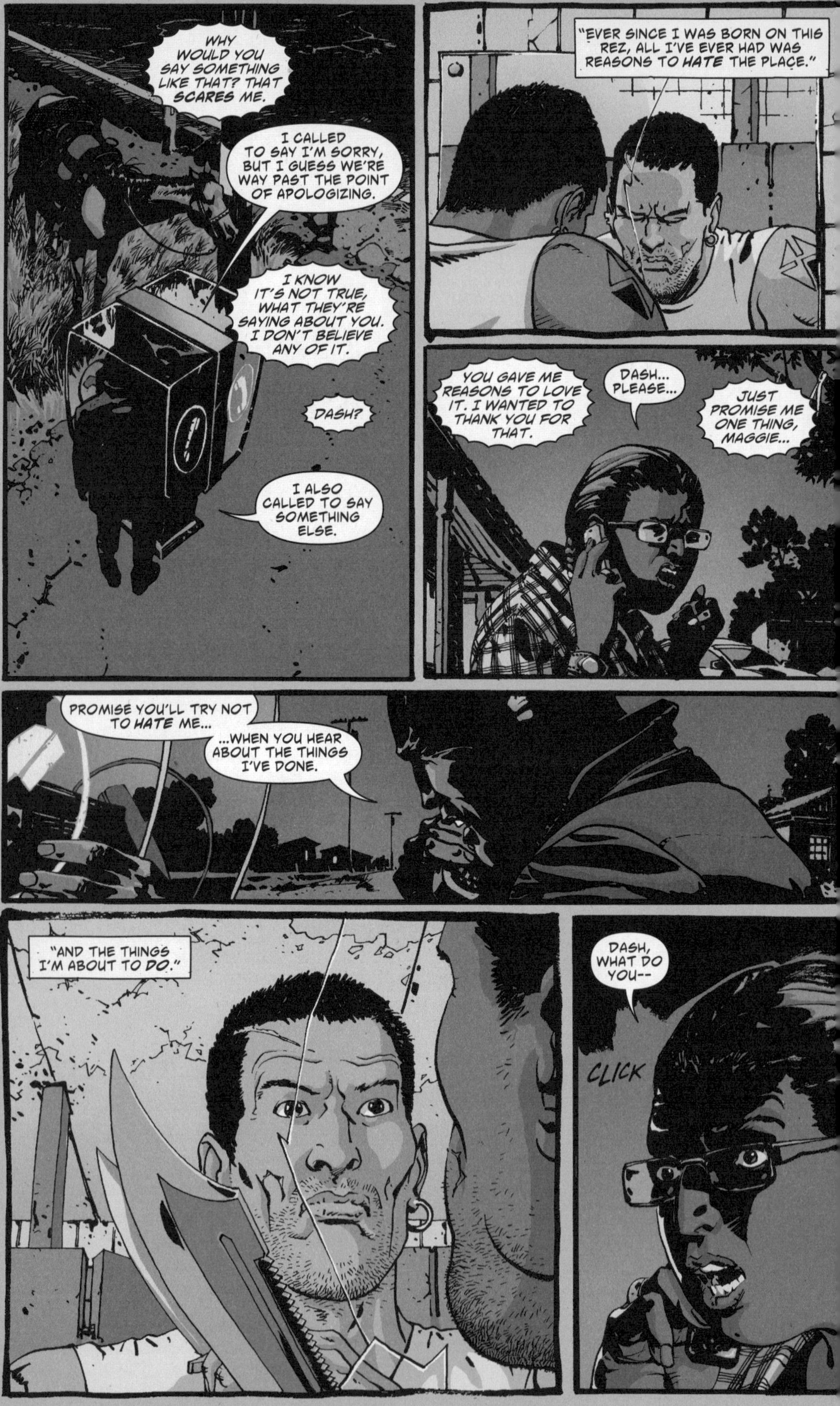
WHY WOULD YOU SAY SOMETHING LIKE THAT? THAT SCARES ME.
I CALLED TO SAY I'M SORRY, BUT I GUESS WE'RE WAY PAST THE POINT OF APOLOGIZING.
I KNOW IT'S NOT TRUE, WHAT THEY'RE SAYING ABOUT YOU. I DON'T BELIEVE ANY OF IT.
DASH?
I ALSO CALLED TO SAY SOMETHING ELSE.
"EVER SINCE I WAS BORN ON THIS REZ, ALL I'VE EVER HAD WAS REASONS TO HATE THE PLACE."
YOU GAVE ME REASONS TO LOVE IT. I WANTED TO THANK YOU FOR THAT.
DASH... PLEASE...
JUST PROMISE ME ONE THING, MAGGIE...
PROMISE YOU'LL TRY NOT TO HATE ME...
...WHEN YOU HEAR ABOUT THE THINGS I'VE DONE.
"AND THE THINGS I'M ABOUT TO DO."
DASH, WHAT DO YOU--
CLICK

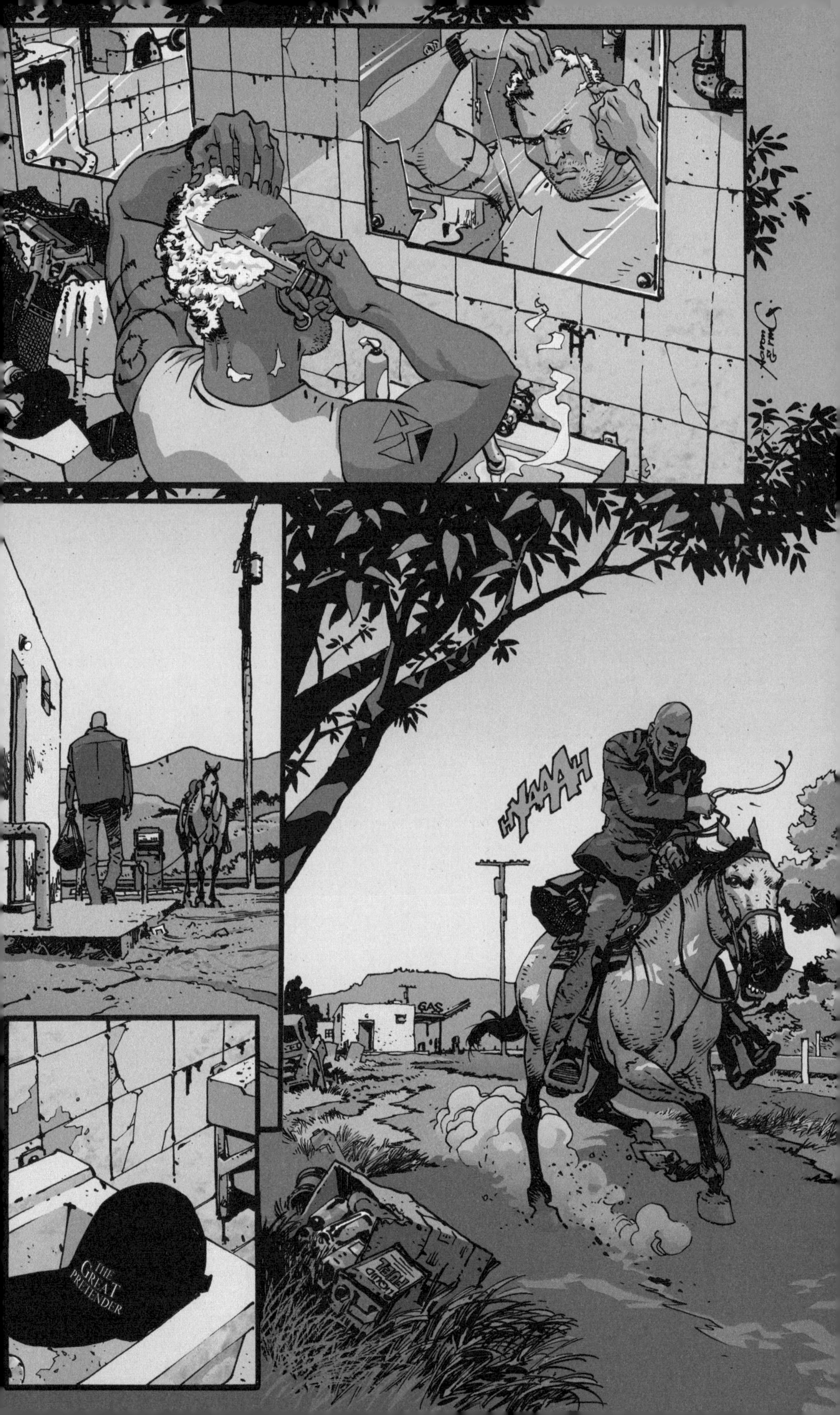
THE GREAT PRETENDER
GAS
HYAAAH
LIQUID FUEL

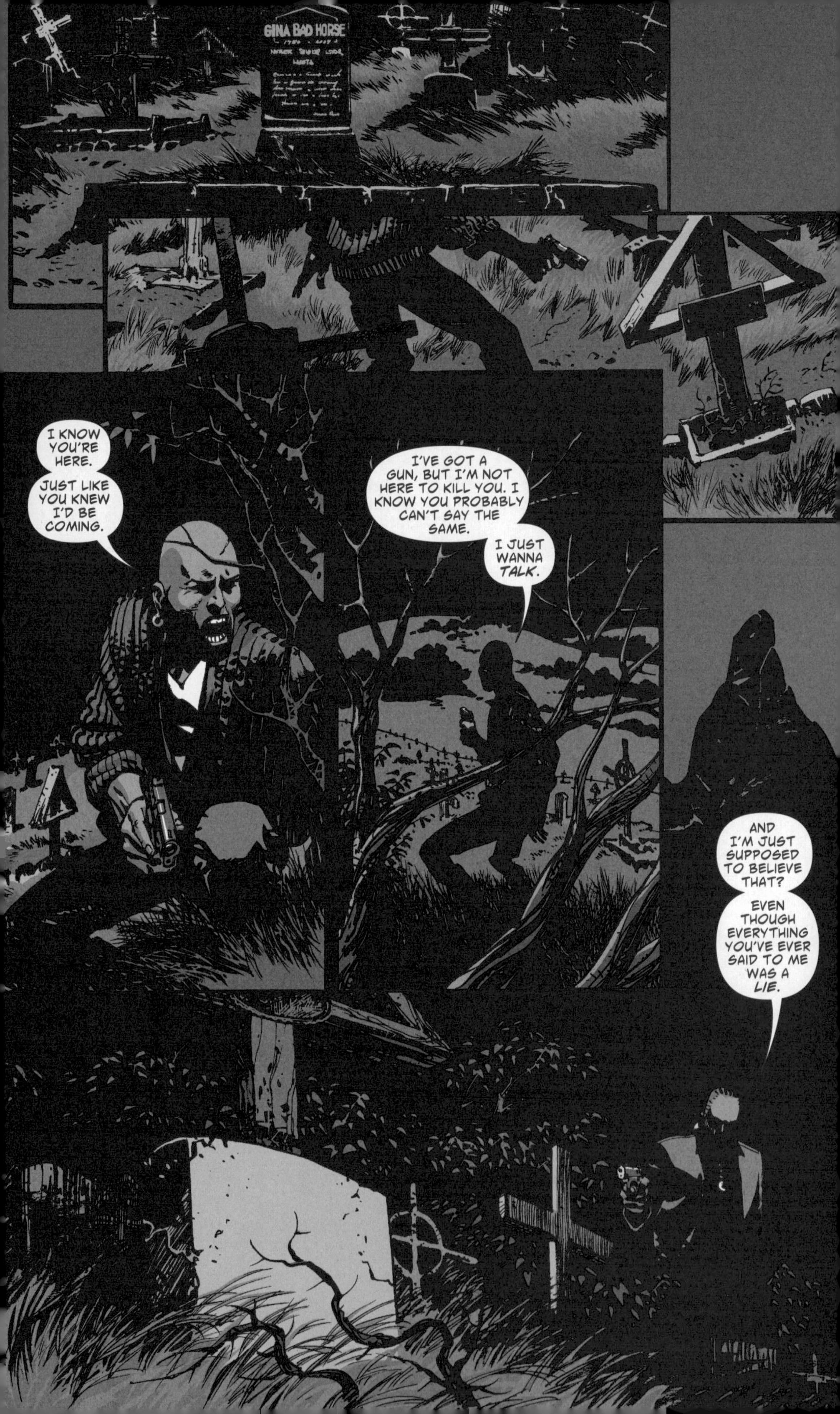
GINA BAD HORSE
I KNOW YOU'RE HERE.
JUST LIKE YOU KNEW I'D BE COMING.
I'VE GOT A GUN, BUT I'M NOT HERE TO KILL YOU. I KNOW YOU PROBABLY CAN'T SAY THE SAME.
I JUST WANNA *TALK*.
AND I'M JUST SUPPOSED TO BELIEVE THAT?
EVEN THOUGH EVERYTHING YOU'VE EVER SAID TO ME WAS A *LIE*.

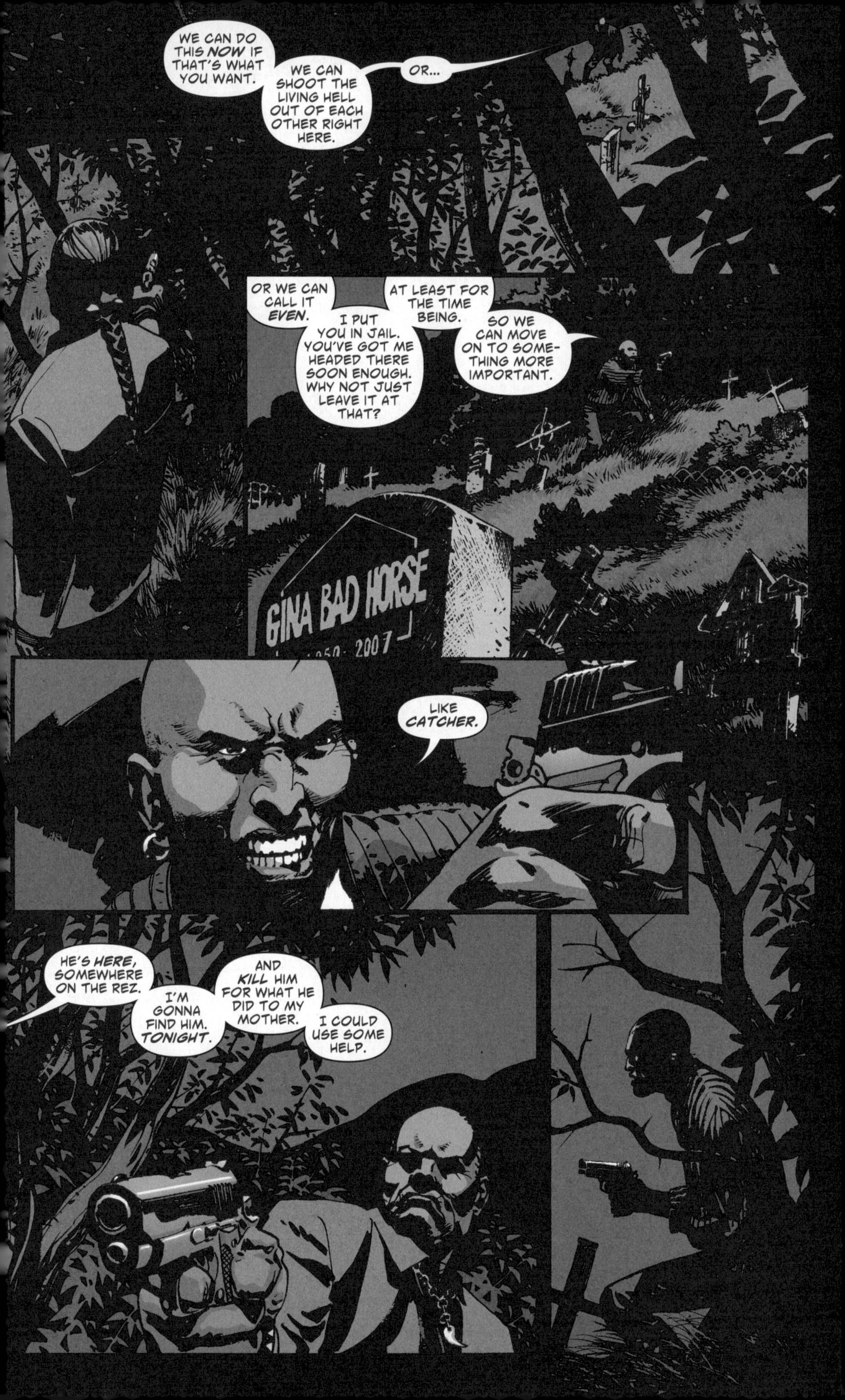

WE CAN DO THIS NOW IF THAT'S WHAT YOU WANT.
WE CAN SHOOT THE LIVING HELL OUT OF EACH OTHER RIGHT HERE.
OR...
OR WE CAN CALL IT EVEN.
I PUT YOU IN JAIL. YOU'VE GOT ME HEADED THERE SOON ENOUGH. WHY NOT JUST LEAVE IT AT THAT?
AT LEAST FOR THE TIME BEING.
SO WE CAN MOVE ON TO SOMETHING MORE IMPORTANT.
GINA BAD HORSE
LIKE CATCHER.
HE'S HERE, SOMEWHERE ON THE REZ.
I'M GONNA FIND HIM. TONIGHT.
AND KILL HIM FOR WHAT HE DID TO MY MOTHER.
I COULD USE SOME HELP.

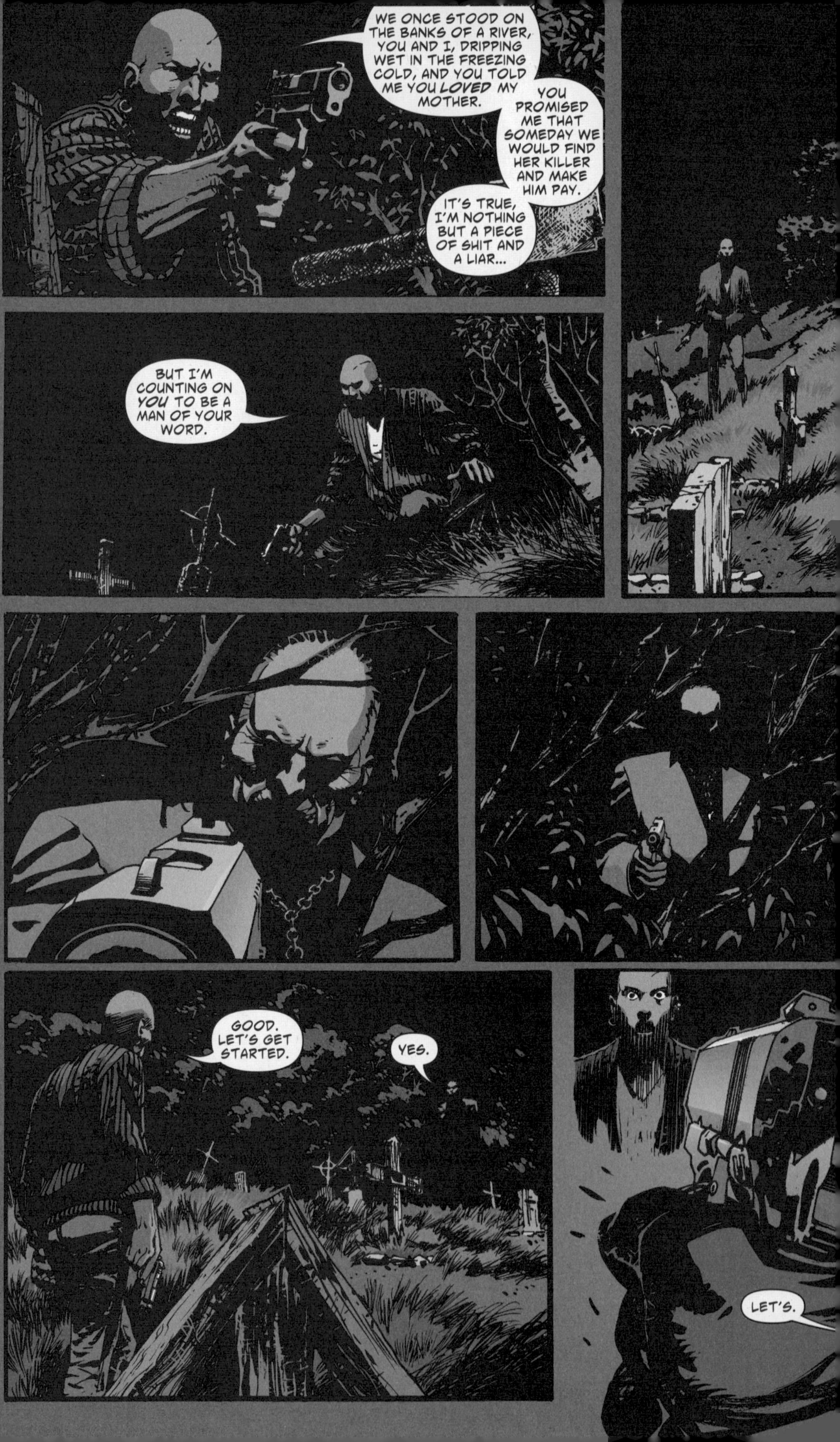
WE ONCE STOOD ON THE BANKS OF A RIVER, YOU AND I, DRIPPING WET IN THE FREEZING COLD, AND YOU TOLD ME YOU *LOVED* MY MOTHER.
YOU PROMISED ME THAT SOMEDAY WE WOULD FIND HER KILLER AND MAKE HIM PAY.
IT'S TRUE, I'M NOTHING BUT A PIECE OF SHIT AND A LIAR...
BUT I'M COUNTING ON *YOU* TO BE A MAN OF YOUR WORD.
GOOD. LET'S GET STARTED.
YES.
LET'S.

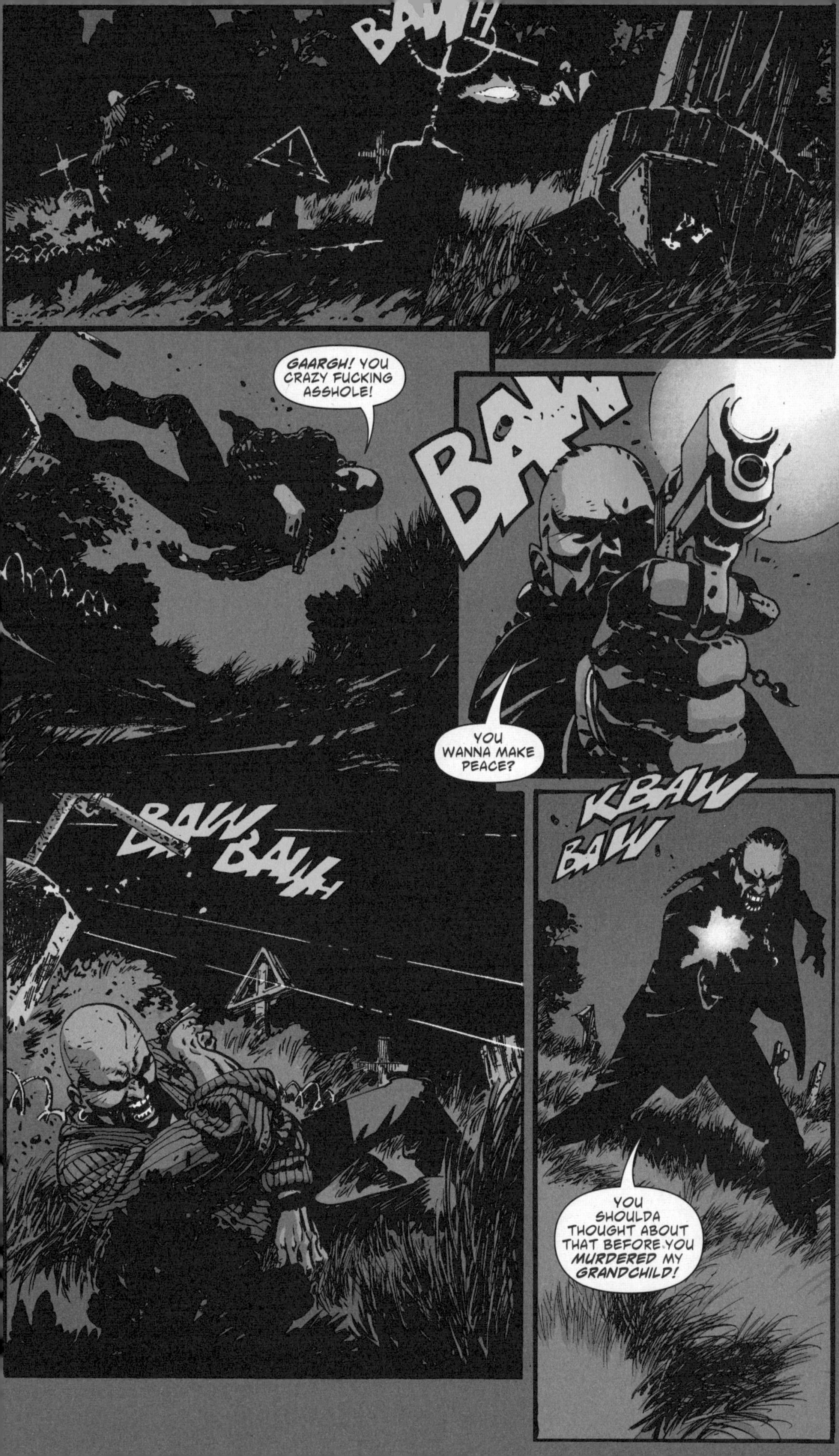
BAWH
GAARGH! YOU CRAZY FUCKING ASSHOLE!
BAW
YOU WANNA MAKE PEACE?
BAW BAWH
KBAW
BAW
YOU SHOULDA THOUGHT ABOUT THAT BEFORE YOU MURDERED MY GRANDCHILD!

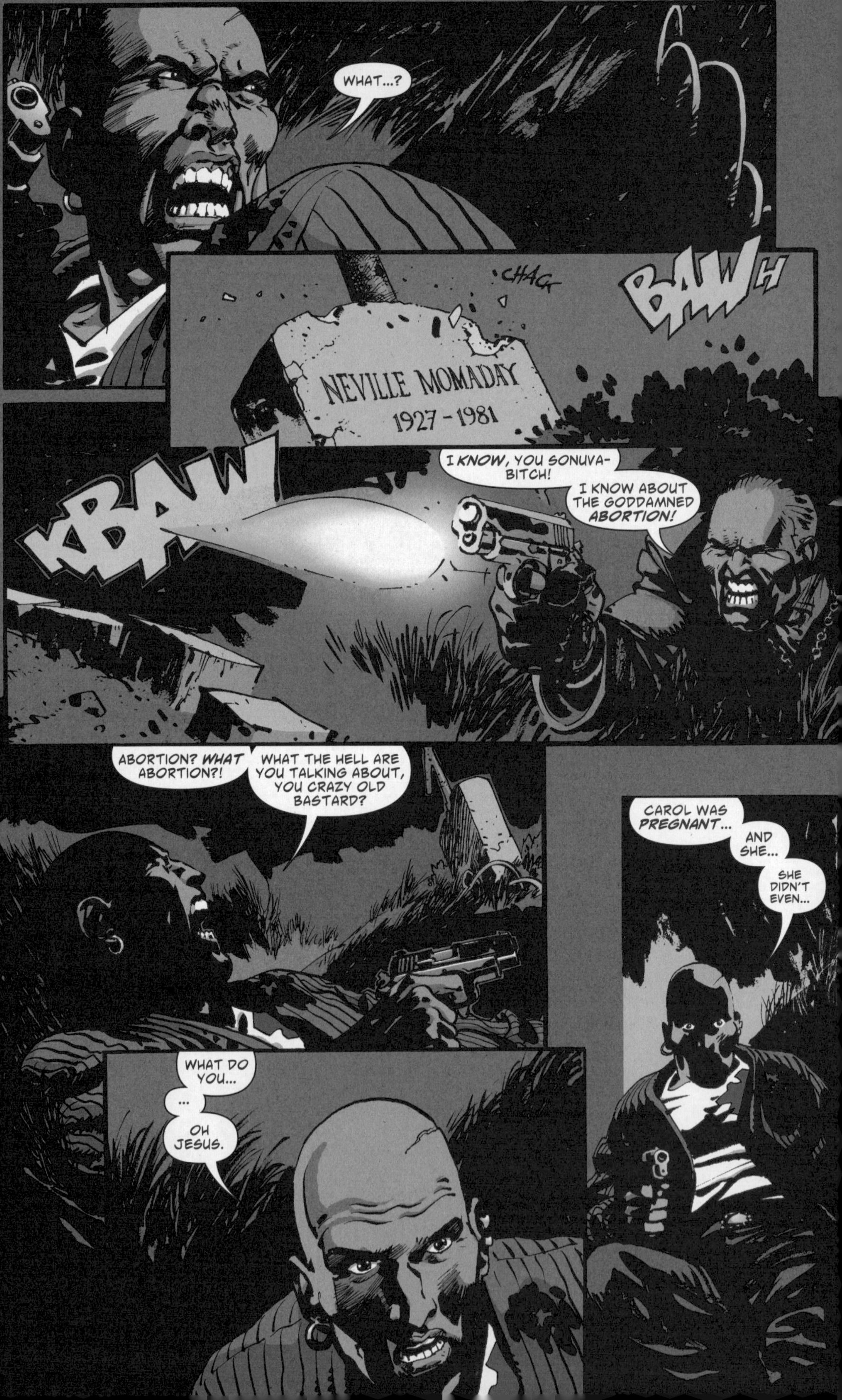

WHAT...?
CHACK
BAWH
NEVILLE MOMADAY
1927 - 1981
KBAW
I KNOW, YOU SONUVA-BITCH!
I KNOW ABOUT THE GODDAMNED ABORTION!
ABORTION? WHAT ABORTION?!
WHAT THE HELL ARE YOU TALKING ABOUT, YOU CRAZY OLD BASTARD?
CAROL WAS PREGNANT...
AND SHE...
SHE DIDN'T EVEN...
WHAT DO YOU...
...
OH JESUS.

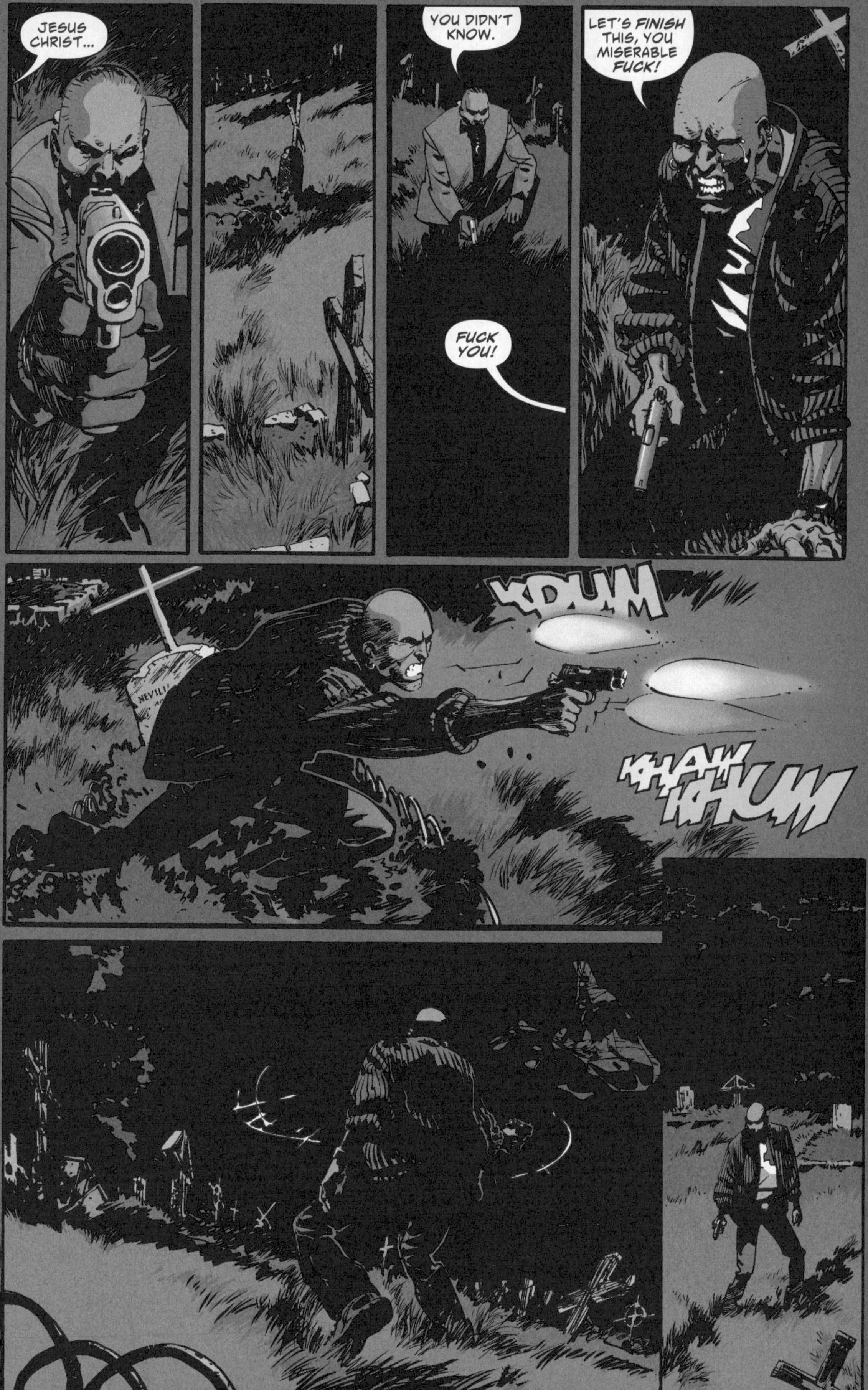
JESUS CHRIST...
YOU DIDN'T KNOW.
FUCK YOU!
LET'S FINISH THIS, YOU MISERABLE FUCK!
KDUM
KHAW KHUM

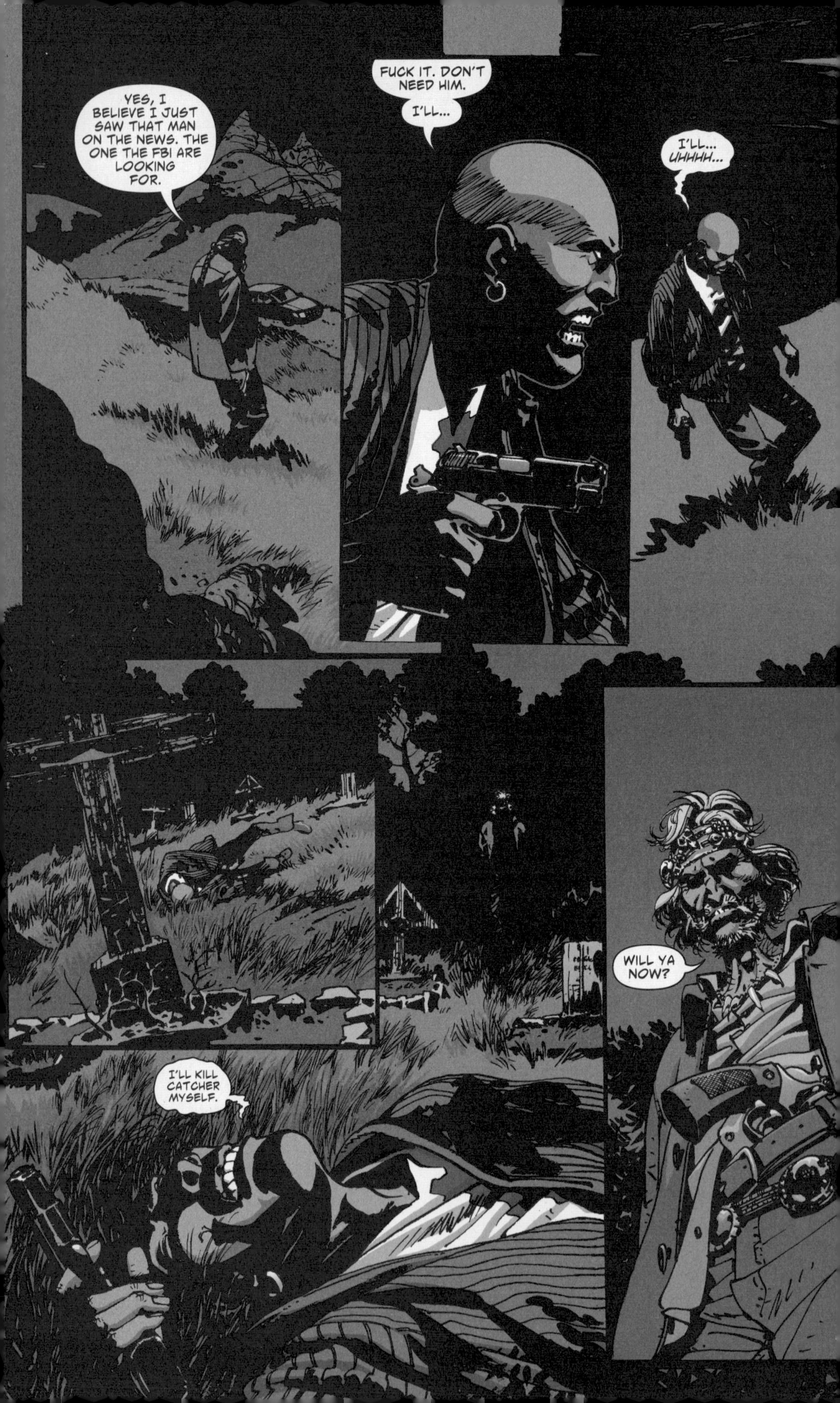
YES, I BELIEVE I JUST SAW THAT MAN ON THE NEWS. THE ONE THE FBI ARE LOOKING FOR.
FUCK IT. DON'T NEED HIM.
I'LL...
I'LL... UHHHH...
I'LL KILL CATCHER MYSELF.
WILL YA NOW?

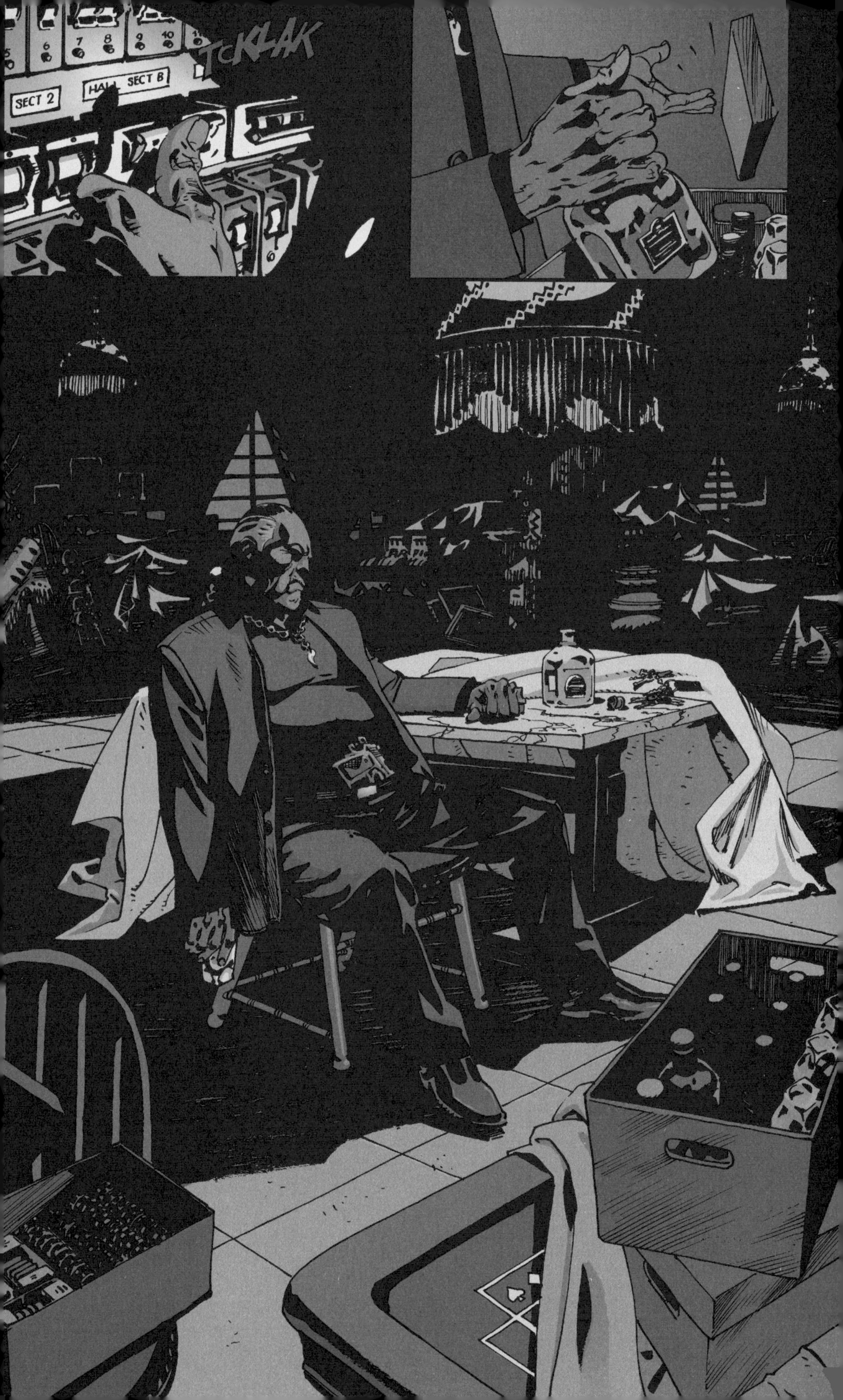
TCKLAK
SECT 2
HALL SECT B

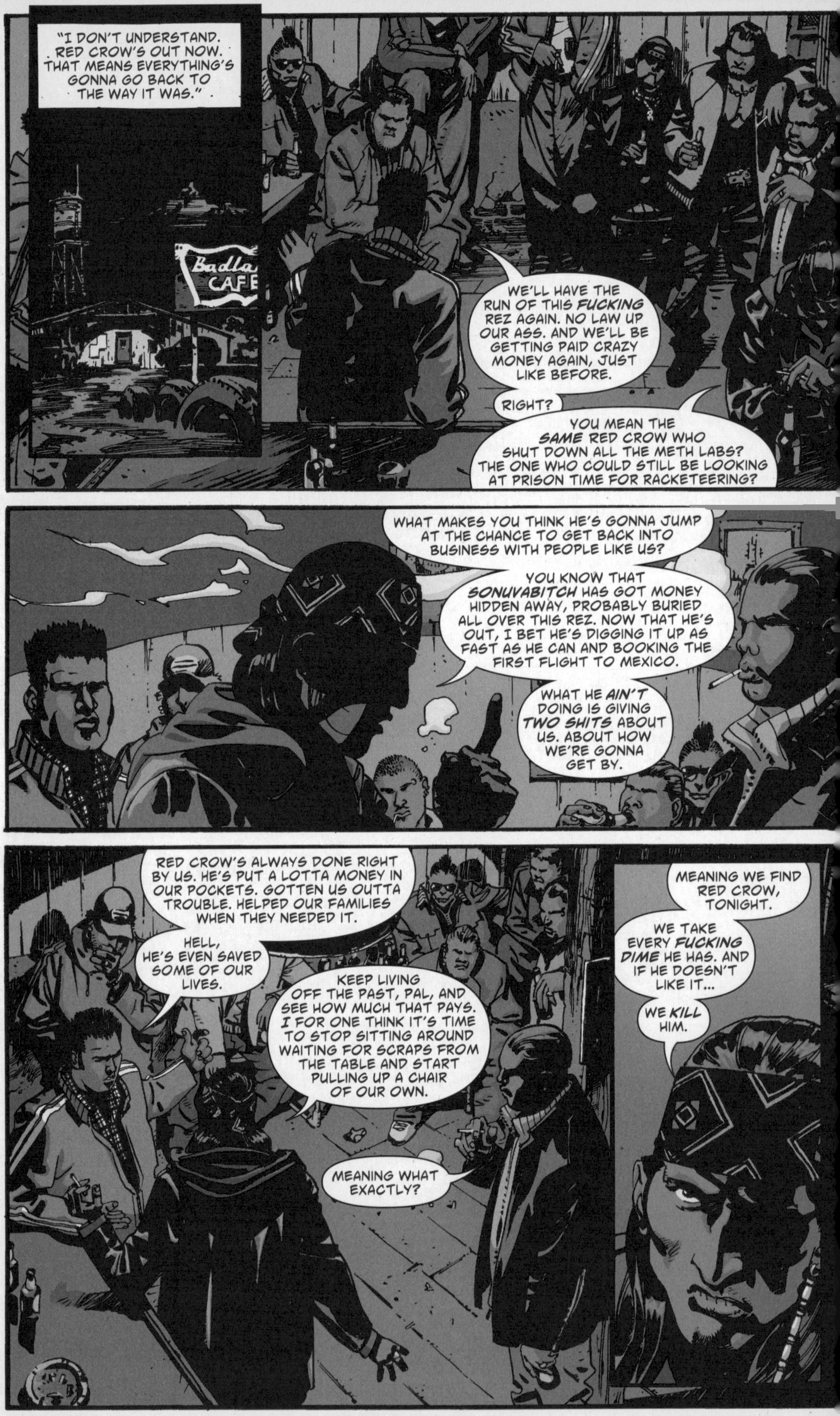
"I DON'T UNDERSTAND. RED CROW'S OUT NOW. THAT MEANS EVERYTHING'S GONNA GO BACK TO THE WAY IT WAS."
Badlands CAFE
WE'LL HAVE THE RUN OF THIS FUCKING REZ AGAIN. NO LAW UP OUR ASS. AND WE'LL BE GETTING PAID CRAZY MONEY AGAIN, JUST LIKE BEFORE.
RIGHT?
YOU MEAN THE SAME RED CROW WHO SHUT DOWN ALL THE METH LABS? THE ONE WHO COULD STILL BE LOOKING AT PRISON TIME FOR RACKETEERING?
WHAT MAKES YOU THINK HE'S GONNA JUMP AT THE CHANCE TO GET BACK INTO BUSINESS WITH PEOPLE LIKE US?
YOU KNOW THAT SONUVABITCH HAS GOT MONEY HIDDEN AWAY, PROBABLY BURIED ALL OVER THIS REZ. NOW THAT HE'S OUT, I BET HE'S DIGGING IT UP AS FAST AS HE CAN AND BOOKING THE FIRST FLIGHT TO MEXICO.
WHAT HE AIN'T DOING IS GIVING TWO SHITS ABOUT US. ABOUT HOW WE'RE GONNA GET BY.
RED CROW'S ALWAYS DONE RIGHT BY US. HE'S PUT A LOTTA MONEY IN OUR POCKETS. GOTTEN US OUTTA TROUBLE. HELPED OUR FAMILIES WHEN THEY NEEDED IT.
HELL, HE'S EVEN SAVED SOME OF OUR LIVES.
KEEP LIVING OFF THE PAST, PAL, AND SEE HOW MUCH THAT PAYS. I FOR ONE THINK IT'S TIME TO STOP SITTING AROUND WAITING FOR SCRAPS FROM THE TABLE AND START PULLING UP A CHAIR OF OUR OWN.
MEANING WHAT EXACTLY?
MEANING WE FIND RED CROW, TONIGHT.
WE TAKE EVERY FUCKING DIME HE HAS. AND IF HE DOESN'T LIKE IT...
WE KILL HIM.

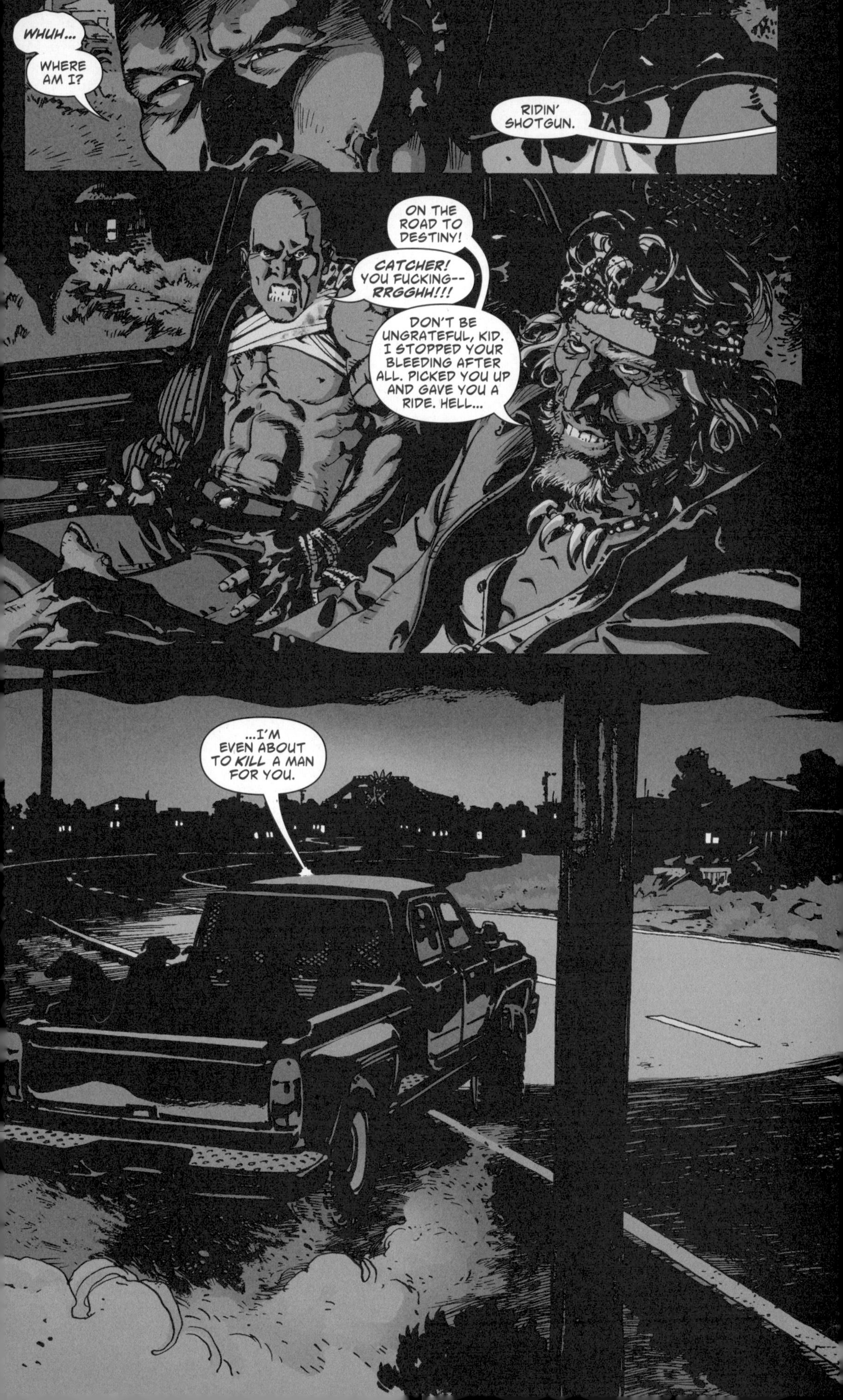
WHUH...
WHERE AM I?
RIDIN' SHOTGUN.
ON THE ROAD TO DESTINY!
CATCHER! YOU FUCKING-- RRGGHH!!!
DON'T BE UNGRATEFUL, KID. I STOPPED YOUR BLEEDING AFTER ALL. PICKED YOU UP AND GAVE YOU A RIDE. HELL...
...I'M EVEN ABOUT TO KILL A MAN FOR YOU.

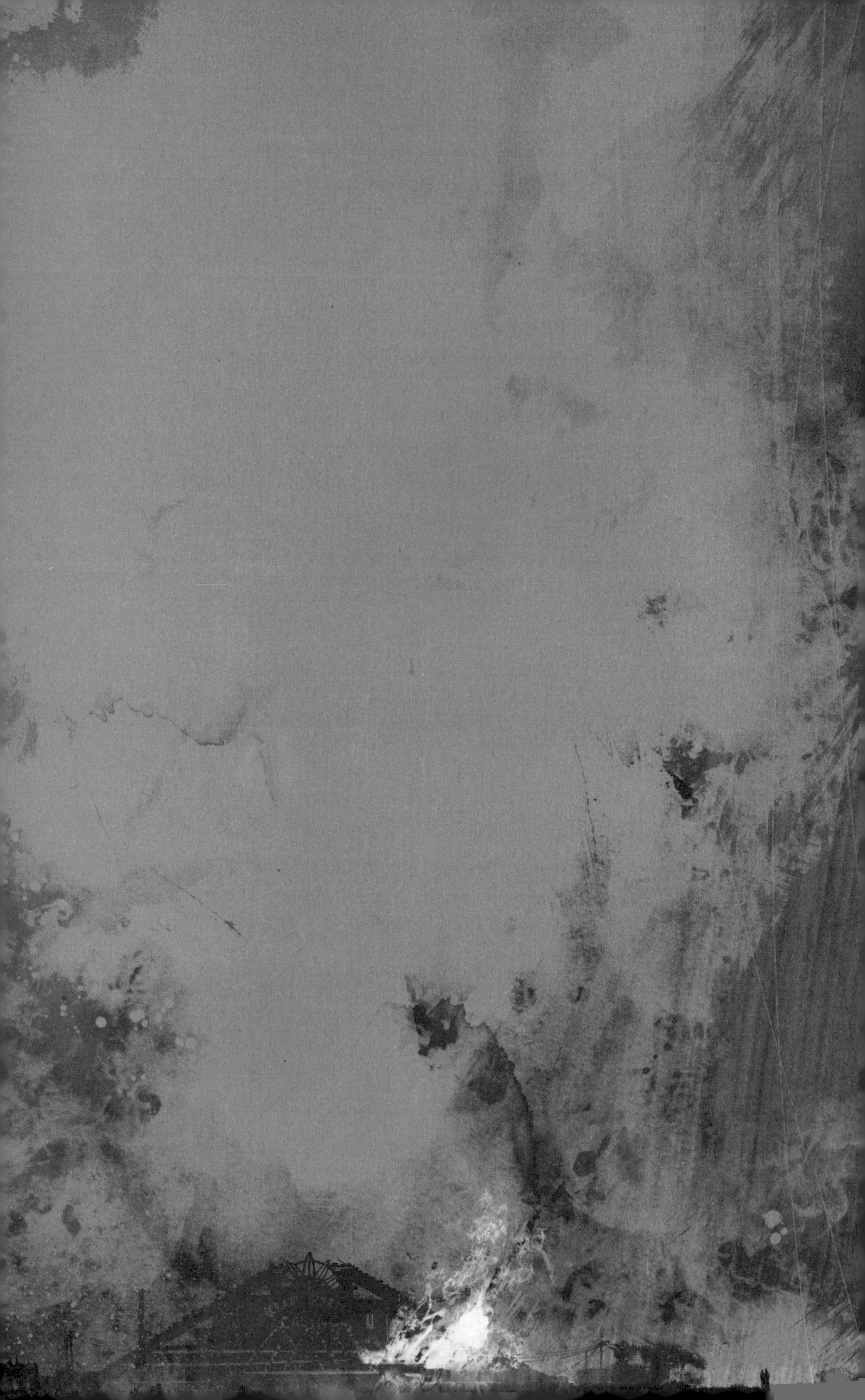

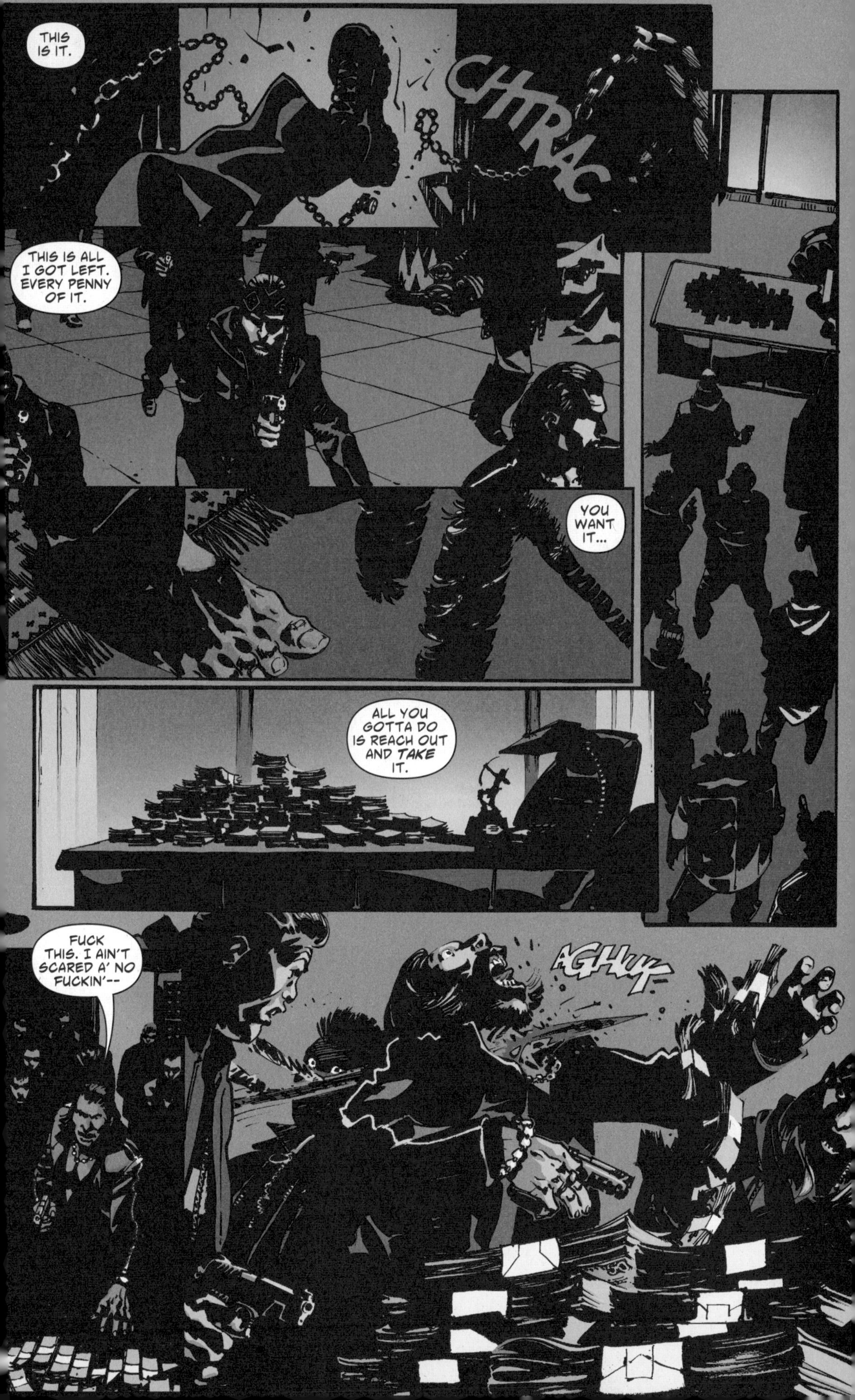
THIS IS IT.
CHTRAC
THIS IS ALL I GOT LEFT. EVERY PENNY OF IT.
YOU WANT IT...
ALL YOU GOTTA DO IS REACH OUT AND *TAKE* IT.
FUCK THIS. I AIN'T SCARED A' NO FUCKIN'--
AGHUK

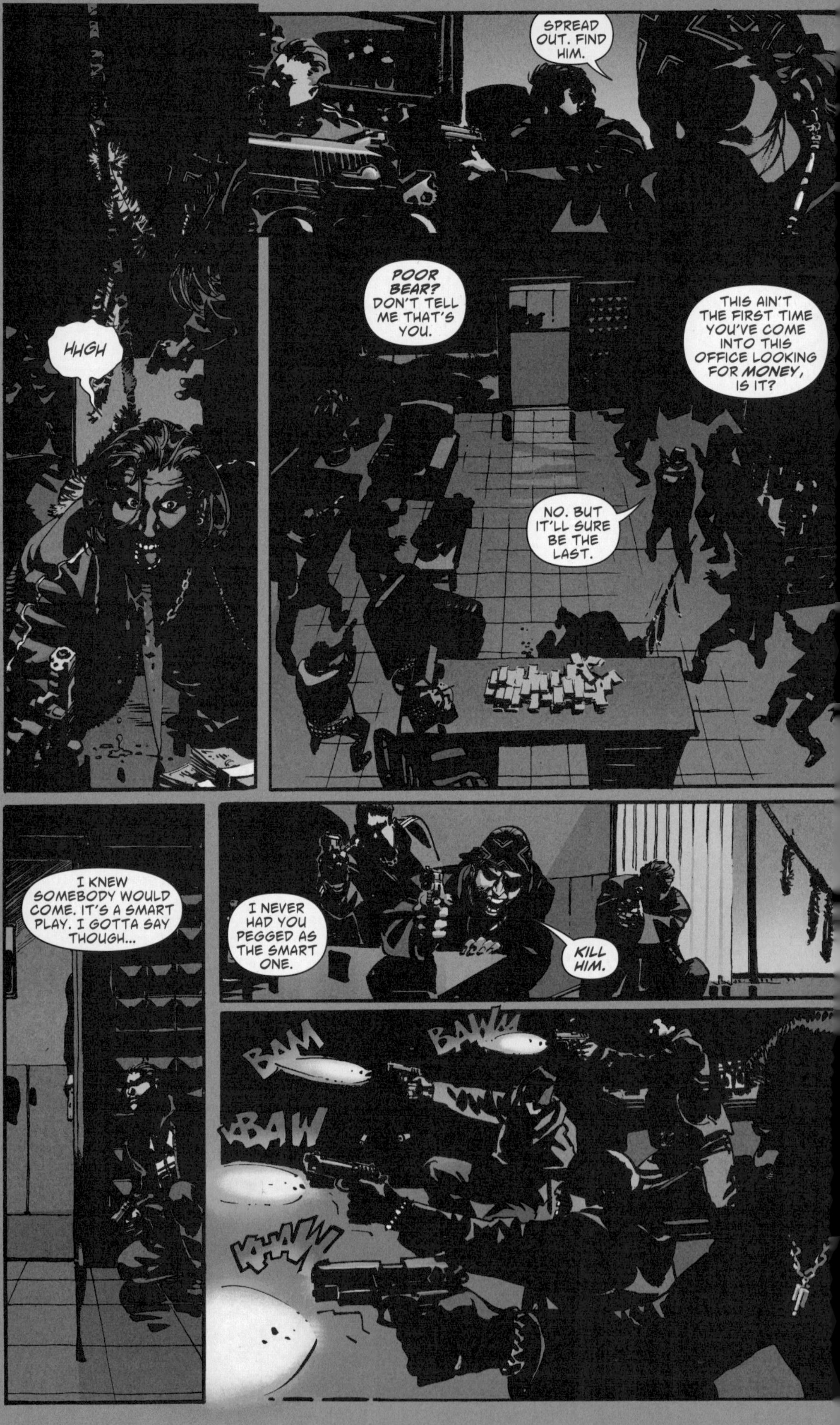

SPREAD OUT. FIND HIM.
HUGH
POOR BEAR? DON'T TELL ME THAT'S YOU.
THIS AIN'T THE FIRST TIME YOU'VE COME INTO THIS OFFICE LOOKING FOR *MONEY*, IS IT?
NO. BUT IT'LL SURE BE THE LAST.
I KNEW SOMEBODY WOULD COME. IT'S A SMART PLAY. I GOTTA SAY THOUGH...
I NEVER HAD YOU PEGGED AS THE SMART ONE.
KILL HIM.
BAM
BAW
BAW
KHAW

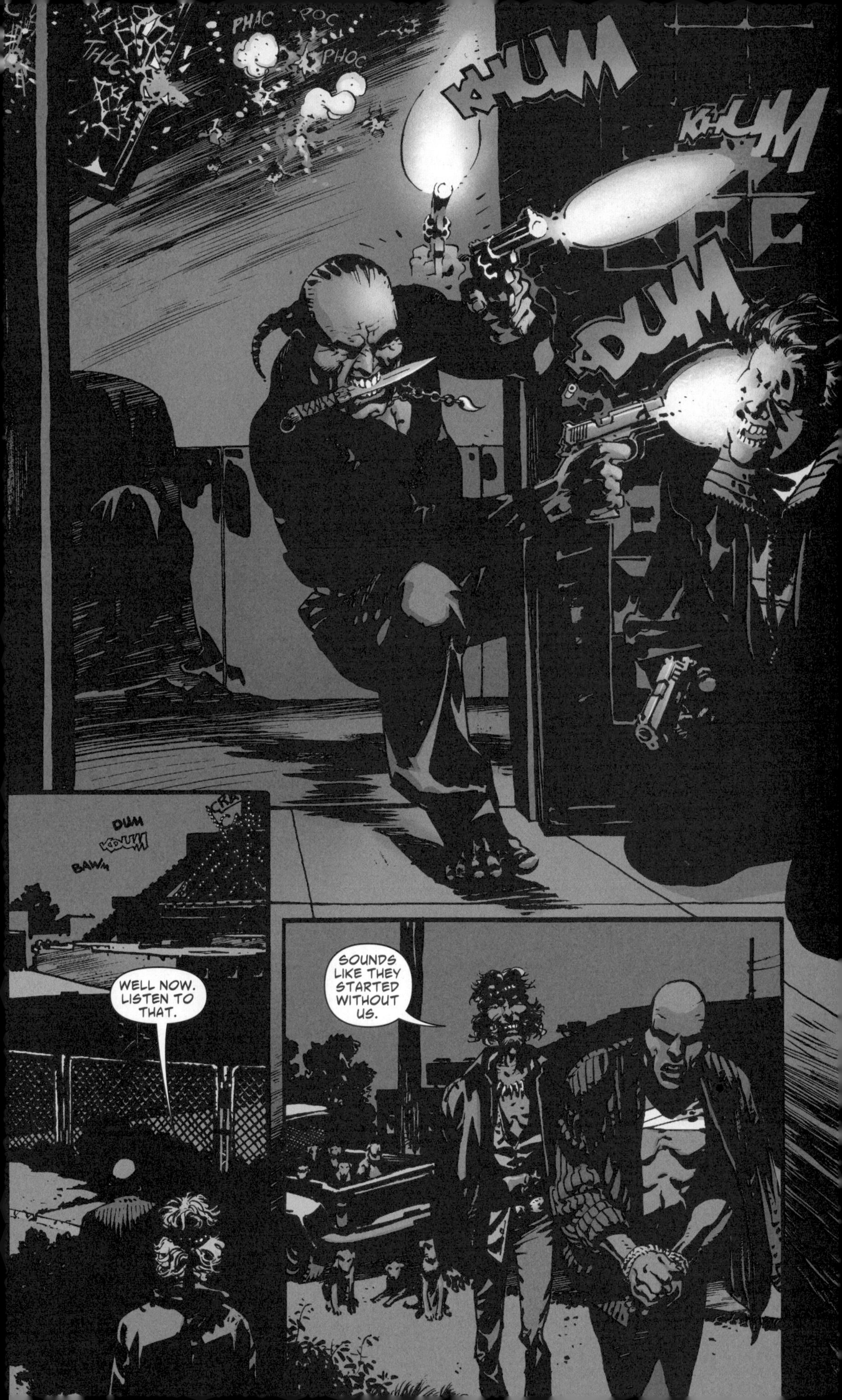

PHAC
POC
PHOC
THUC
KHUM
KHUM
KDUM
DUM
KDUM
BAWM
WELL NOW. LISTEN TO THAT.
SOUNDS LIKE THEY STARTED WITHOUT US.

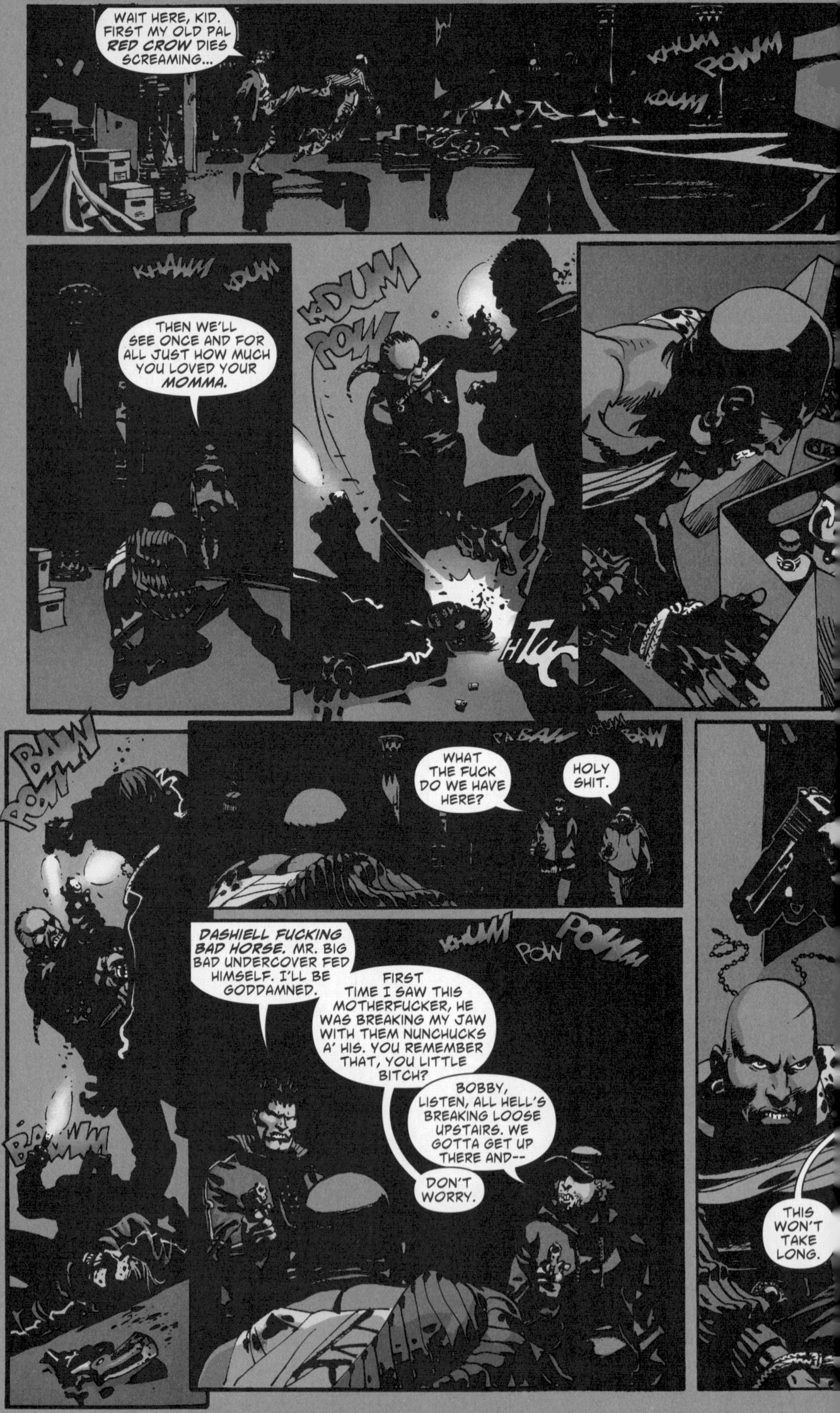
WAIT HERE, KID. FIRST MY OLD PAL RED CROW DIES SCREAMING...
KHUM POWM
KDUM
KHAWM KDUM
THEN WE'LL SEE ONCE AND FOR ALL JUST HOW MUCH YOU LOVED YOUR MOMMA.
KDUM POW
HTUC
BAWM POW
PA'BAW KHUM BAW
WHAT THE FUCK DO WE HAVE HERE?
HOLY SHIT.
DASHIELL FUCKING BAD HORSE. MR. BIG BAD UNDERCOVER FED HIMSELF. I'LL BE GODDAMNED.
KHUM POW POWM
FIRST TIME I SAW THIS MOTHERFUCKER, HE WAS BREAKING MY JAW WITH THEM NUNCHUCKS A' HIS. YOU REMEMBER THAT, YOU LITTLE BITCH?
BOBBY, LISTEN, ALL HELL'S BREAKING LOOSE UPSTAIRS. WE GOTTA GET UP THERE AND--
DON'T WORRY.
BAWM
THIS WON'T TAKE LONG.

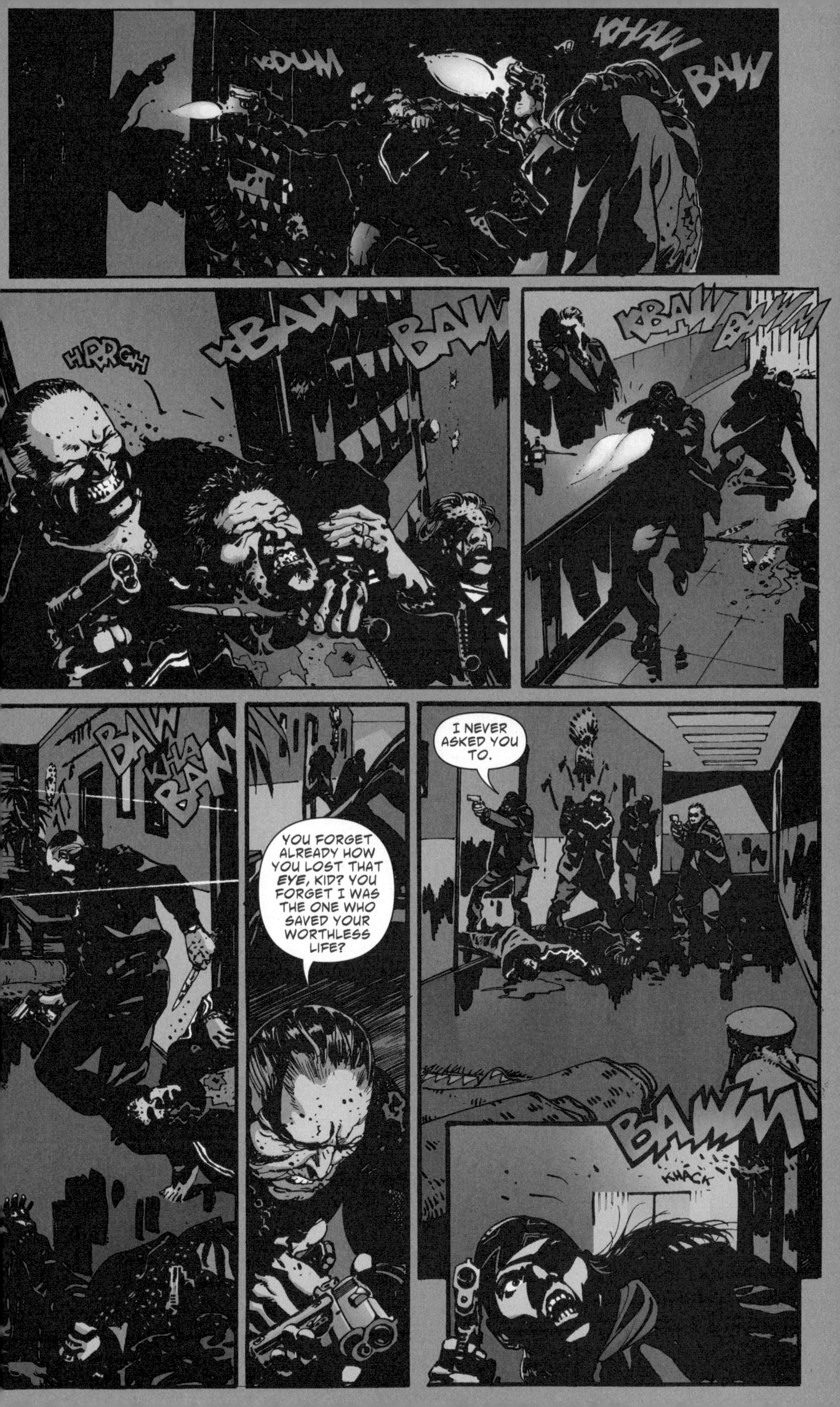
KDUM
KKHAW
BAW
HRRRGH
KBAW
BAW
KBAW
BAWM
BAW
KHA
BAM
YOU FORGET ALREADY HOW YOU LOST THAT EYE, KID? YOU FORGET I WAS THE ONE WHO SAVED YOUR WORTHLESS LIFE?
I NEVER ASKED YOU TO.
BAWM
KNACK

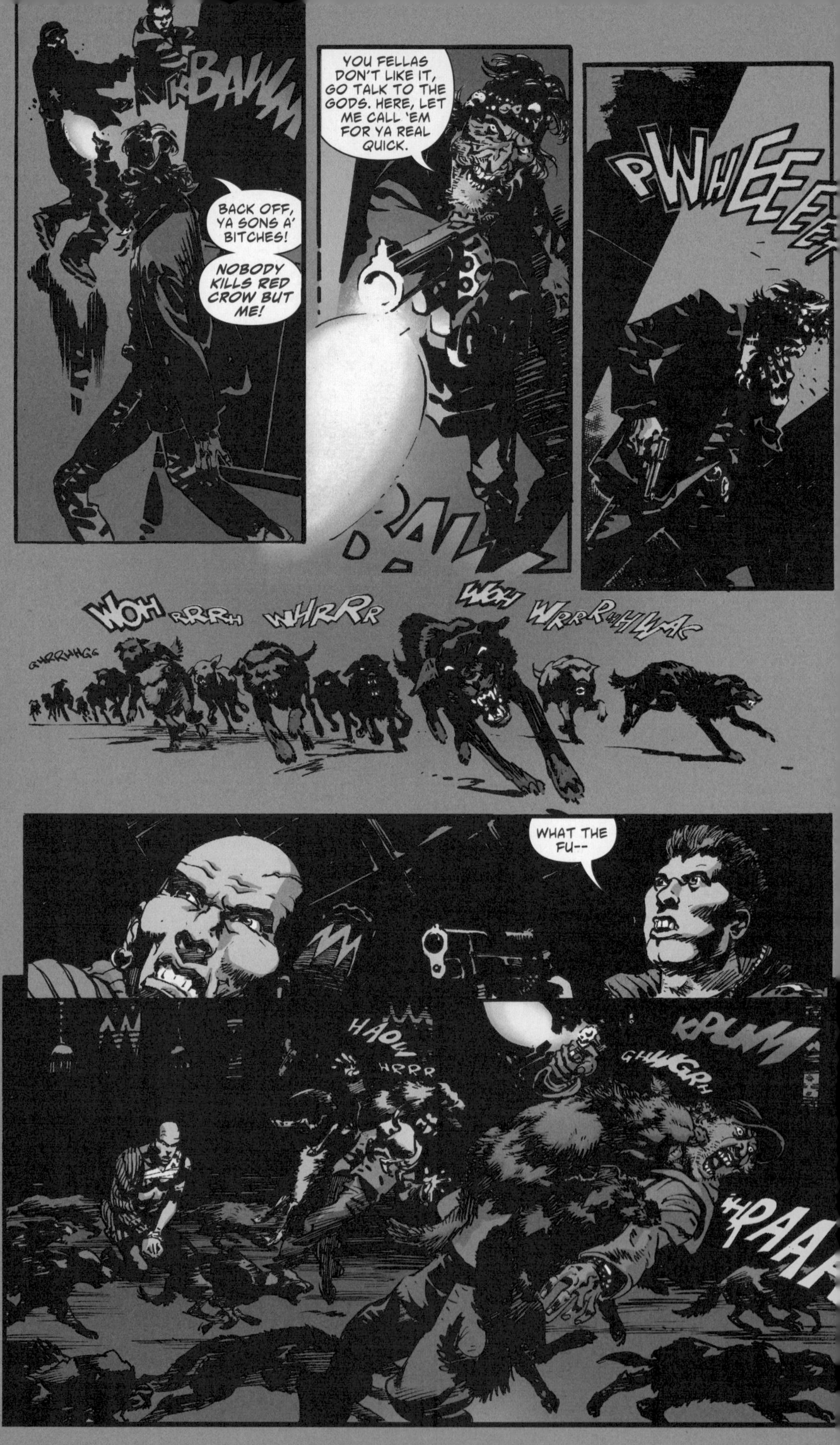
KBAWM
BACK OFF, YA SONS A' BITCHES!
NOBODY KILLS RED CROW BUT ME!
YOU FELLAS DON'T LIKE IT, GO TALK TO THE GODS. HERE, LET ME CALL 'EM FOR YA REAL QUICK.
DAM
PWHEEEET
GHRRWHAG
WOH RRRH WHRRR WOH WRRRHHWAC
WHAT THE FU--
HAOW HRRR
KPUM
GHWGRH
KPAAF

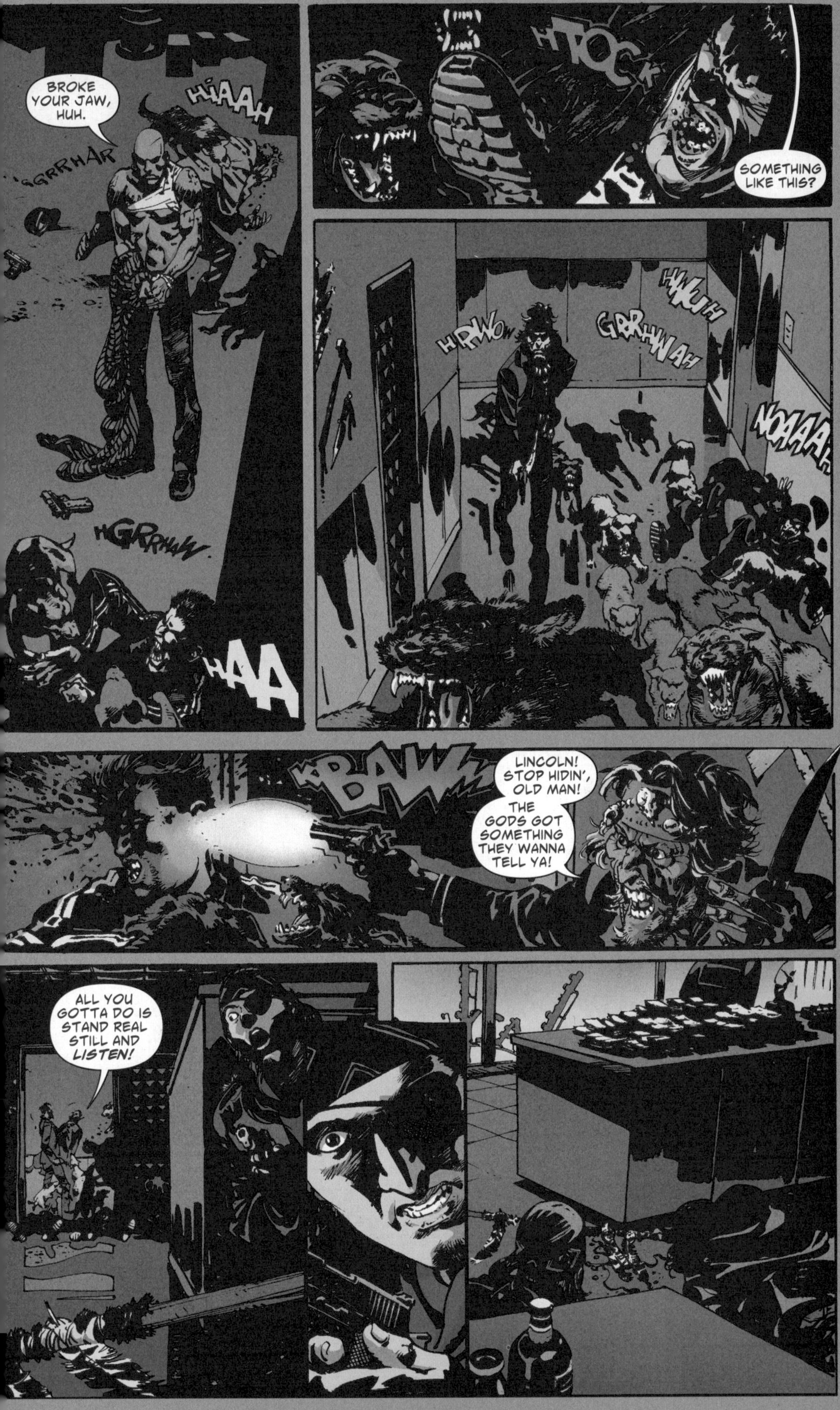
BROKE YOUR JAW, HUH.
HiAAH
GRRHAR
HGRRHAW
HAA
HTOCK
SOMETHING LIKE THIS?
HAWUH
GRRHWAH
NOAAAR
BAW
LINCOLN! STOP HIDIN', OLD MAN!
THE GODS GOT SOMETHING THEY WANNA TELL YA!
ALL YOU GOTTA DO IS STAND REAL STILL AND *LISTEN!*

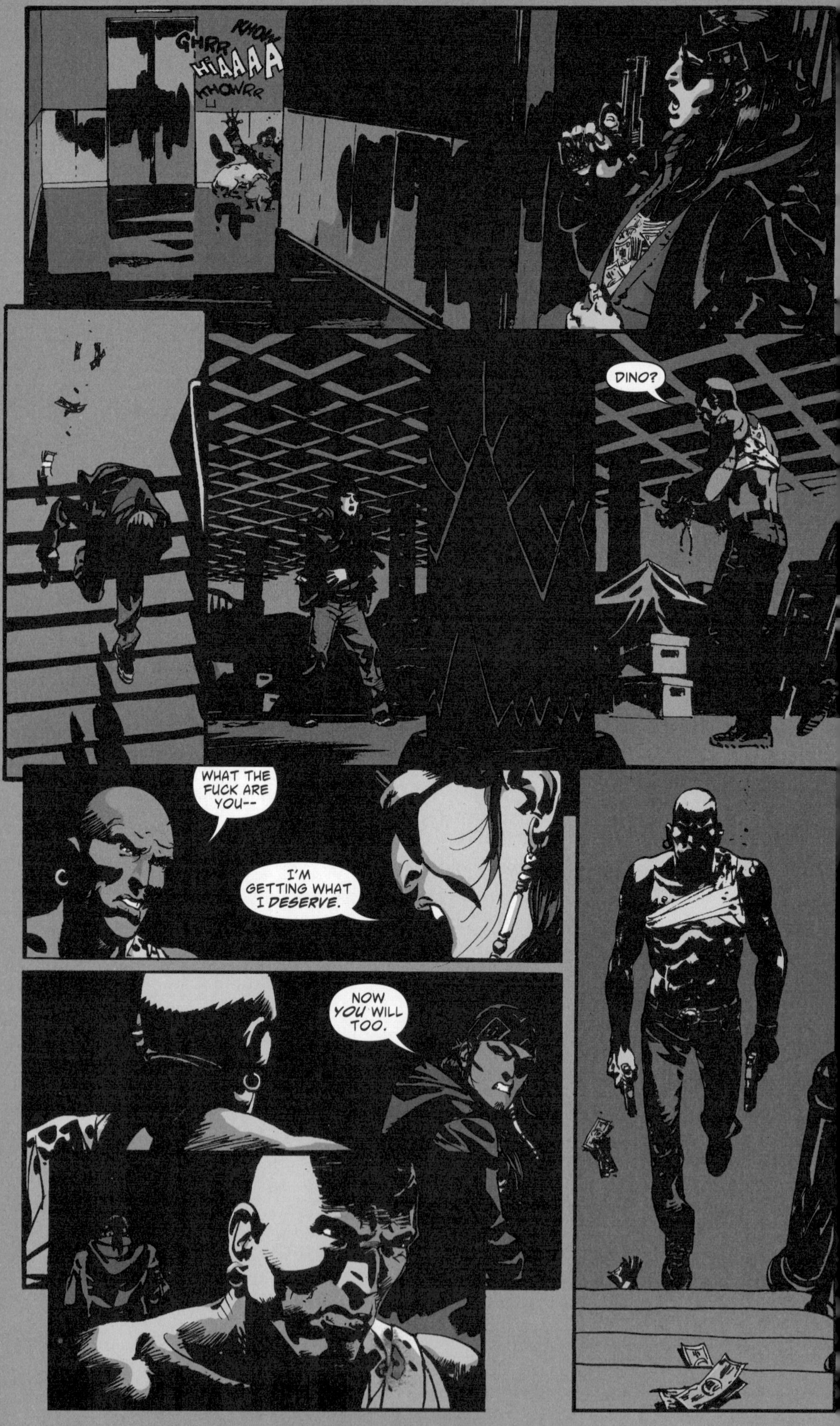
KHOW
GHRR
HiAAAA
KHOWRR
DINO?
WHAT THE FUCK ARE YOU--
I'M GETTING WHAT I DESERVE.
NOW YOU WILL TOO.

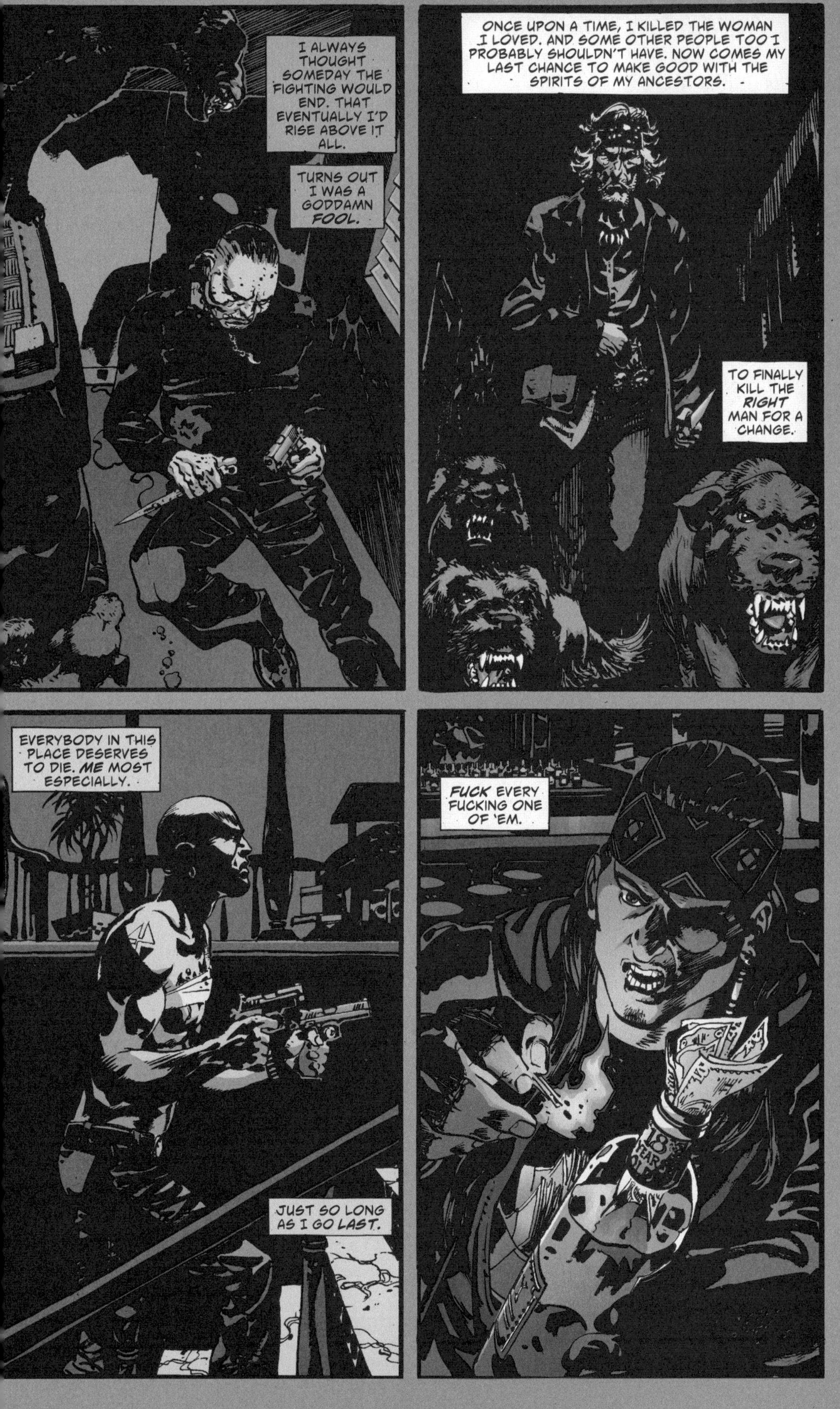
I ALWAYS THOUGHT SOMEDAY THE FIGHTING WOULD END. THAT EVENTUALLY I'D RISE ABOVE IT ALL.
TURNS OUT I WAS A GODDAMN *FOOL*.
ONCE UPON A TIME, I KILLED THE WOMAN I LOVED. AND SOME OTHER PEOPLE TOO I PROBABLY SHOULDN'T HAVE. NOW COMES MY LAST CHANCE TO MAKE GOOD WITH THE SPIRITS OF MY ANCESTORS.
TO FINALLY KILL THE *RIGHT* MAN FOR A CHANGE.
EVERYBODY IN THIS PLACE DESERVES TO DIE. *ME* MOST ESPECIALLY.
JUST SO LONG AS I GO *LAST*.
FUCK EVERY FUCKING ONE OF 'EM.

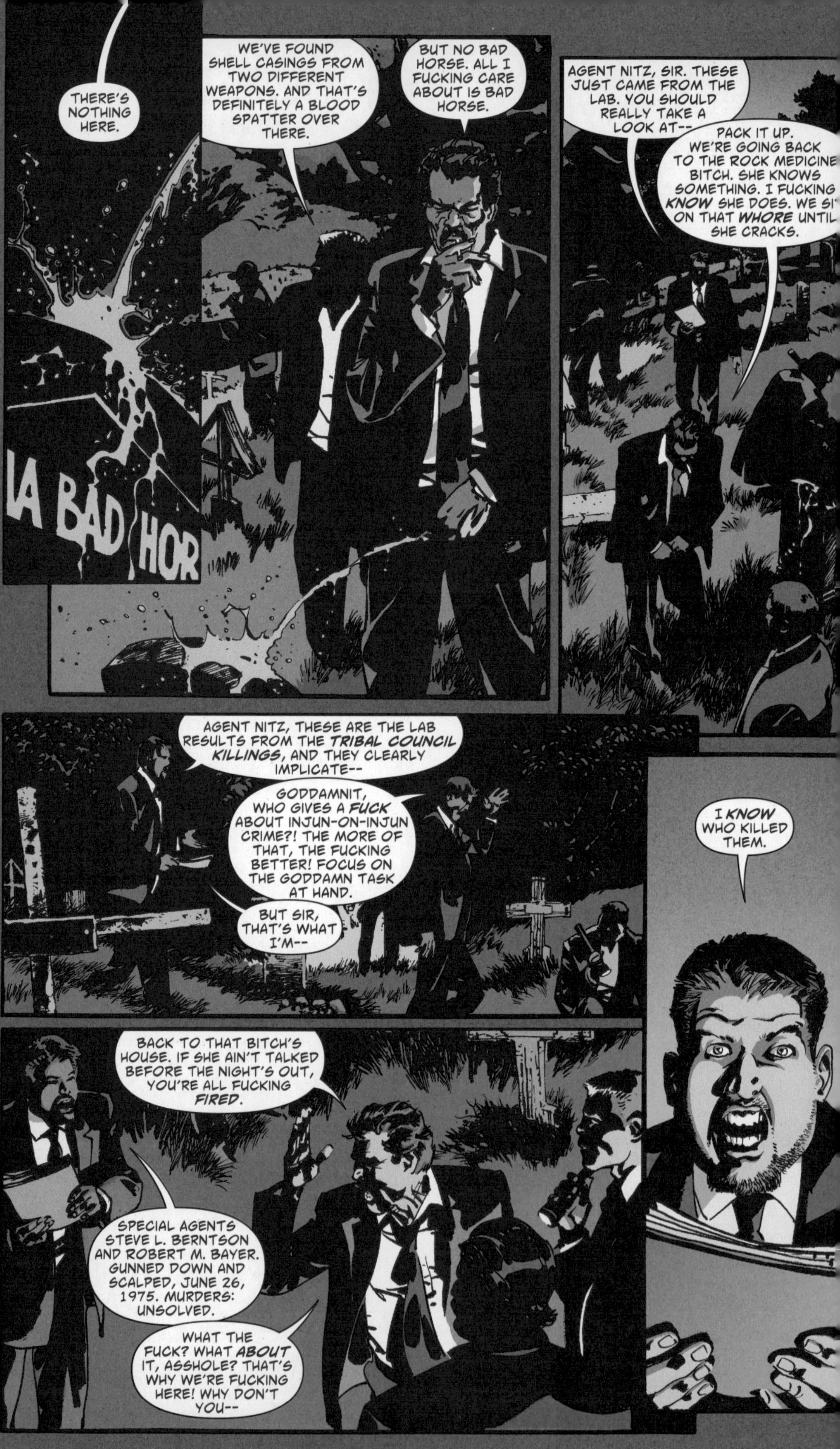
THERE'S NOTHING HERE.
WE'VE FOUND SHELL CASINGS FROM TWO DIFFERENT WEAPONS. AND THAT'S DEFINITELY A BLOOD SPATTER OVER THERE.
BUT NO BAD HORSE. ALL I FUCKING CARE ABOUT IS BAD HORSE.
IA BAD HOR
AGENT NITZ, SIR. THESE JUST CAME FROM THE LAB. YOU SHOULD REALLY TAKE A LOOK AT--
PACK IT UP. WE'RE GOING BACK TO THE ROCK MEDICINE BITCH. SHE KNOWS SOMETHING. I FUCKING KNOW SHE DOES. WE SI ON THAT WHORE UNTIL SHE CRACKS.
AGENT NITZ, THESE ARE THE LAB RESULTS FROM THE TRIBAL COUNCIL KILLINGS, AND THEY CLEARLY IMPLICATE--
GODDAMNIT, WHO GIVES A FUCK ABOUT INJUN-ON-INJUN CRIME?! THE MORE OF THAT, THE FUCKING BETTER! FOCUS ON THE GODDAMN TASK AT HAND.
BUT SIR, THAT'S WHAT I'M--
BACK TO THAT BITCH'S HOUSE. IF SHE AIN'T TALKED BEFORE THE NIGHT'S OUT, YOU'RE ALL FUCKING FIRED.
SPECIAL AGENTS STEVE L. BERNTSON AND ROBERT M. BAYER. GUNNED DOWN AND SCALPED, JUNE 26, 1975. MURDERS: UNSOLVED.
WHAT THE FUCK? WHAT ABOUT IT, ASSHOLE? THAT'S WHY WE'RE FUCKING HERE! WHY DON'T YOU--
I KNOW WHO KILLED THEM.

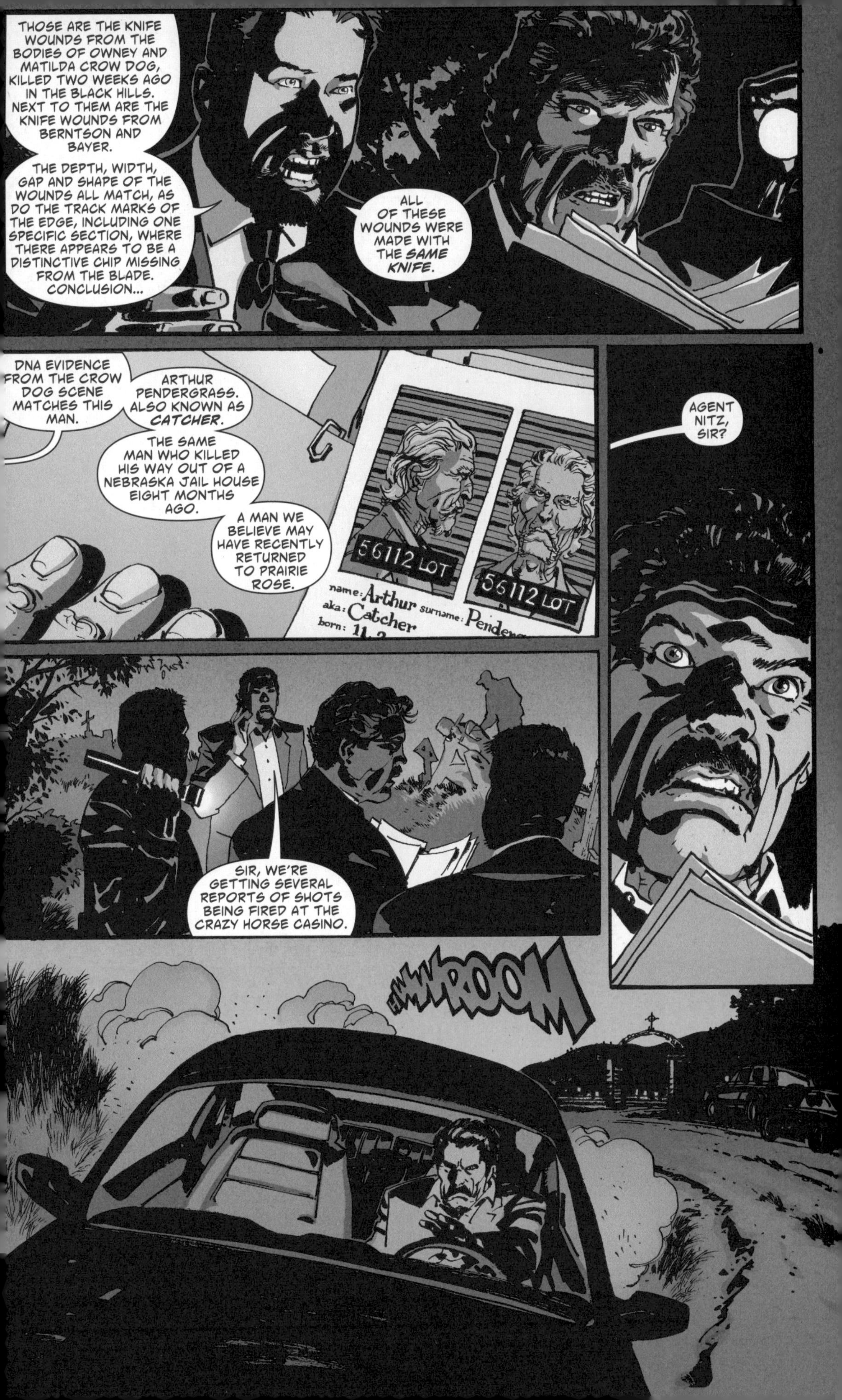

THOSE ARE THE KNIFE WOUNDS FROM THE BODIES OF OWNEY AND MATILDA CROW DOG, KILLED TWO WEEKS AGO IN THE BLACK HILLS. NEXT TO THEM ARE THE KNIFE WOUNDS FROM BERNTSON AND BAYER.
THE DEPTH, WIDTH, GAP AND SHAPE OF THE WOUNDS ALL MATCH, AS DO THE TRACK MARKS OF THE EDGE, INCLUDING ONE SPECIFIC SECTION, WHERE THERE APPEARS TO BE A DISTINCTIVE CHIP MISSING FROM THE BLADE. CONCLUSION...
ALL OF THESE WOUNDS WERE MADE WITH THE SAME KNIFE.
DNA EVIDENCE FROM THE CROW DOG SCENE MATCHES THIS MAN.
ARTHUR PENDERGRASS. ALSO KNOWN AS CATCHER.
THE SAME MAN WHO KILLED HIS WAY OUT OF A NEBRASKA JAIL HOUSE EIGHT MONTHS AGO.
A MAN WE BELIEVE MAY HAVE RECENTLY RETURNED TO PRAIRIE ROSE.
56112 LOT
56112 LOT
name: Arthur surname: Penderg
aka: Catcher
born: 11.2
AGENT NITZ, SIR?
SIR, WE'RE GETTING SEVERAL REPORTS OF SHOTS BEING FIRED AT THE CRAZY HORSE CASINO.
VVROOM

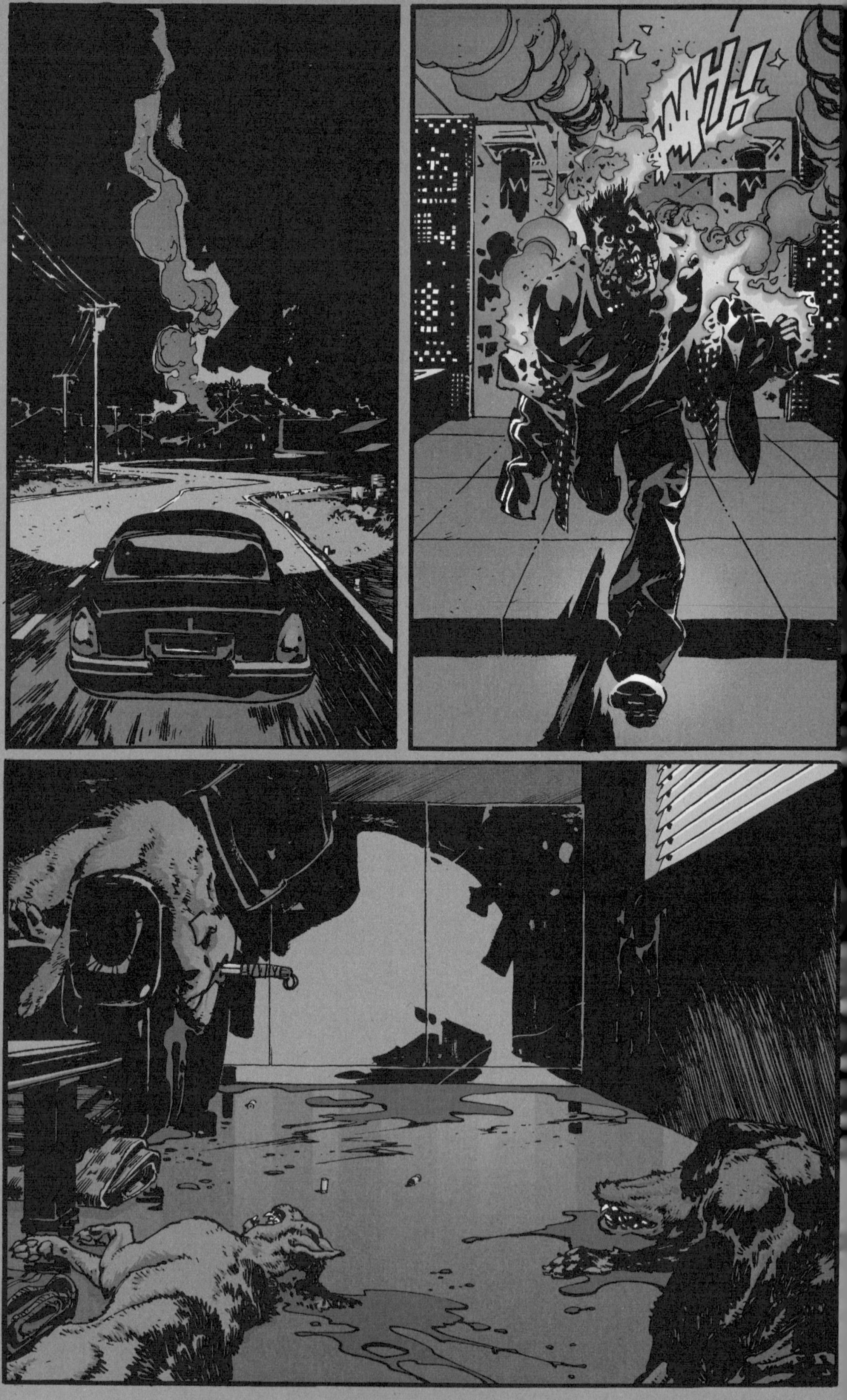

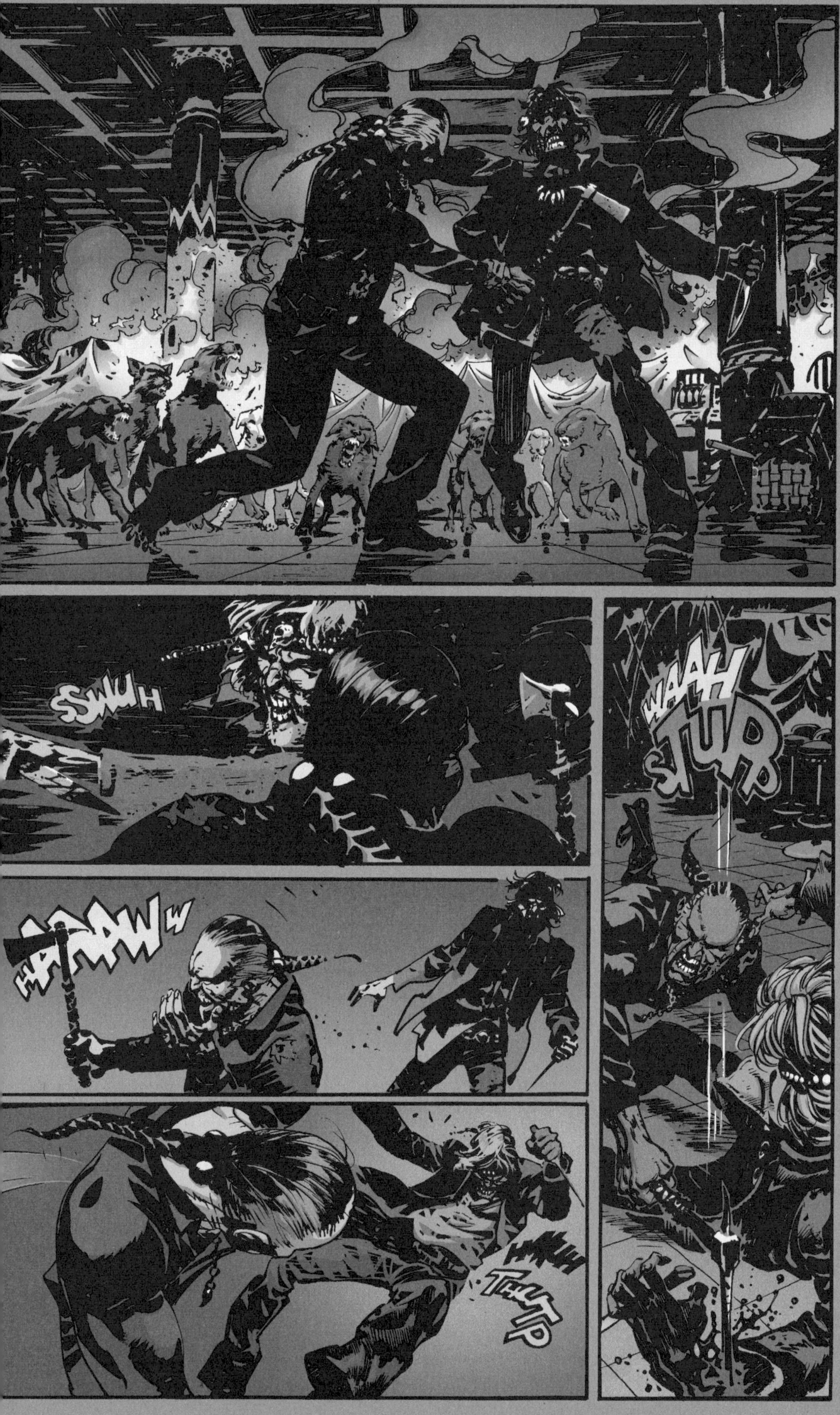
SWUH
HRAWW
WAAH
STUP
HWUH
THUTP

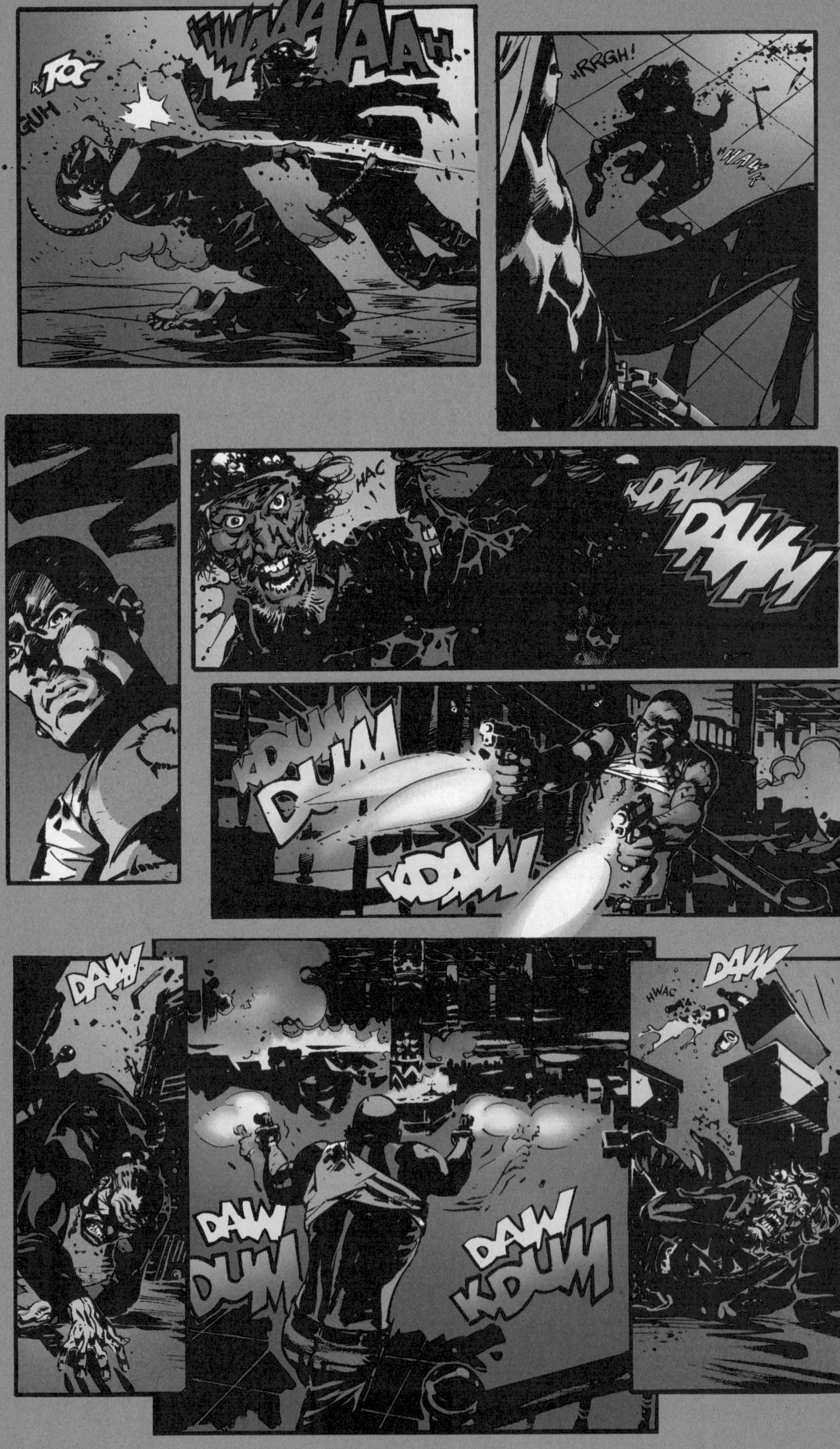

KTOC
GUH
iiWAAAAAAH
MRRGH!
HWAK
HAC
KDAW
DAWM
KDUM
DUM
KDAW
DAW
DAW
DUM
DAW
KDUM
DAW
HWAC

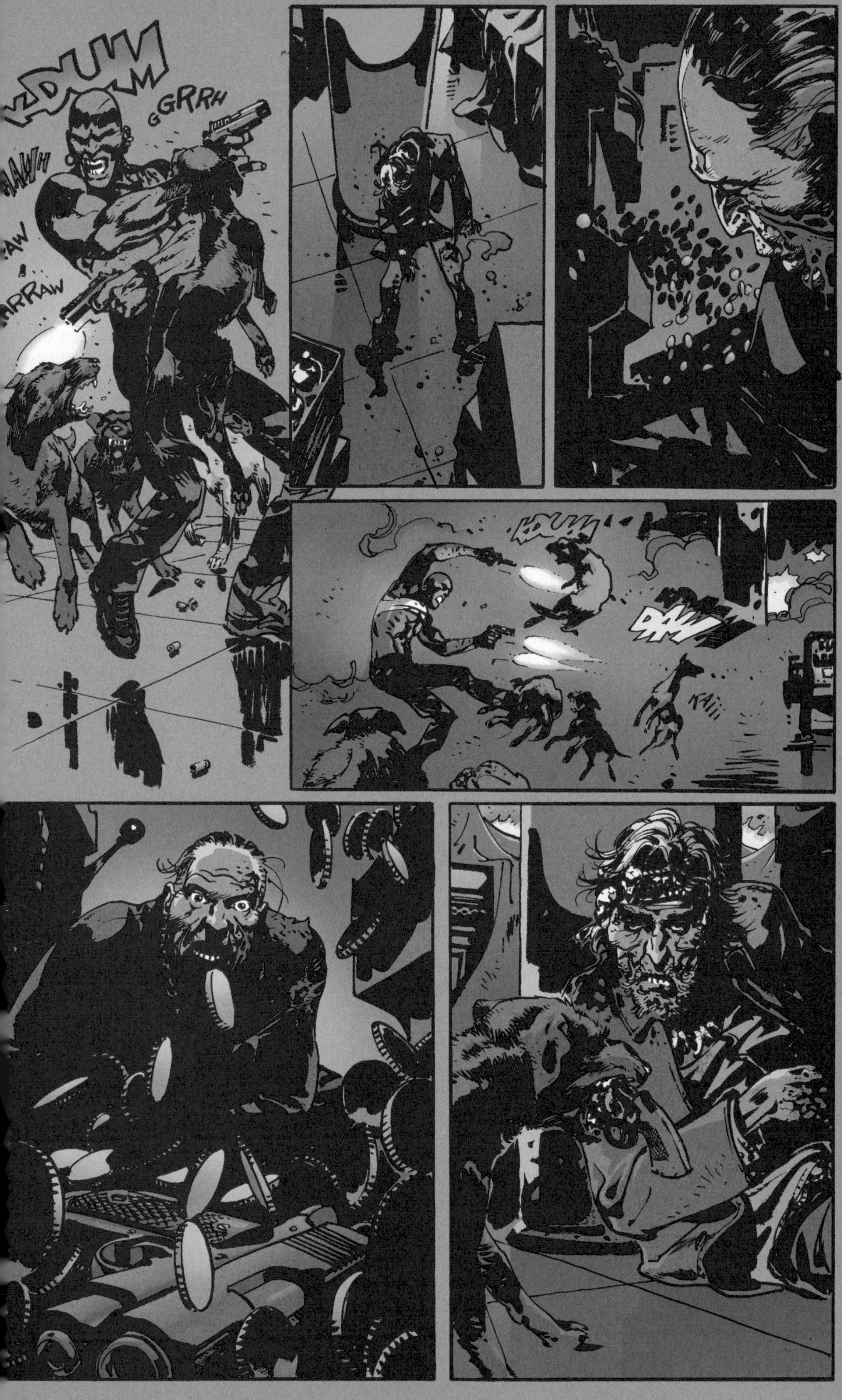

KDUM
GGRRH
AWH
AW
ARRAW
KDUM
DAW
KAIII

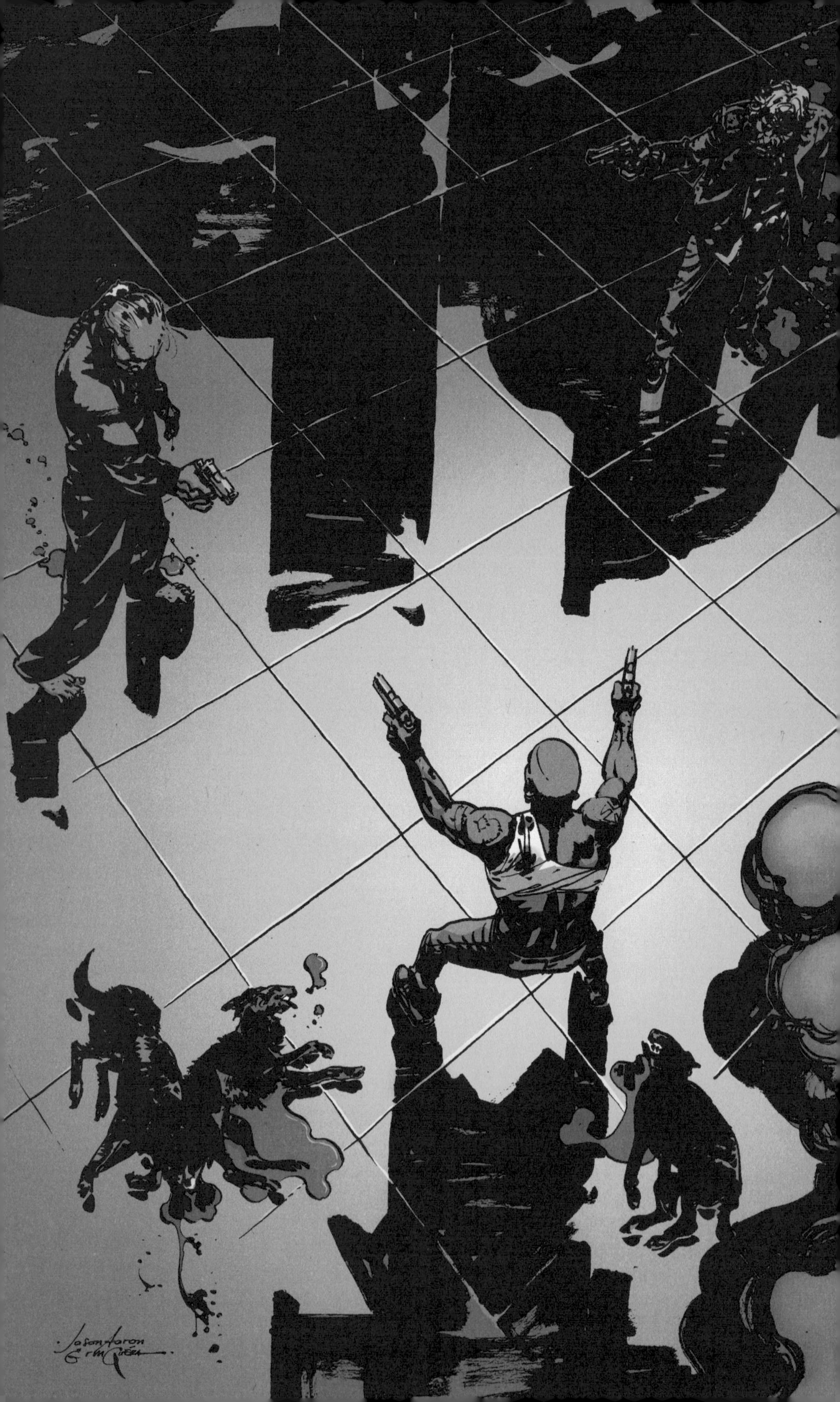

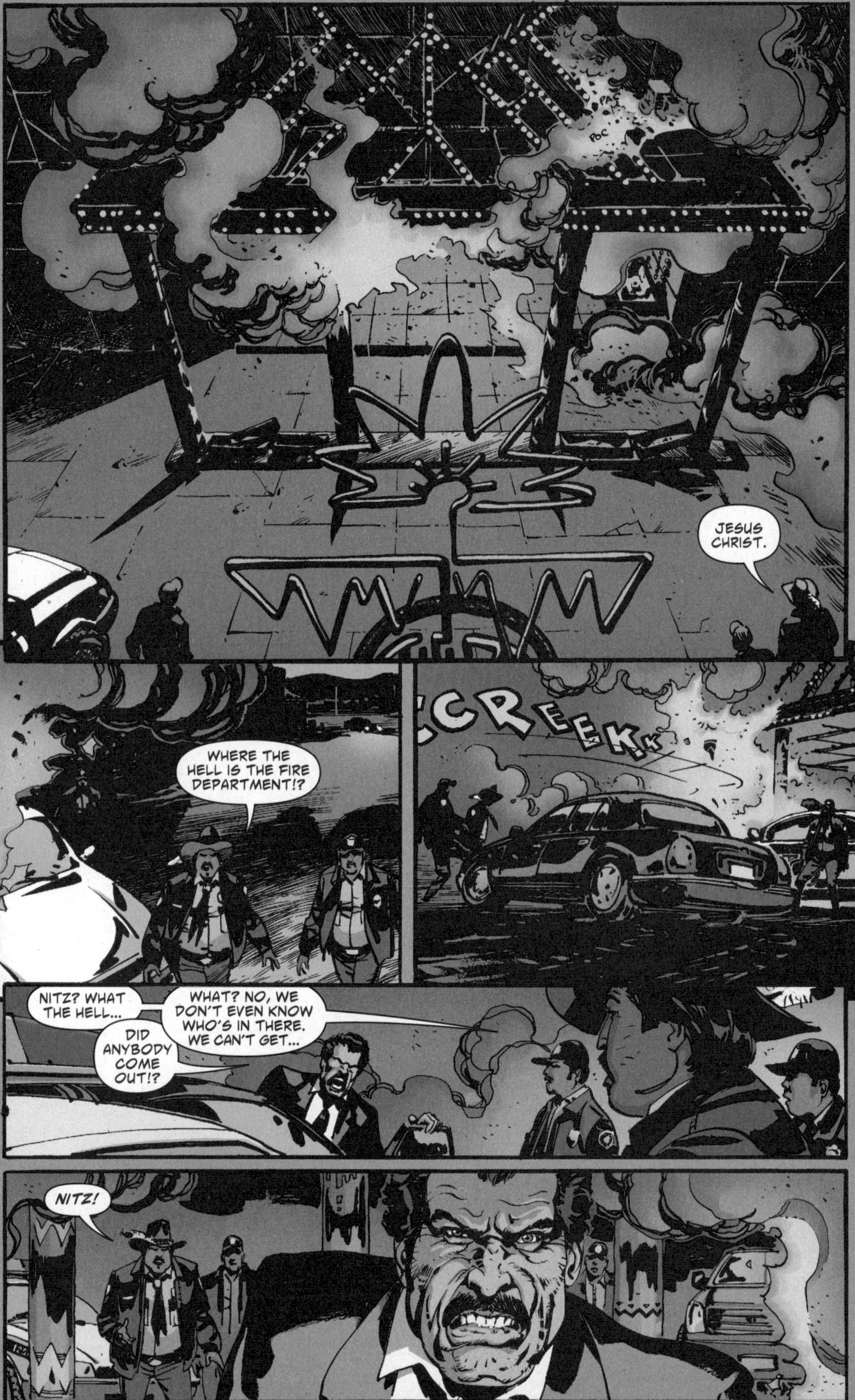

PAC
POC
JESUS CHRIST.
WHERE THE HELL IS THE FIRE DEPARTMENT!?
CREEEKKK
NITZ? WHAT THE HELL...
WHAT? NO, WE DON'T EVEN KNOW WHO'S IN THERE. WE CAN'T GET...
DID ANYBODY COME OUT!?
NITZ!

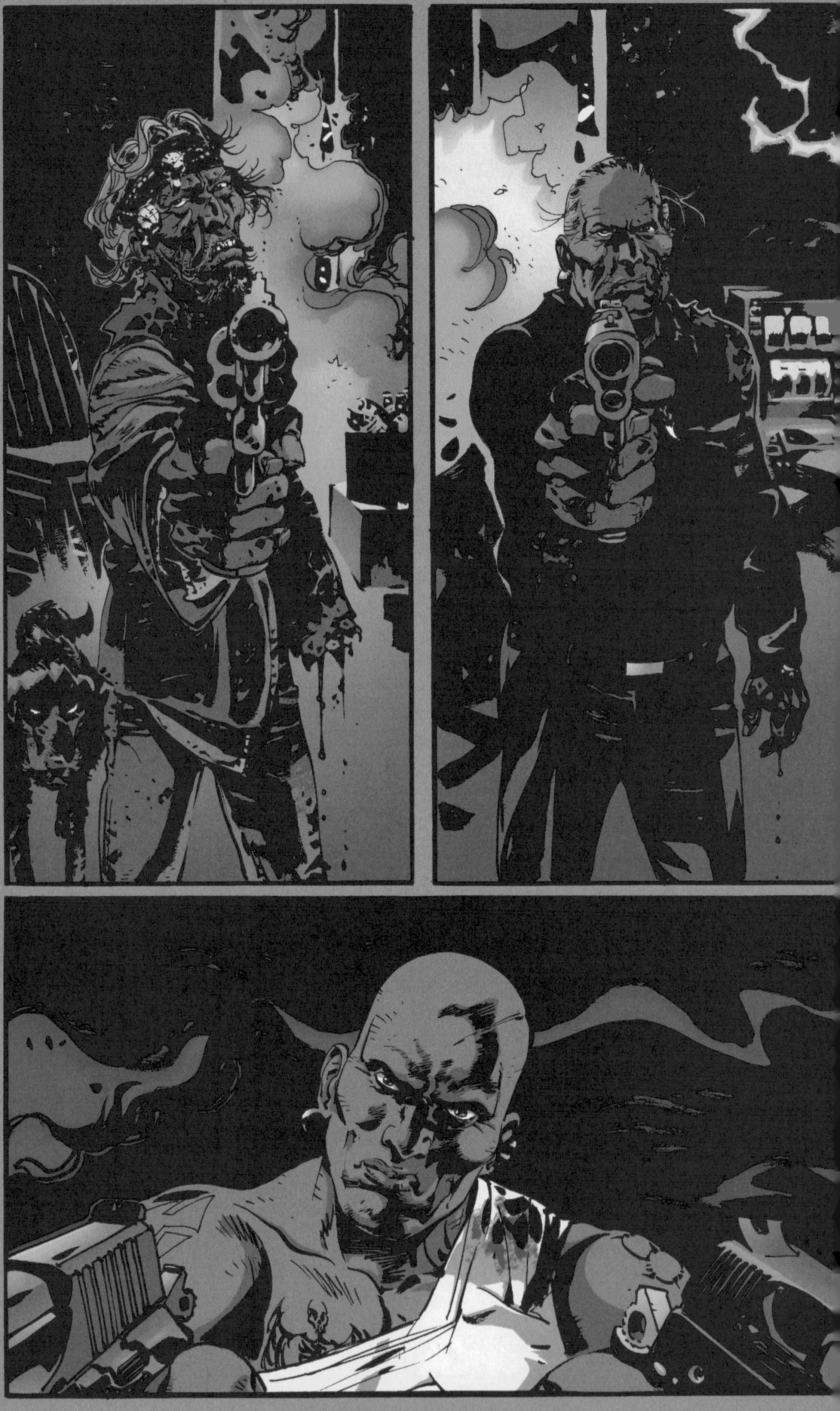

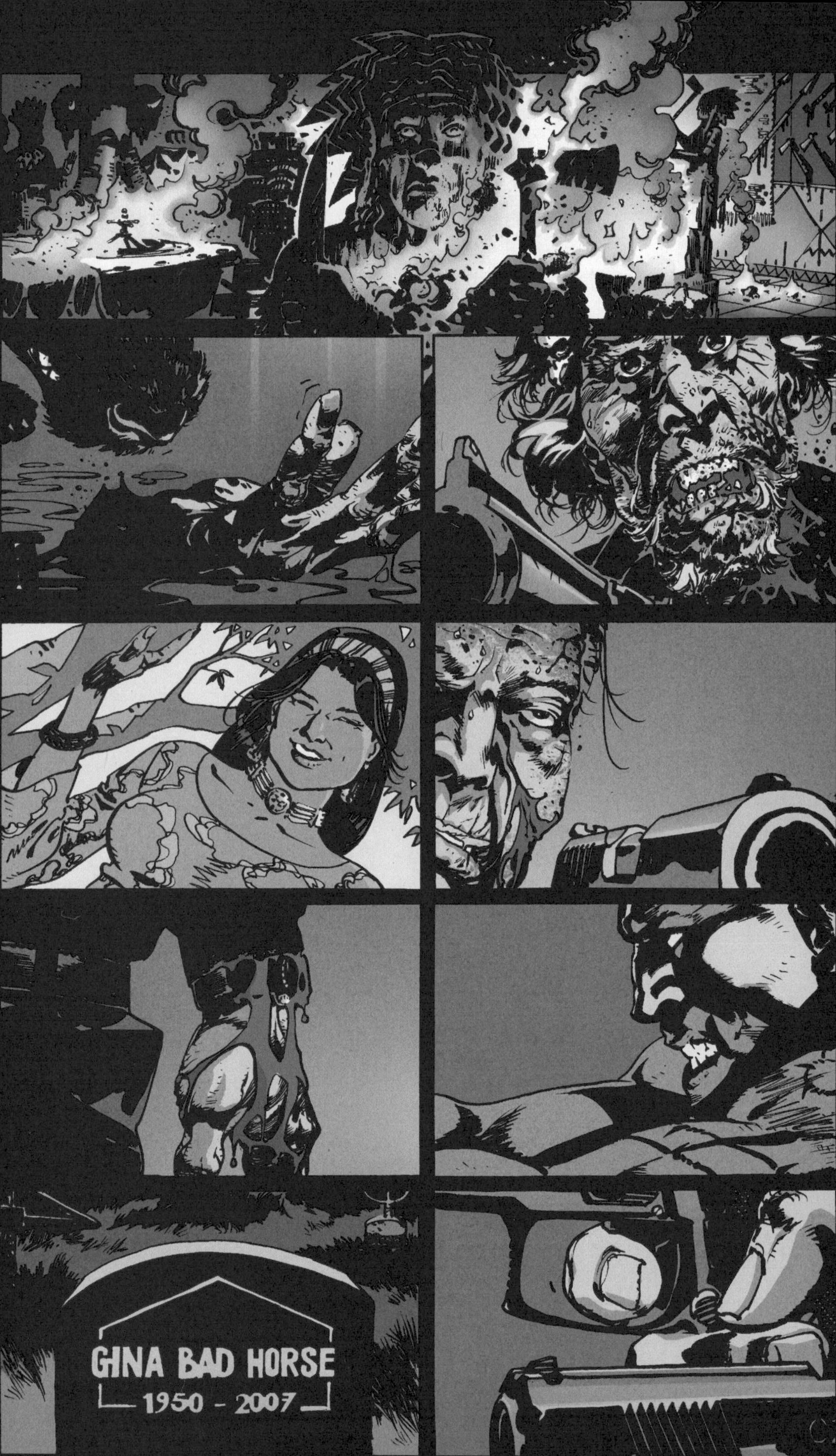
GINA BAD HORSE
1950 - 2007

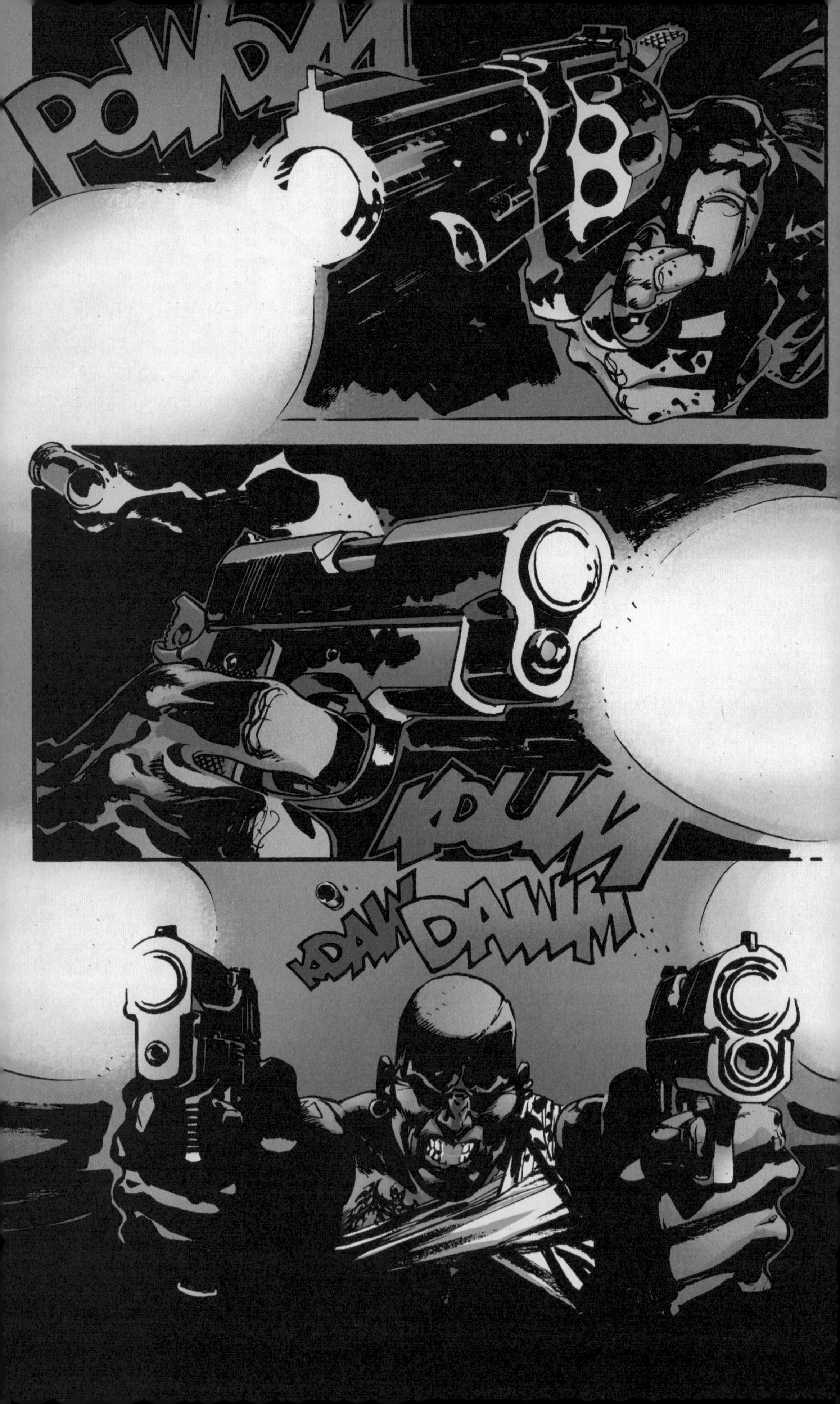

POWDAM
KDUM
KDAW
DAWM

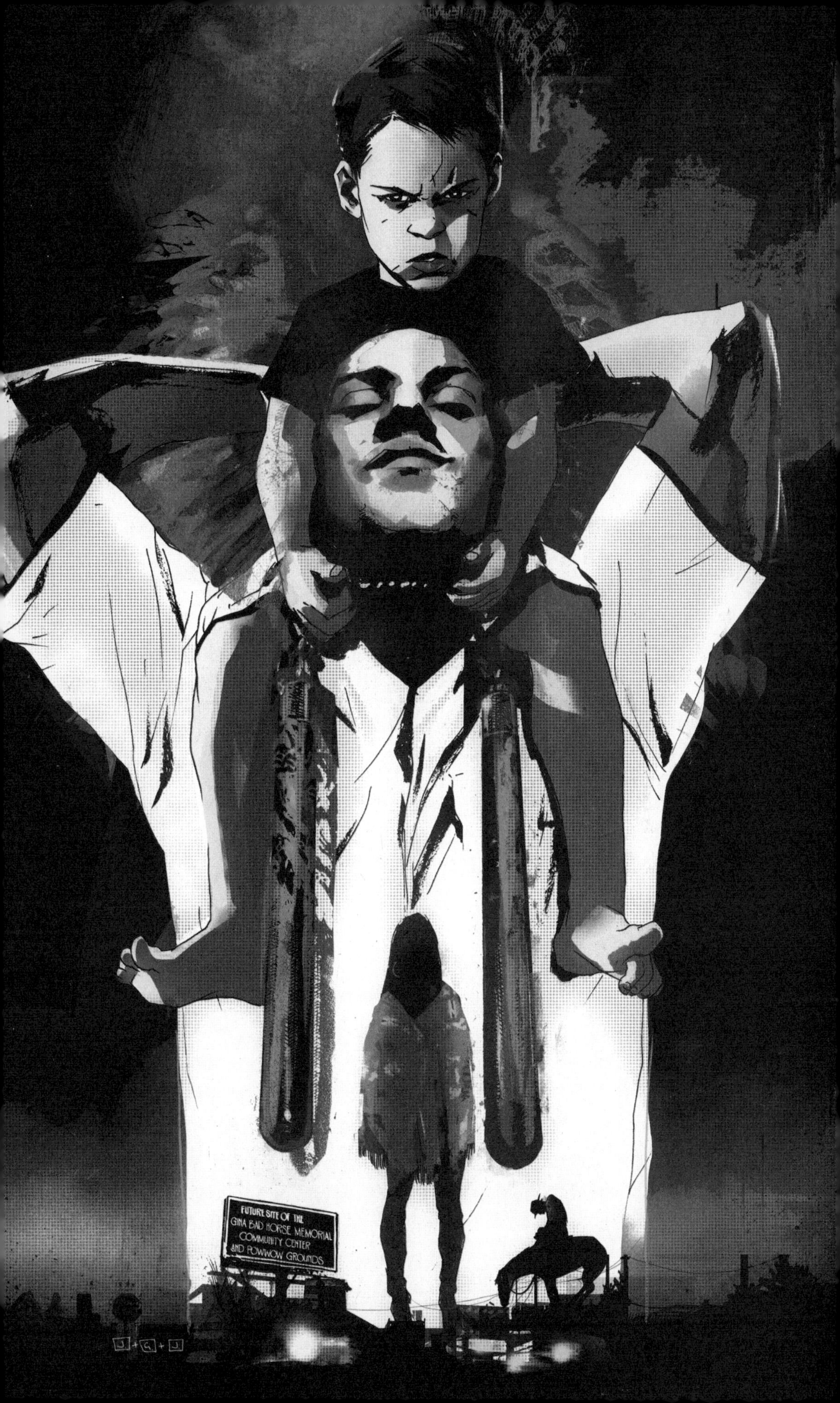
FUTURE SITE OF THE
GINA BAD HORSE MEMORIAL
COMMUNITY CENTER
AND POWWOW GROUNDS

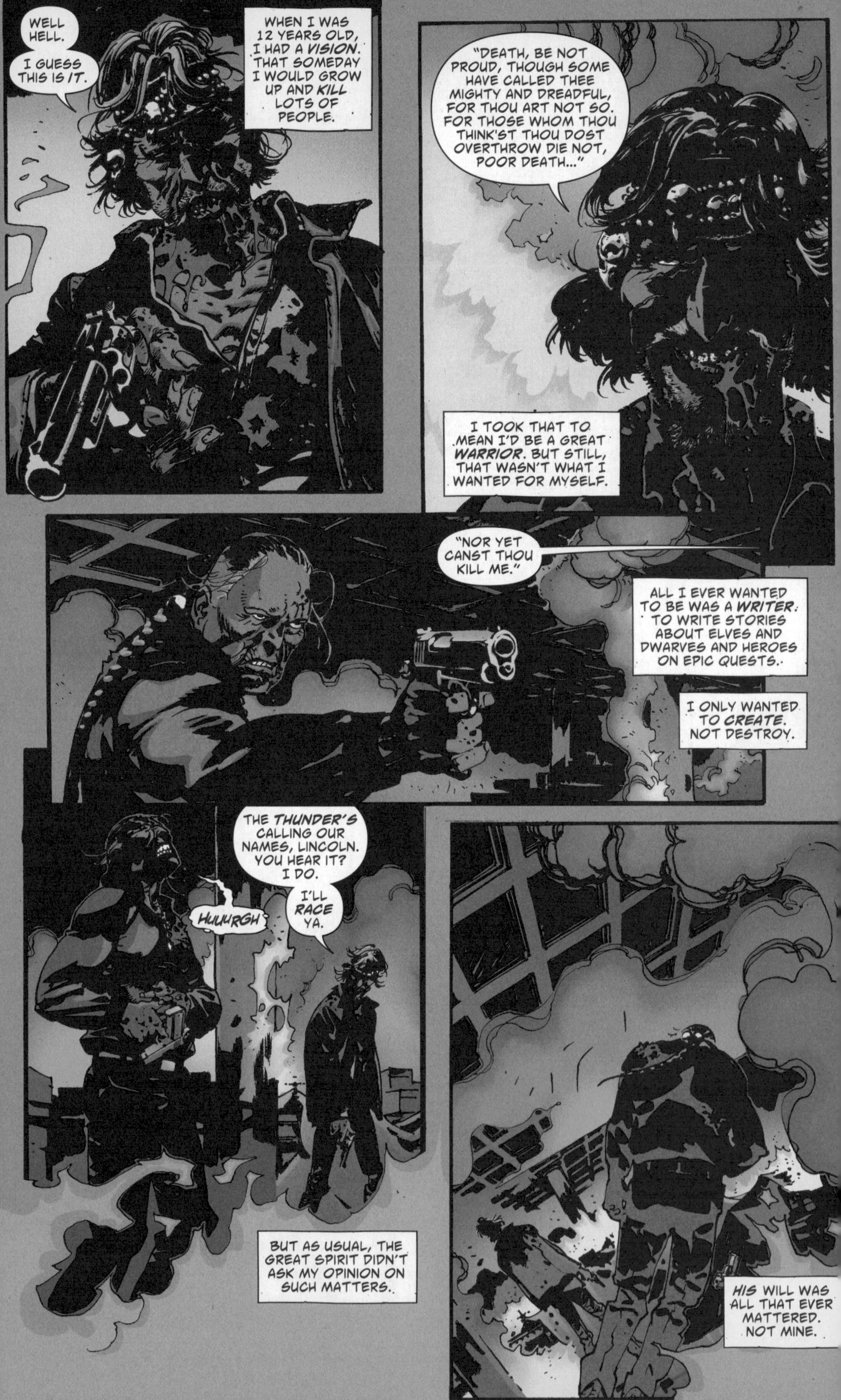
WELL HELL.
I GUESS THIS IS *IT*.
WHEN I WAS 12 YEARS OLD, I HAD A *VISION*. THAT SOMEDAY I WOULD GROW UP AND *KILL* LOTS OF PEOPLE.
"DEATH, BE NOT PROUD, THOUGH SOME HAVE CALLED THEE MIGHTY AND DREADFUL, FOR THOU ART NOT SO. FOR THOSE WHOM THOU THINK'ST THOU DOST OVERTHROW DIE NOT, POOR DEATH..."
I TOOK THAT TO MEAN I'D BE A GREAT *WARRIOR*. BUT STILL, THAT WASN'T WHAT I WANTED FOR MYSELF.
"NOR YET CANST THOU KILL ME."
ALL I EVER WANTED TO BE WAS A *WRITER*. TO WRITE STORIES ABOUT ELVES AND DWARVES AND HEROES ON EPIC QUESTS.
I ONLY WANTED TO *CREATE*. NOT DESTROY.
THE *THUNDER'S* CALLING OUR NAMES, LINCOLN. YOU HEAR IT? I DO.
I'LL *RACE* YA.
HUUURGH
BUT AS USUAL, THE GREAT SPIRIT DIDN'T ASK MY OPINION ON SUCH MATTERS.
HIS WILL WAS ALL THAT EVER MATTERED. NOT MINE.

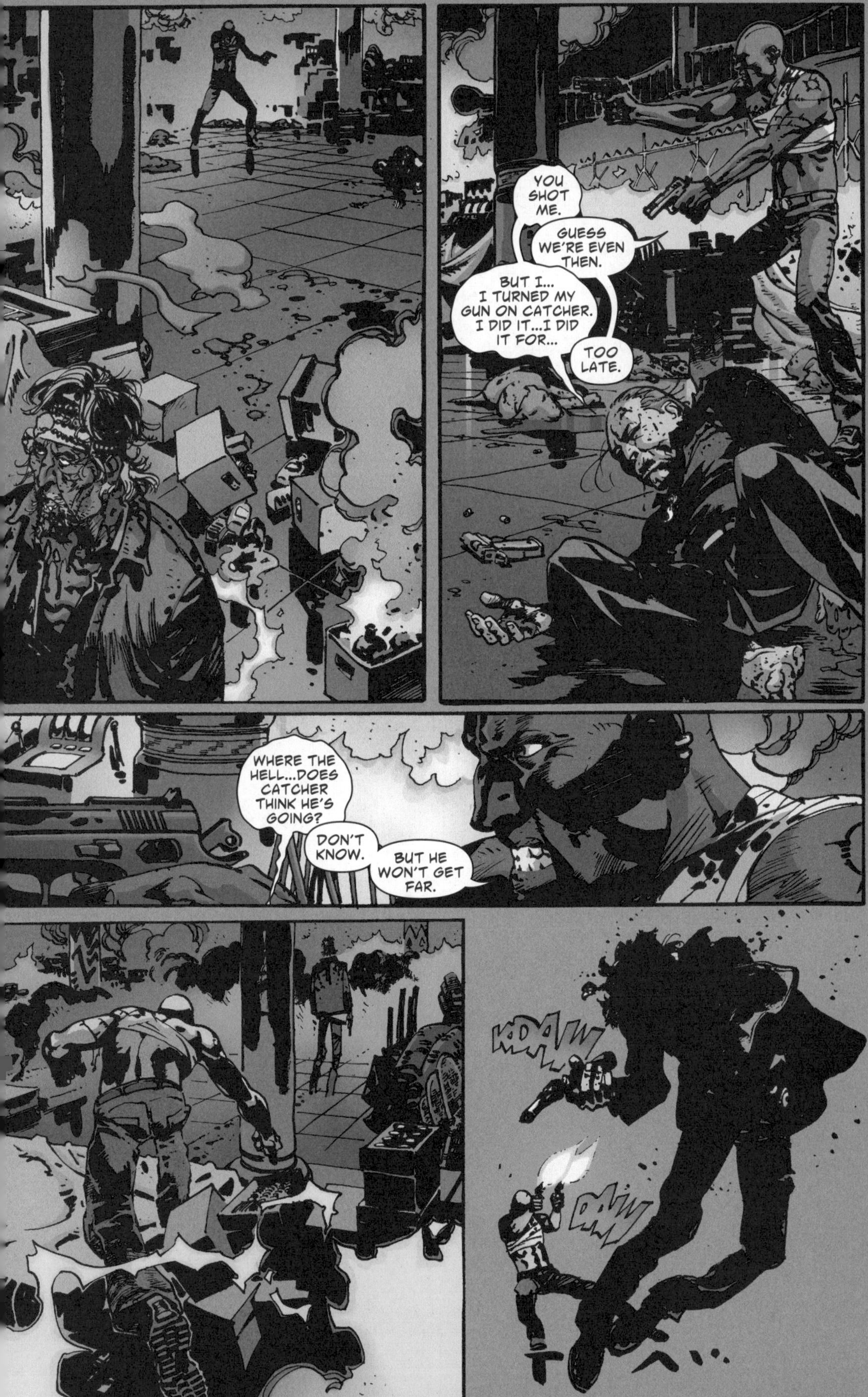
YOU SHOT ME.
GUESS WE'RE EVEN THEN.
BUT I... I TURNED MY GUN ON CATCHER. I DID IT...I DID IT FOR...
TOO LATE.
WHERE THE HELL...DOES CATCHER THINK HE'S GOING?
DON'T KNOW.
BUT HE WON'T GET FAR.
KDAW
DAW

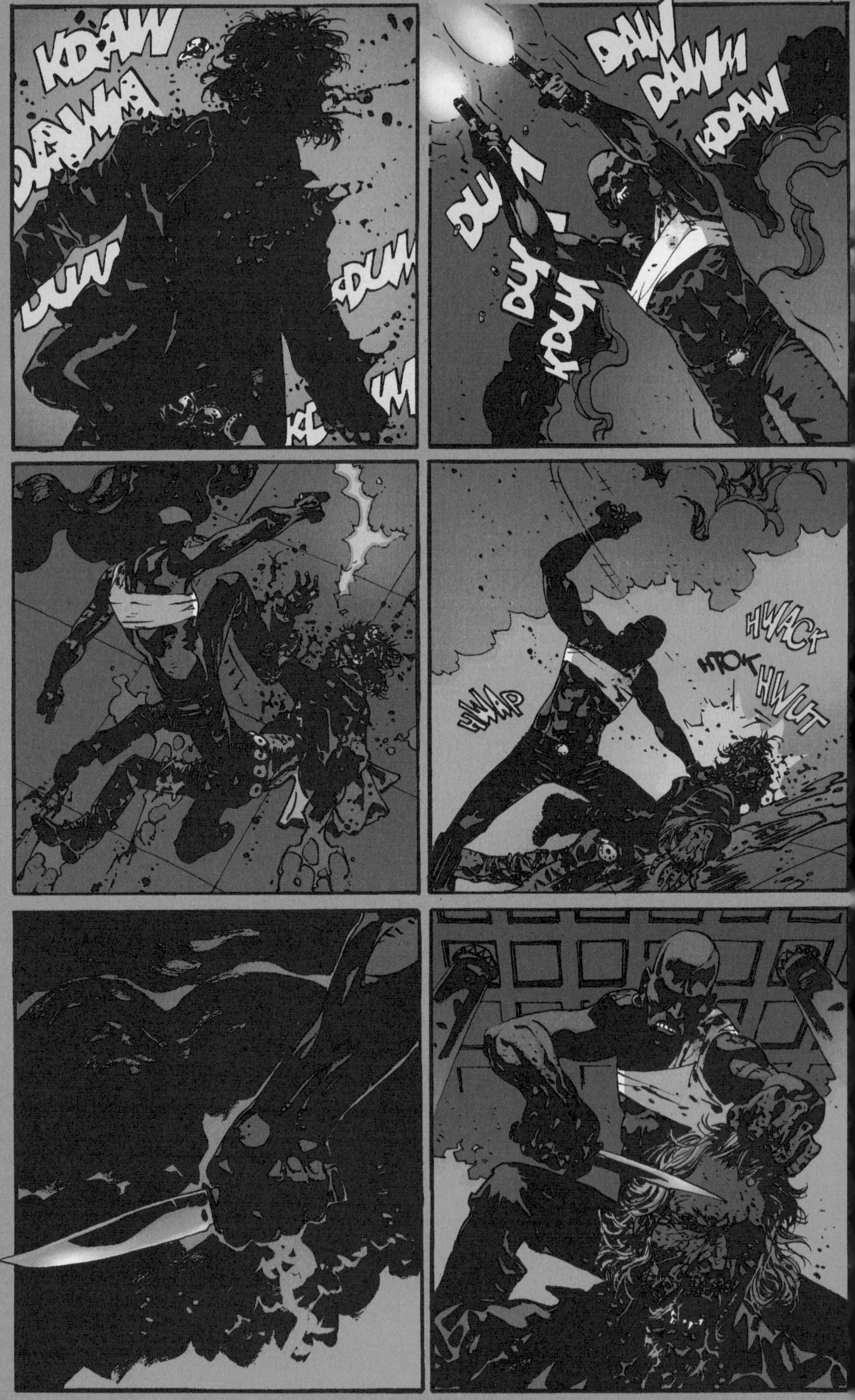
KDAW
DUW
KDUM
DAW
DAWM
KDAW
KDAW
HWACK
HTOK
HWUT
HWAP

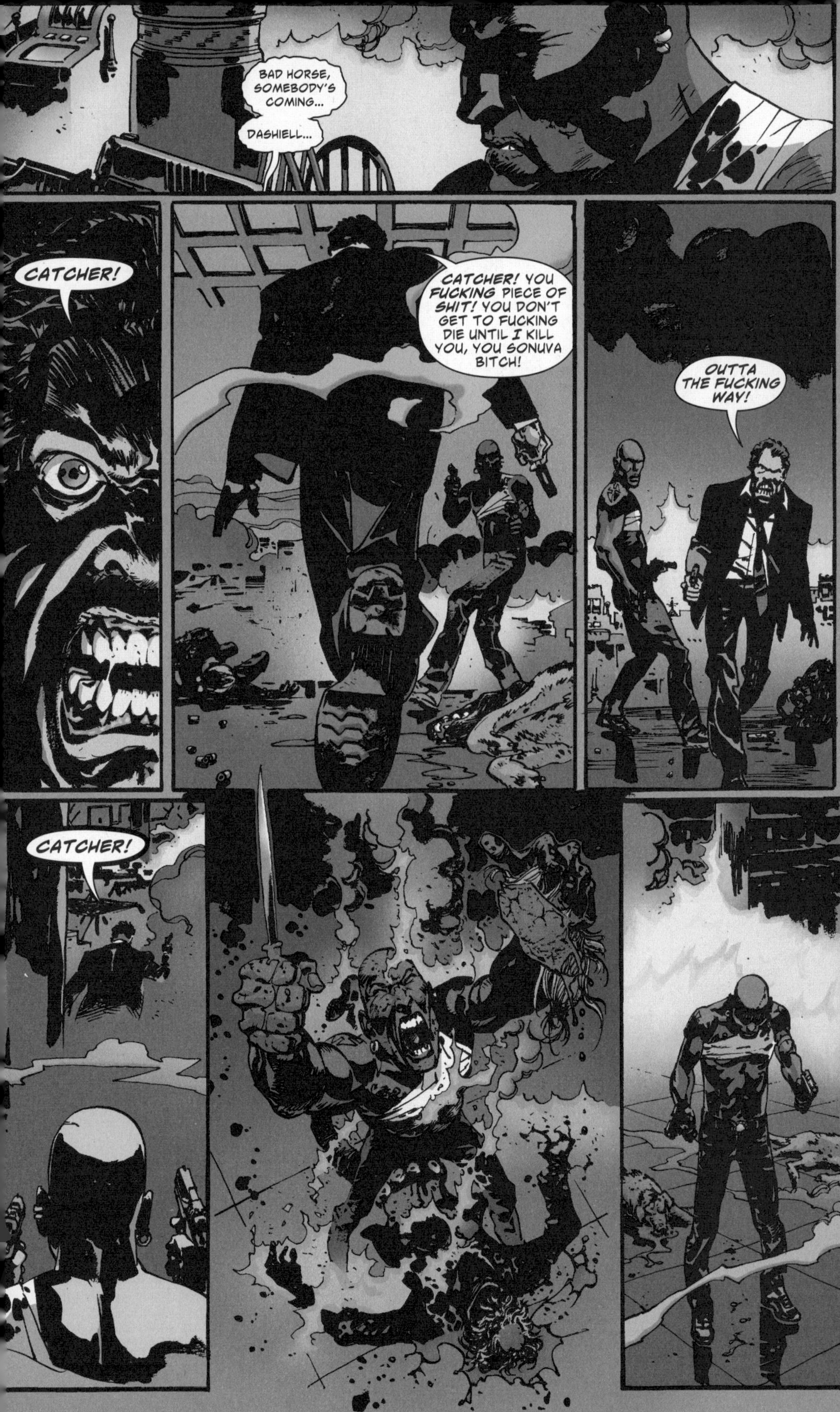

BAD HORSE, SOMEBODY'S COMING...
DASHIELL...
CATCHER!
CATCHER! YOU FUCKING PIECE OF SHIT! YOU DON'T GET TO FUCKING DIE UNTIL I KILL YOU, YOU SONUVA BITCH!
OUTTA THE FUCKING WAY!
CATCHER!

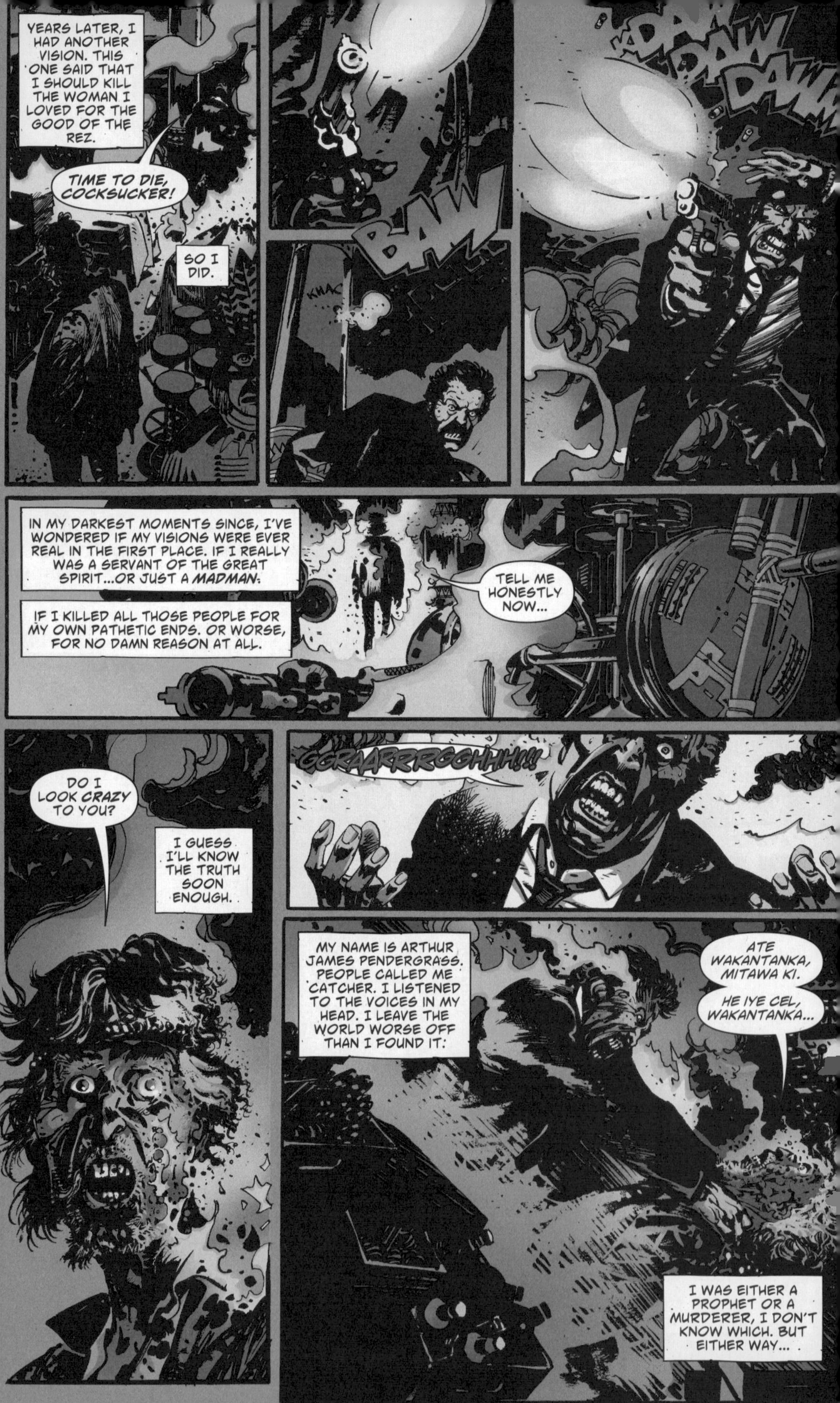

YEARS LATER, I HAD ANOTHER VISION. THIS ONE SAID THAT I SHOULD KILL THE WOMAN I LOVED FOR THE GOOD OF THE REZ.
TIME TO DIE, COCKSUCKER!
SO I DID.
BAW
KHAC
DAW DAW DAW
IN MY DARKEST MOMENTS SINCE, I'VE WONDERED IF MY VISIONS WERE EVER REAL IN THE FIRST PLACE. IF I REALLY WAS A SERVANT OF THE GREAT SPIRIT...OR JUST A MADMAN.
IF I KILLED ALL THOSE PEOPLE FOR MY OWN PATHETIC ENDS. OR WORSE, FOR NO DAMN REASON AT ALL.
TELL ME HONESTLY NOW...
DO I LOOK CRAZY TO YOU?
I GUESS I'LL KNOW THE TRUTH SOON ENOUGH.
GGRAARRRGGHHH!!!
MY NAME IS ARTHUR JAMES PENDERGRASS. PEOPLE CALLED ME CATCHER. I LISTENED TO THE VOICES IN MY HEAD. I LEAVE THE WORLD WORSE OFF THAN I FOUND IT.
ATE WAKANTANKA, MITAWA KI.
HE IYE CEL, WAKANTANKA...
I WAS EITHER A PROPHET OR A MURDERER, I DON'T KNOW WHICH. BUT EITHER WAY...

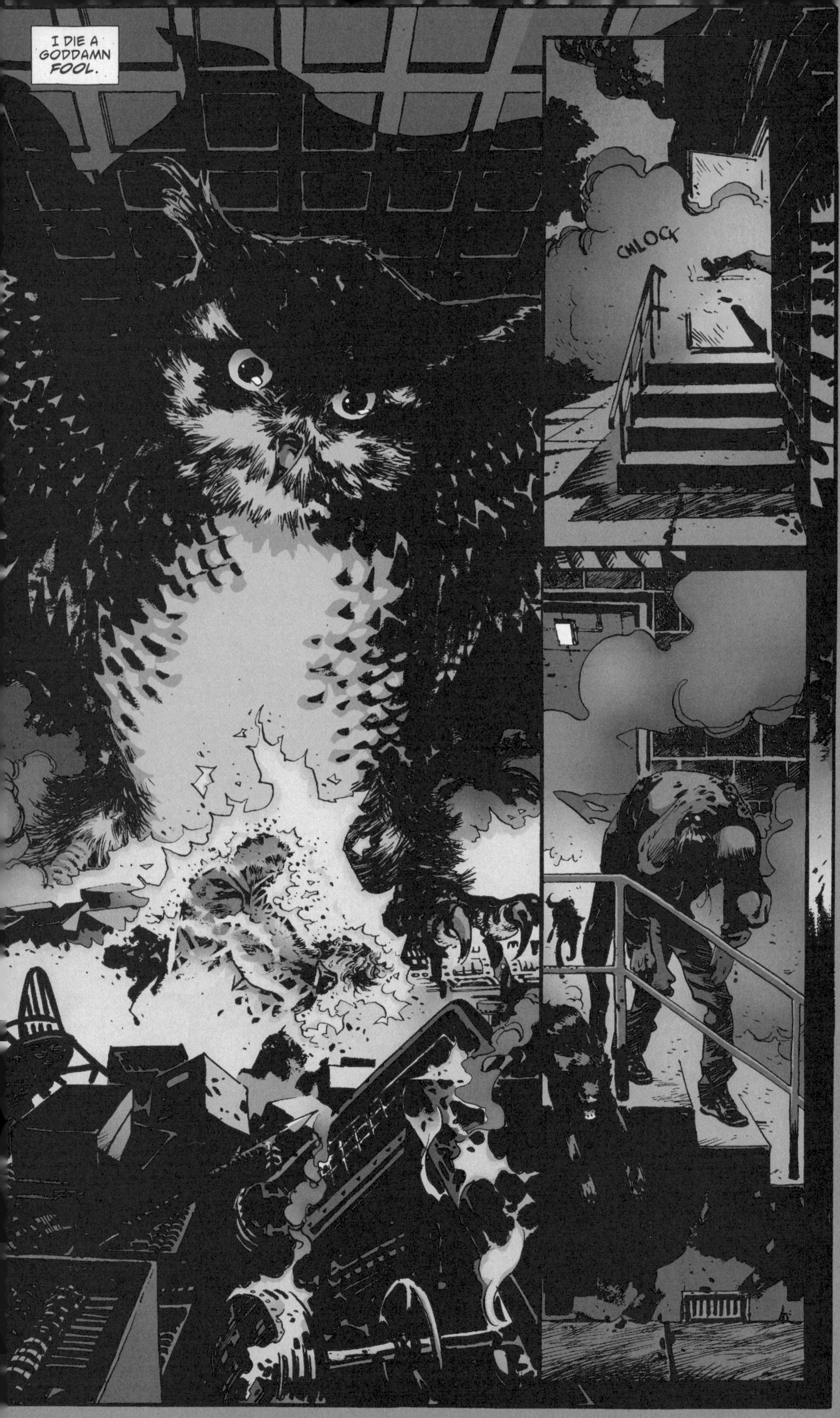
I DIE A GODDAMN FOOL.
CHLOCK

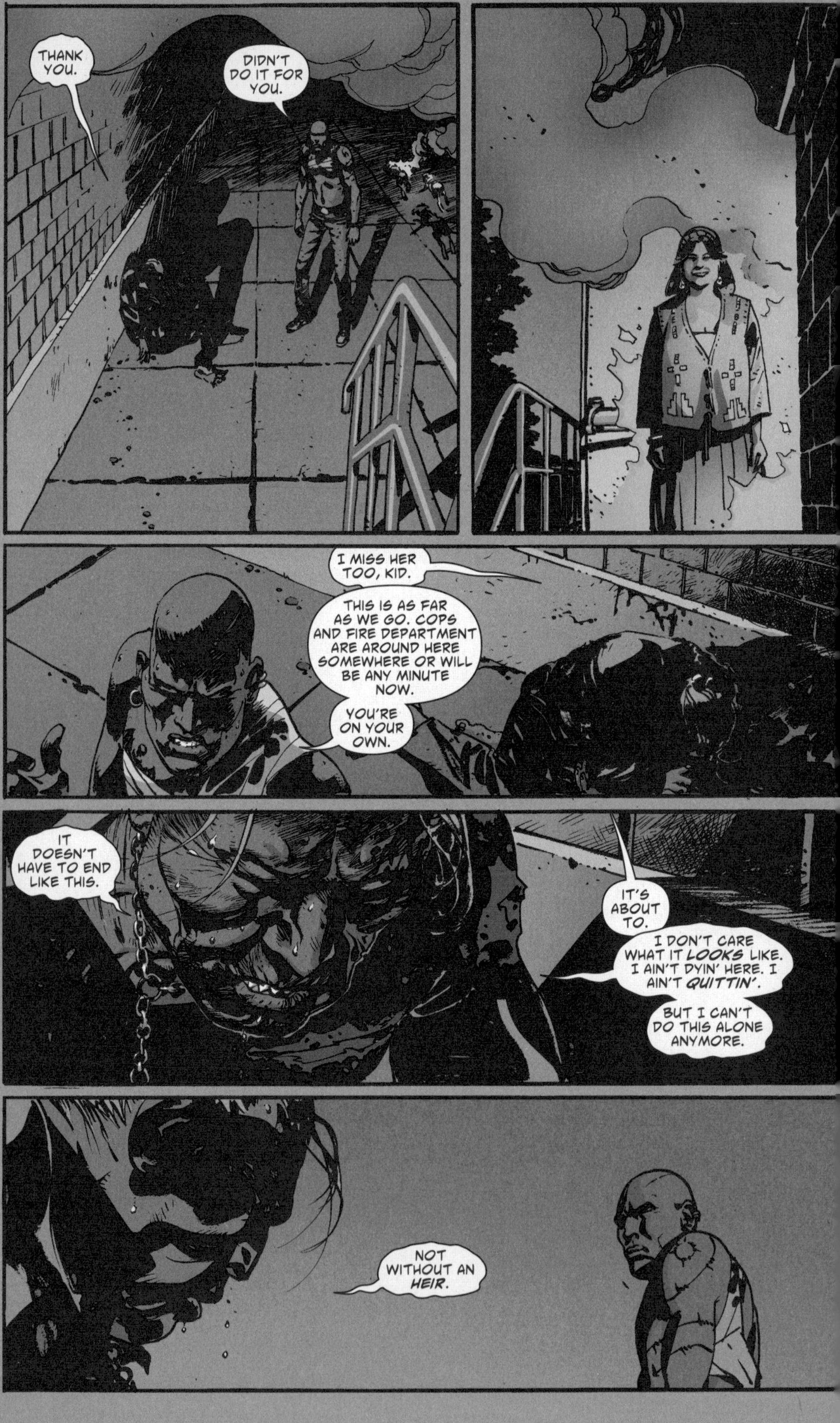
THANK YOU.
DIDN'T DO IT FOR YOU.
I MISS HER TOO, KID.
THIS IS AS FAR AS WE GO. COPS AND FIRE DEPARTMENT ARE AROUND HERE SOMEWHERE OR WILL BE ANY MINUTE NOW.
YOU'RE ON YOUR OWN.
IT DOESN'T HAVE TO END LIKE THIS.
IT'S ABOUT TO.
I DON'T CARE WHAT IT LOOKS LIKE. I AIN'T DYIN' HERE. I AIN'T QUITTIN'.
BUT I CAN'T DO THIS ALONE ANYMORE.
NOT WITHOUT AN HEIR.

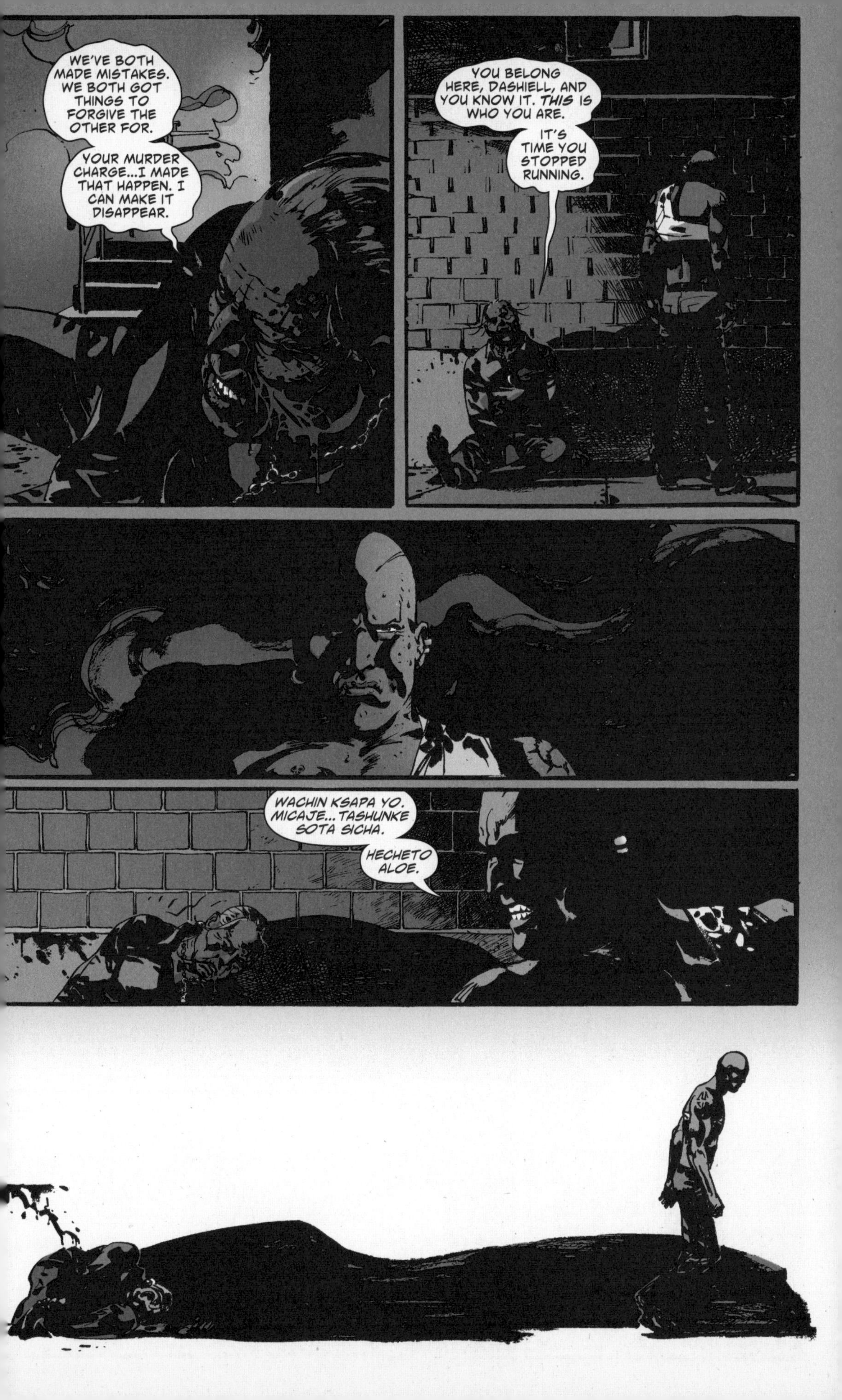
WE'VE BOTH MADE MISTAKES. WE BOTH GOT THINGS TO FORGIVE THE OTHER FOR.
YOUR MURDER CHARGE...I MADE THAT HAPPEN. I CAN MAKE IT DISAPPEAR.
YOU BELONG HERE, DASHIELL, AND YOU KNOW IT. *THIS* IS WHO YOU ARE.
IT'S TIME YOU STOPPED RUNNING.
WACHIN KSAPA YO. MICAJE... TASHUNKE SOTA SICHA.
HECHETO ALOE.

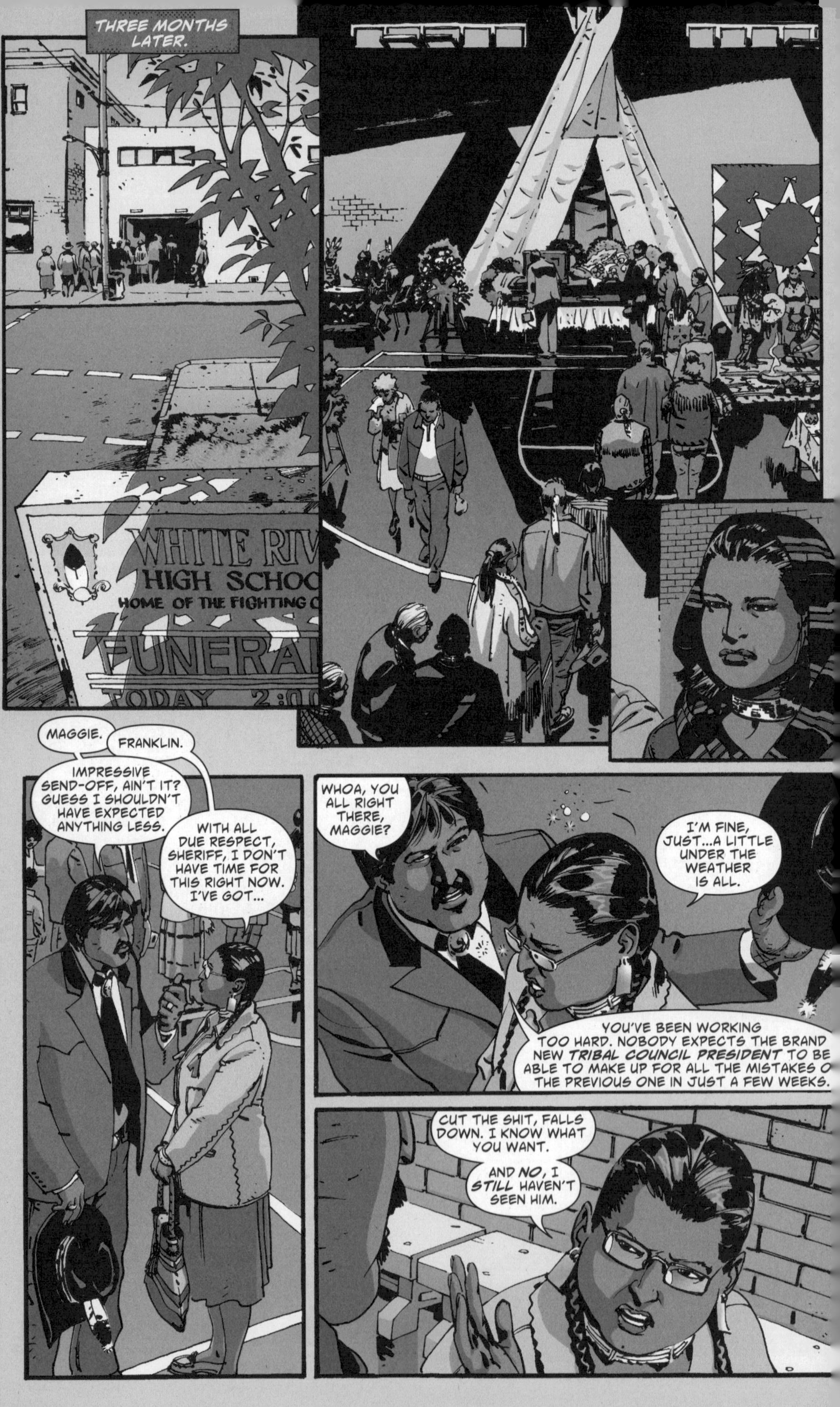
THREE MONTHS LATER.
WHITE RIV
HIGH SCHOO
HOME OF THE FIGHTING
FUNERAL
TODAY 2:0
MAGGIE.
FRANKLIN.
IMPRESSIVE SEND-OFF, AIN'T IT? GUESS I SHOULDN'T HAVE EXPECTED ANYTHING LESS.
WITH ALL DUE RESPECT, SHERIFF, I DON'T HAVE TIME FOR THIS RIGHT NOW. I'VE GOT...
WHOA, YOU ALL RIGHT THERE, MAGGIE?
I'M FINE, JUST...A LITTLE UNDER THE WEATHER IS ALL.
YOU'VE BEEN WORKING TOO HARD. NOBODY EXPECTS THE BRAND NEW *TRIBAL COUNCIL PRESIDENT* TO BE ABLE TO MAKE UP FOR ALL THE MISTAKES O THE PREVIOUS ONE IN JUST A FEW WEEKS.
CUT THE SHIT, FALLS DOWN. I KNOW WHAT YOU WANT.
AND *NO*, I *STILL* HAVEN'T SEEN HIM.

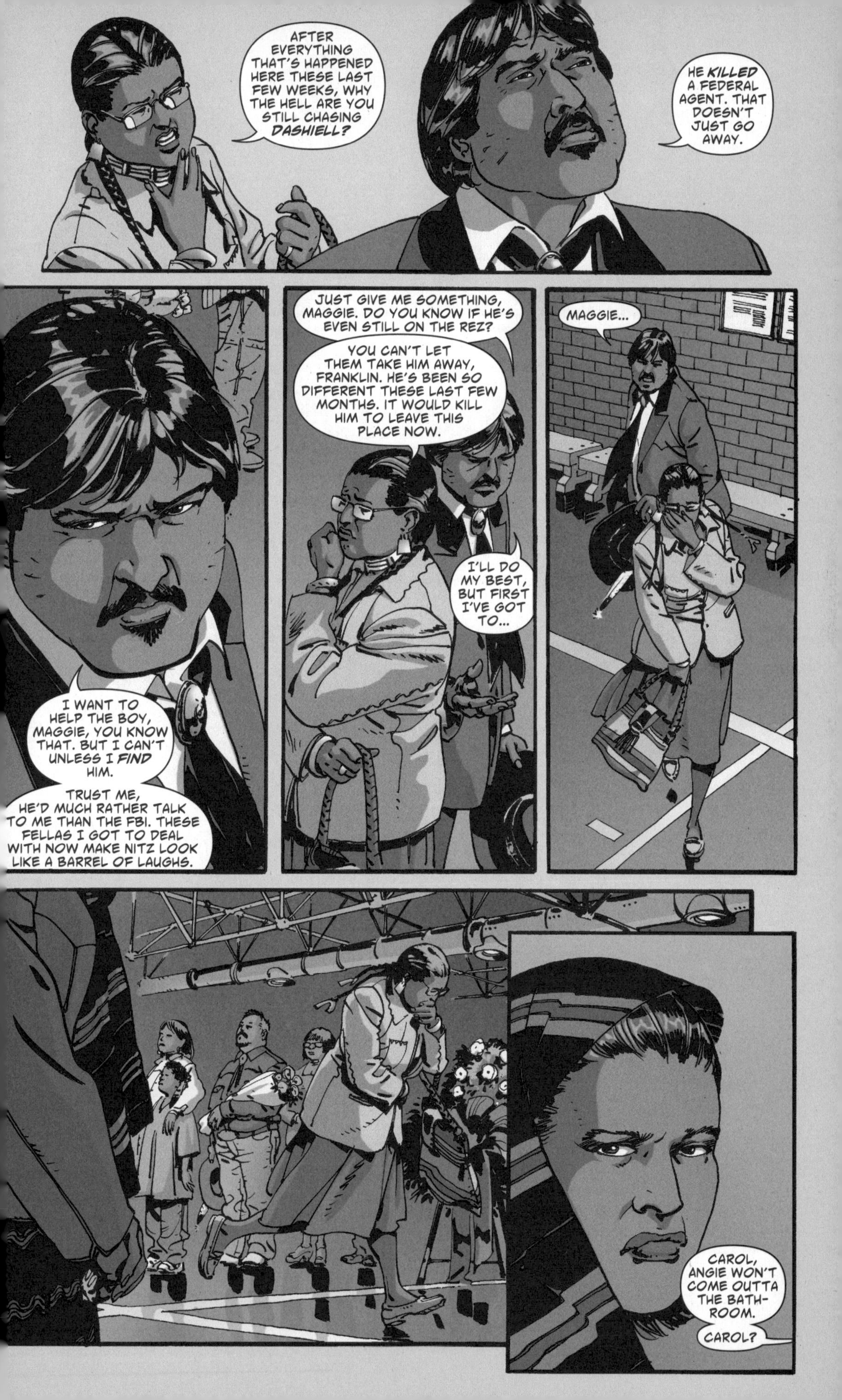
AFTER EVERYTHING THAT'S HAPPENED HERE THESE LAST FEW WEEKS, WHY THE HELL ARE YOU STILL CHASING DASHIELL?
HE KILLED A FEDERAL AGENT. THAT DOESN'T JUST GO AWAY.
I WANT TO HELP THE BOY, MAGGIE, YOU KNOW THAT. BUT I CAN'T UNLESS I FIND HIM.
TRUST ME, HE'D MUCH RATHER TALK TO ME THAN THE FBI. THESE FELLAS I GOT TO DEAL WITH NOW MAKE NITZ LOOK LIKE A BARREL OF LAUGHS.
JUST GIVE ME SOMETHING, MAGGIE. DO YOU KNOW IF HE'S EVEN STILL ON THE REZ?
YOU CAN'T LET THEM TAKE HIM AWAY, FRANKLIN. HE'S BEEN SO DIFFERENT THESE LAST FEW MONTHS. IT WOULD KILL HIM TO LEAVE THIS PLACE NOW.
I'LL DO MY BEST, BUT FIRST I'VE GOT TO...
MAGGIE...
CAROL, ANGIE WON'T COME OUTTA THE BATH-ROOM.
CAROL?

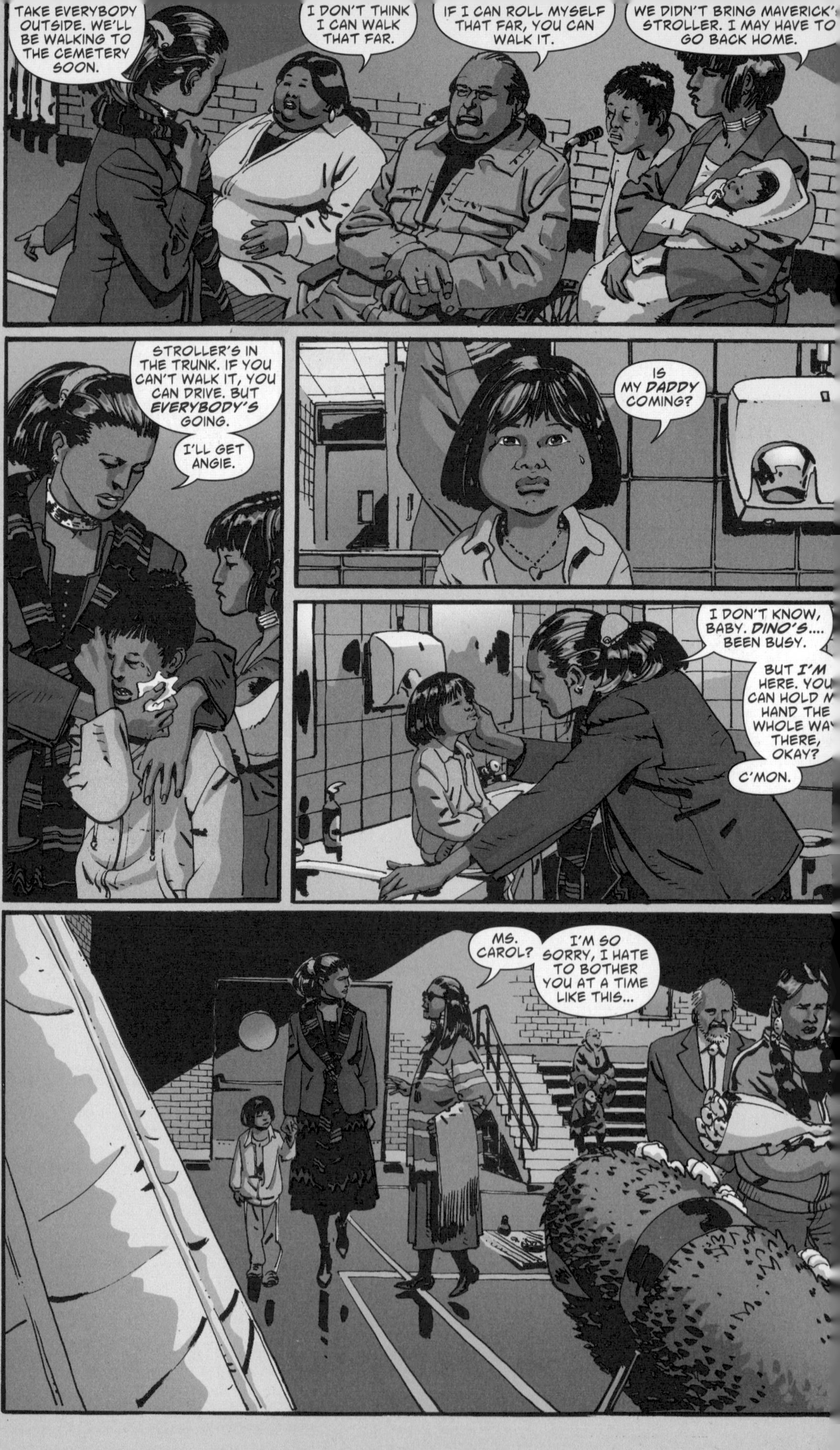
TAKE EVERYBODY OUTSIDE. WE'LL BE WALKING TO THE CEMETERY SOON.
I DON'T THINK I CAN WALK THAT FAR.
IF I CAN ROLL MYSELF THAT FAR, YOU CAN WALK IT.
WE DIDN'T BRING MAVERICK'S STROLLER. I MAY HAVE TO GO BACK HOME.
STROLLER'S IN THE TRUNK. IF YOU CAN'T WALK IT, YOU CAN DRIVE. BUT EVERYBODY'S GOING.
I'LL GET ANGIE.
IS MY DADDY COMING?
I DON'T KNOW, BABY. DINO'S.... BEEN BUSY.
BUT I'M HERE. YOU CAN HOLD MY HAND THE WHOLE WAY THERE, OKAY?
C'MON.
MS. CAROL?
I'M SO SORRY, I HATE TO BOTHER YOU AT A TIME LIKE THIS...

MY SON, MILTON...I.... I THINK HE'S USING *DRUGS*.

I CAN'T GET HIM TO COME TO CHURCH NO MORE. I CAN'T EVEN GET HIM TO TALK TO ME. NOW I THINK HE'S STEALING FROM THE NEIGHBORS. I DON'T KNOW WHAT TO DO.

COME BY THE HOUSE ON TUESDAY. WE'LL MAKE SOME TOBACCO TIES TOGETHER.

THEN YOU CAN TELL ME WHO YOUR SON HANGS OUT WITH. AND *EXACTLY* WHAT HE'S USING, IF YOU CAN FIND OUT. IF YOU CAN'T, JUST BRING SOME OF HIS TRASH AND *I'LL* KNOW.

AFTER THAT COMES THE HARD PART, BUT I'LL DO MY BEST TO HELP YOU. I *PROMISE* YOU THAT.

THANK YOU.

THANK YOU, MAMMA POOR BEAR.

DON'T THANK ME.

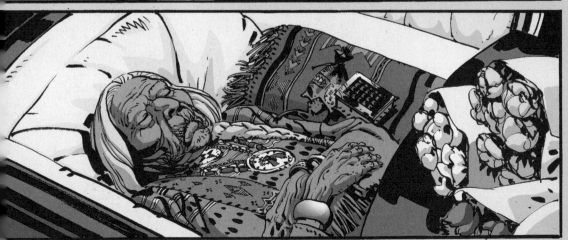

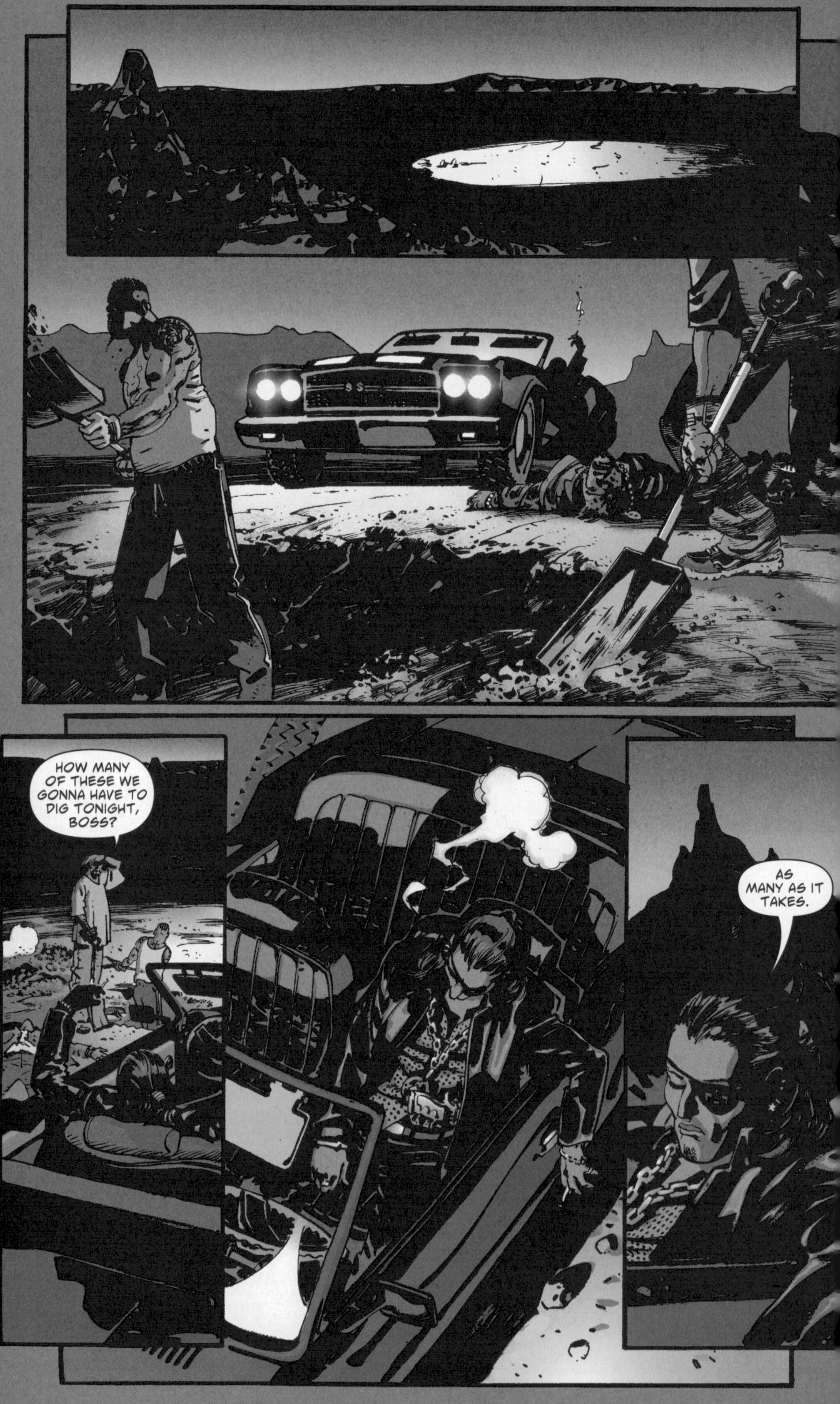

HOW MANY OF THESE WE GONNA HAVE TO DIG TONIGHT, BOSS?
AS MANY AS IT TAKES.

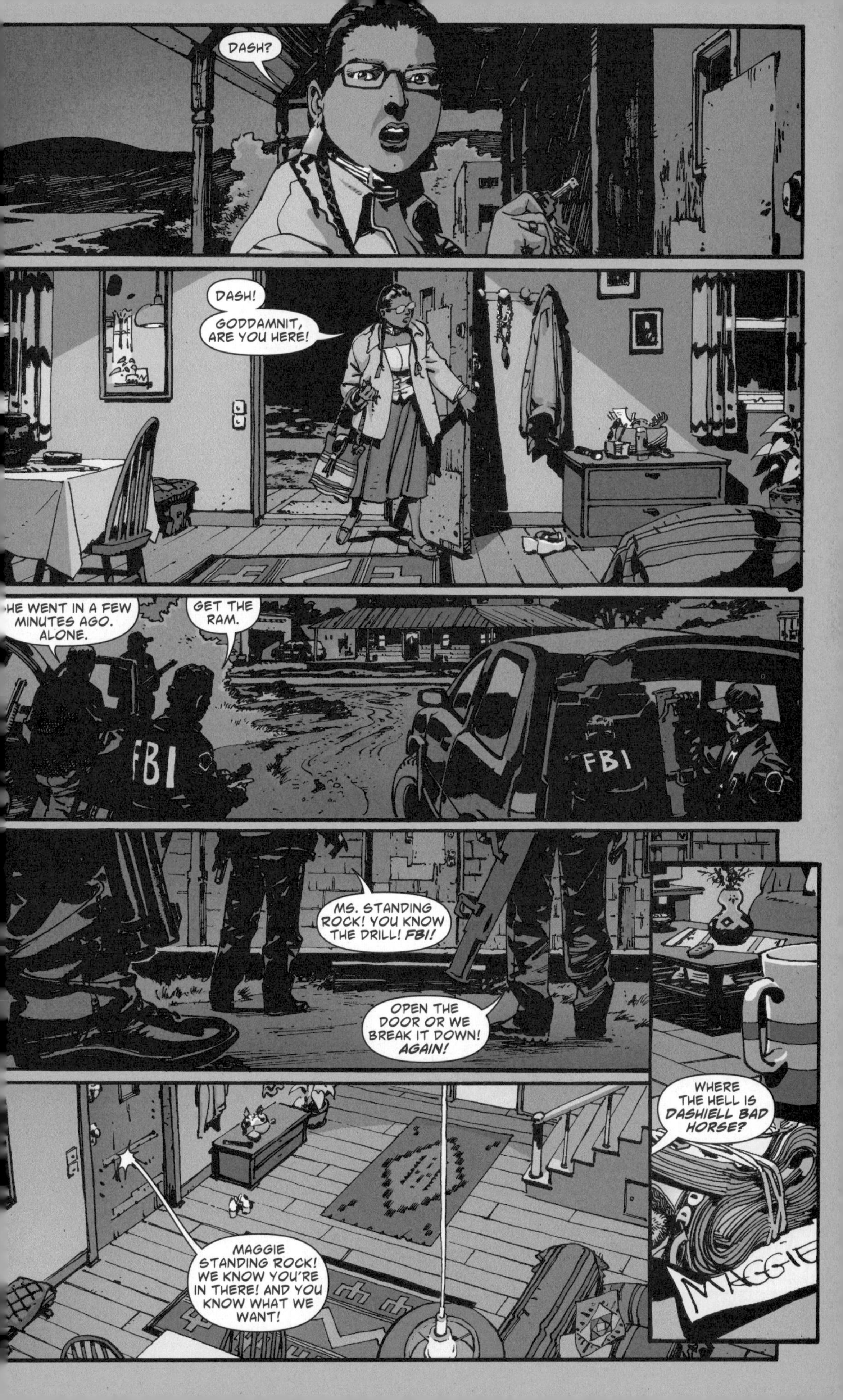
DASH?
DASH!
GODDAMNIT, ARE YOU HERE!
HE WENT IN A FEW MINUTES AGO. ALONE.
GET THE RAM.
MS. STANDING ROCK! YOU KNOW THE DRILL! FBI!
OPEN THE DOOR OR WE BREAK IT DOWN! AGAIN!
WHERE THE HELL IS DASHIELL BAD HORSE?
MAGGIE STANDING ROCK! WE KNOW YOU'RE IN THERE! AND YOU KNOW WHAT WE WANT!
FBI
FBI
MAGGIE

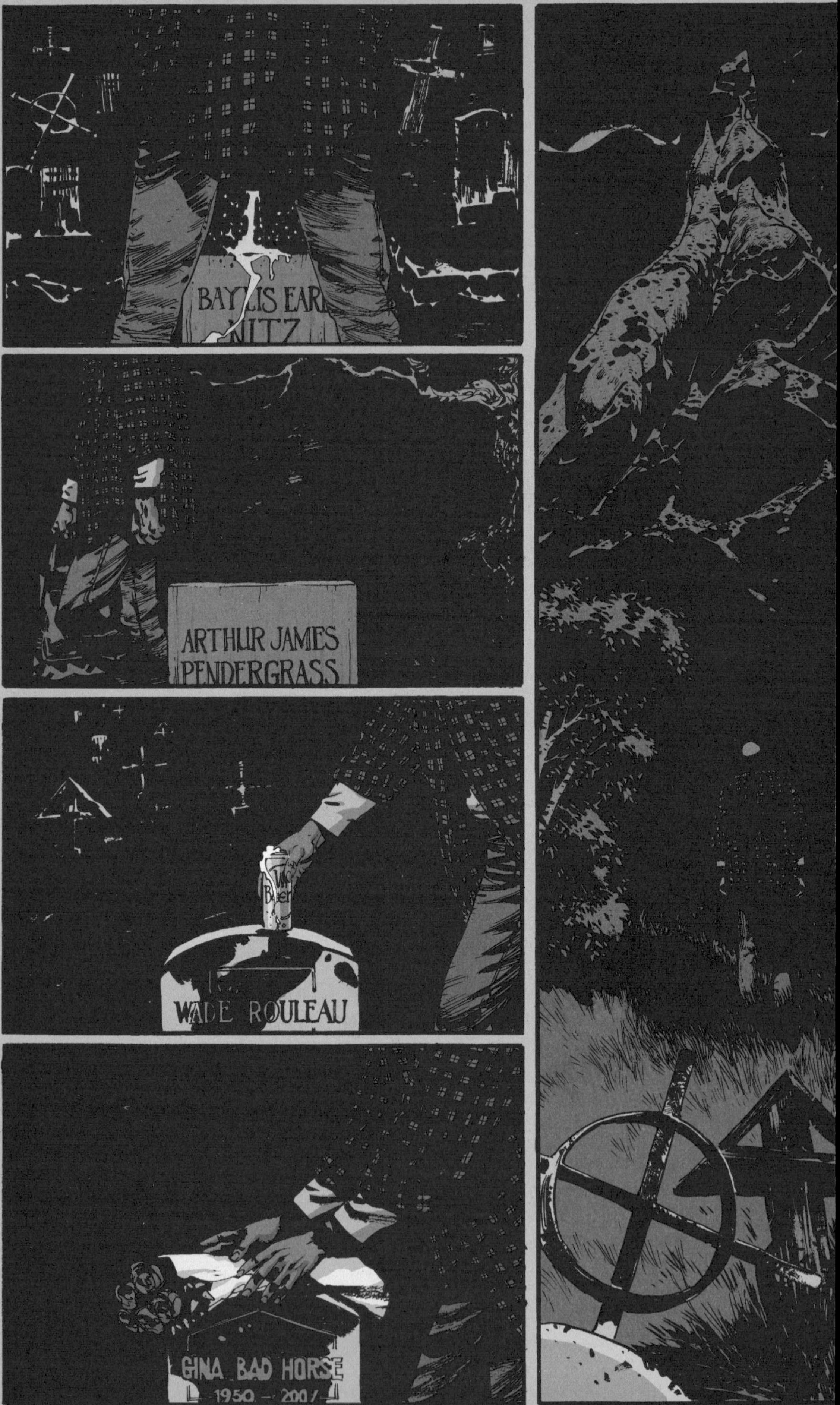
BAYLIS EARL
NITZ
ARTHUR JAMES
PENDERGRASS
WADE ROULEAU
GINA BAD HORSE
1950 – 2007

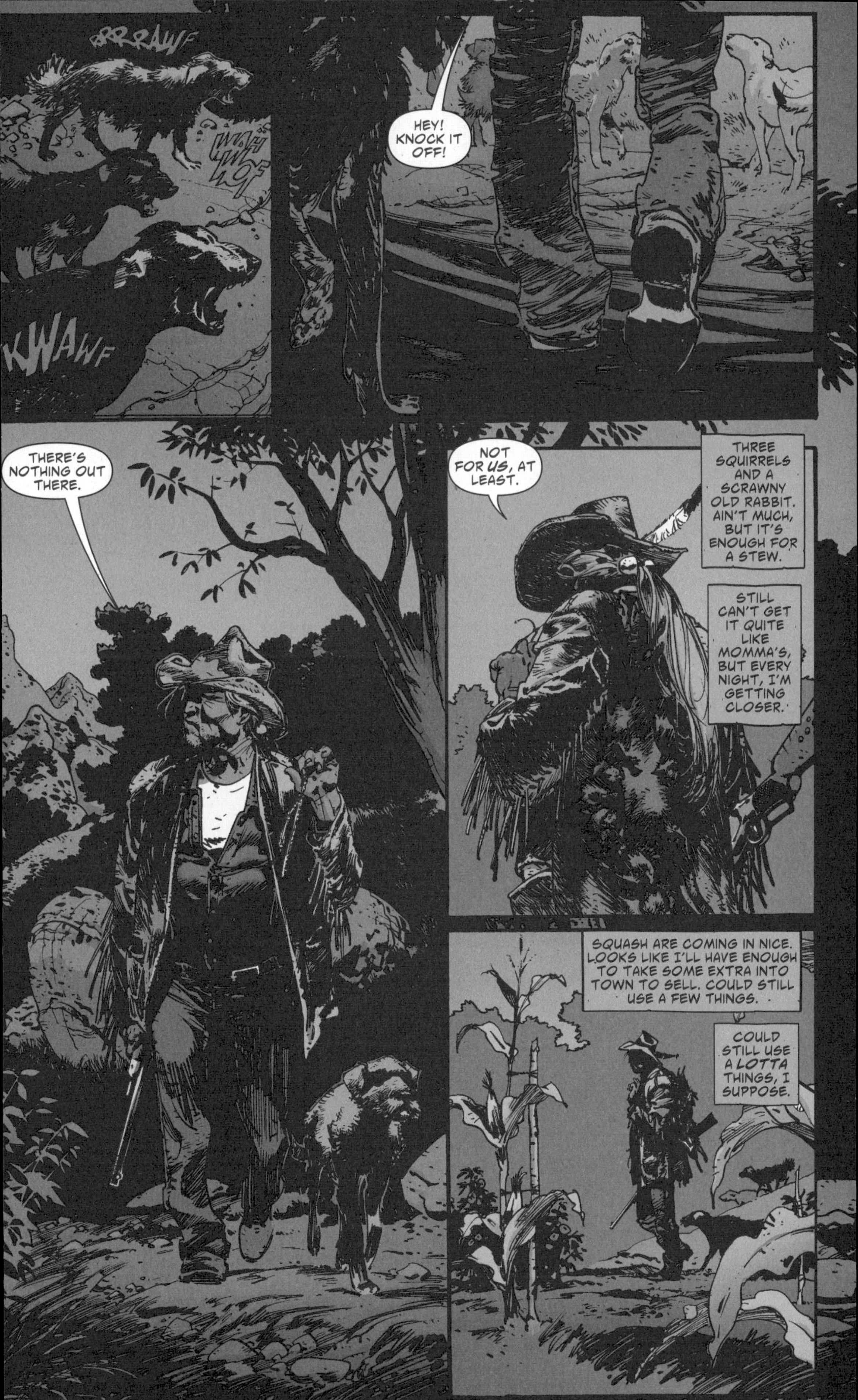
BRRRAWF
WAH WOOF
KWAWF
HEY! KNOCK IT OFF!
THERE'S NOTHING OUT THERE.
NOT FOR *US*, AT LEAST.
THREE SQUIRRELS AND A SCRAWNY OLD RABBIT. AIN'T MUCH, BUT IT'S ENOUGH FOR A STEW.
STILL CAN'T GET IT QUITE LIKE MOMMA'S, BUT EVERY NIGHT, I'M GETTING CLOSER.
SQUASH ARE COMING IN NICE. LOOKS LIKE I'LL HAVE ENOUGH TO TAKE SOME EXTRA INTO TOWN TO SELL. COULD STILL USE A FEW THINGS.
COULD STILL USE A *LOTTA* THINGS, I SUPPOSE.

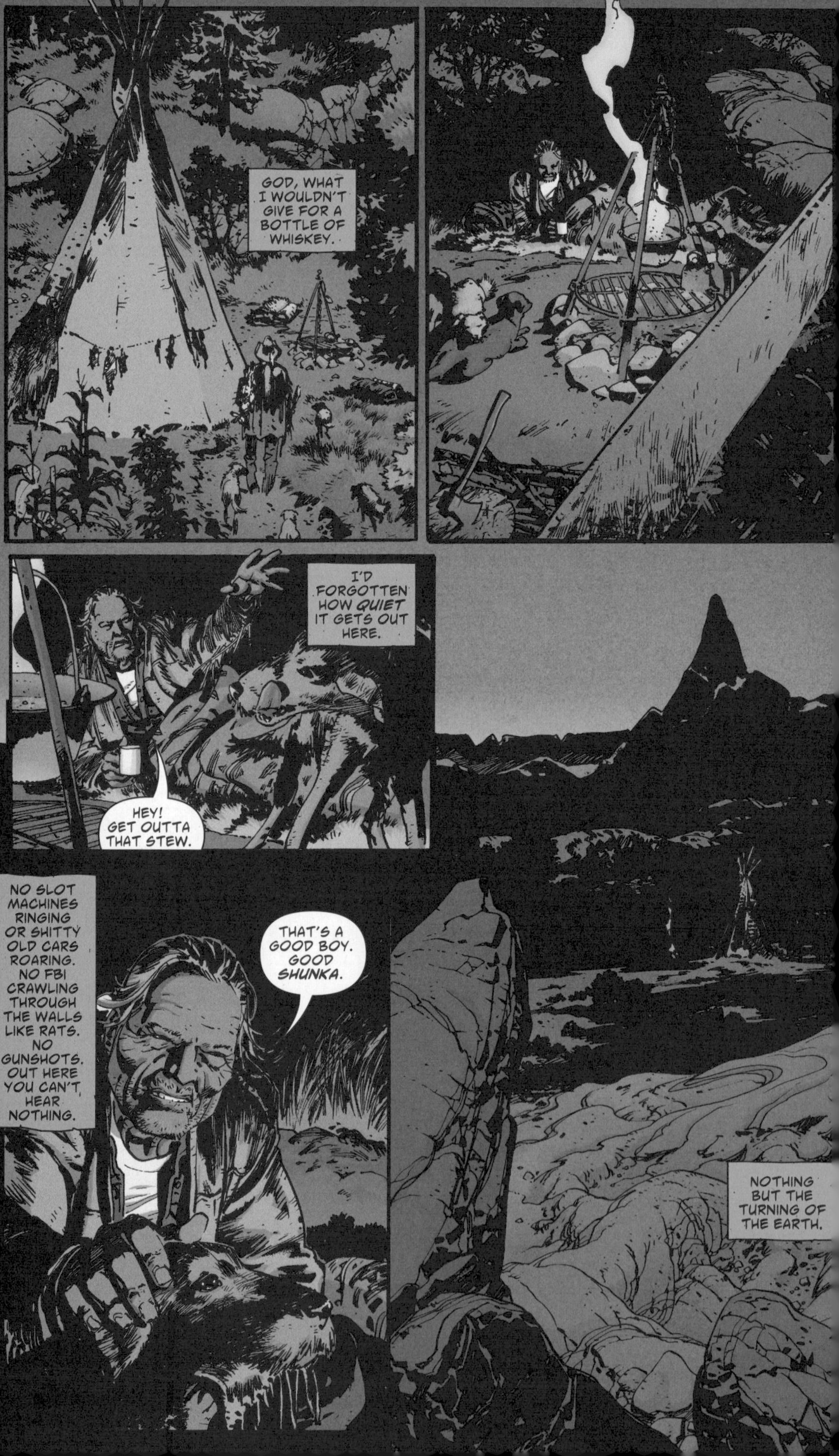
GOD, WHAT I WOULDN'T GIVE FOR A BOTTLE OF WHISKEY.
I'D FORGOTTEN HOW *QUIET* IT GETS OUT HERE.
HEY! GET OUTTA THAT STEW.
NO SLOT MACHINES RINGING OR SHITTY OLD CARS ROARING. NO FBI CRAWLING THROUGH THE WALLS LIKE RATS. NO GUNSHOTS. OUT HERE YOU CAN'T HEAR NOTHING.
THAT'S A GOOD BOY. GOOD *SHUNKA*.
NOTHING BUT THE TURNING OF THE EARTH.

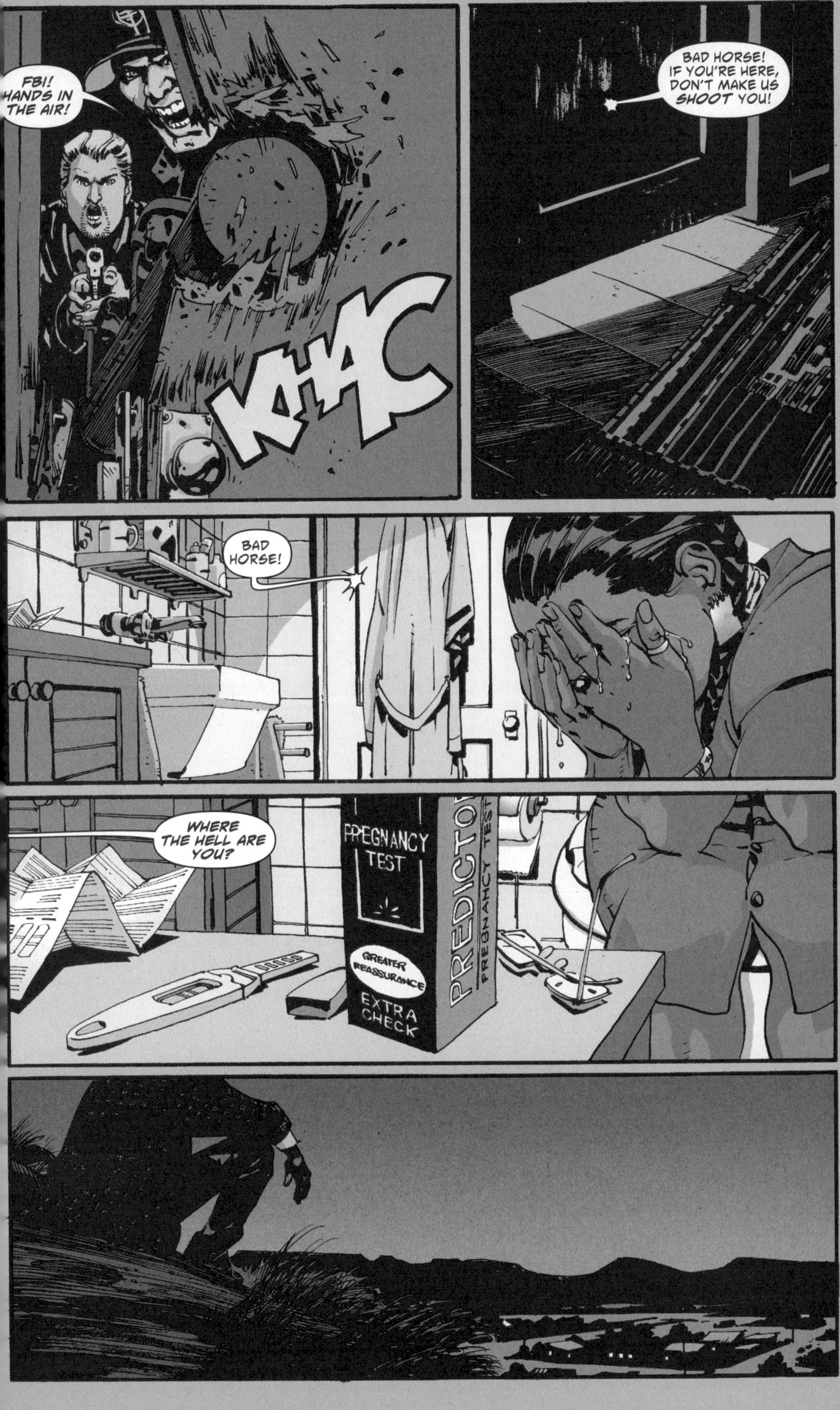
FBI! HANDS IN THE AIR!
KRAC
BAD HORSE! IF YOU'RE HERE, DON'T MAKE US SHOOT YOU!
BAD HORSE!
WHERE THE HELL ARE YOU?
PREGNANCY TEST
PREDICTOR PREGNANCY TEST
GREATER REASSURANCE
EXTRA CHECK

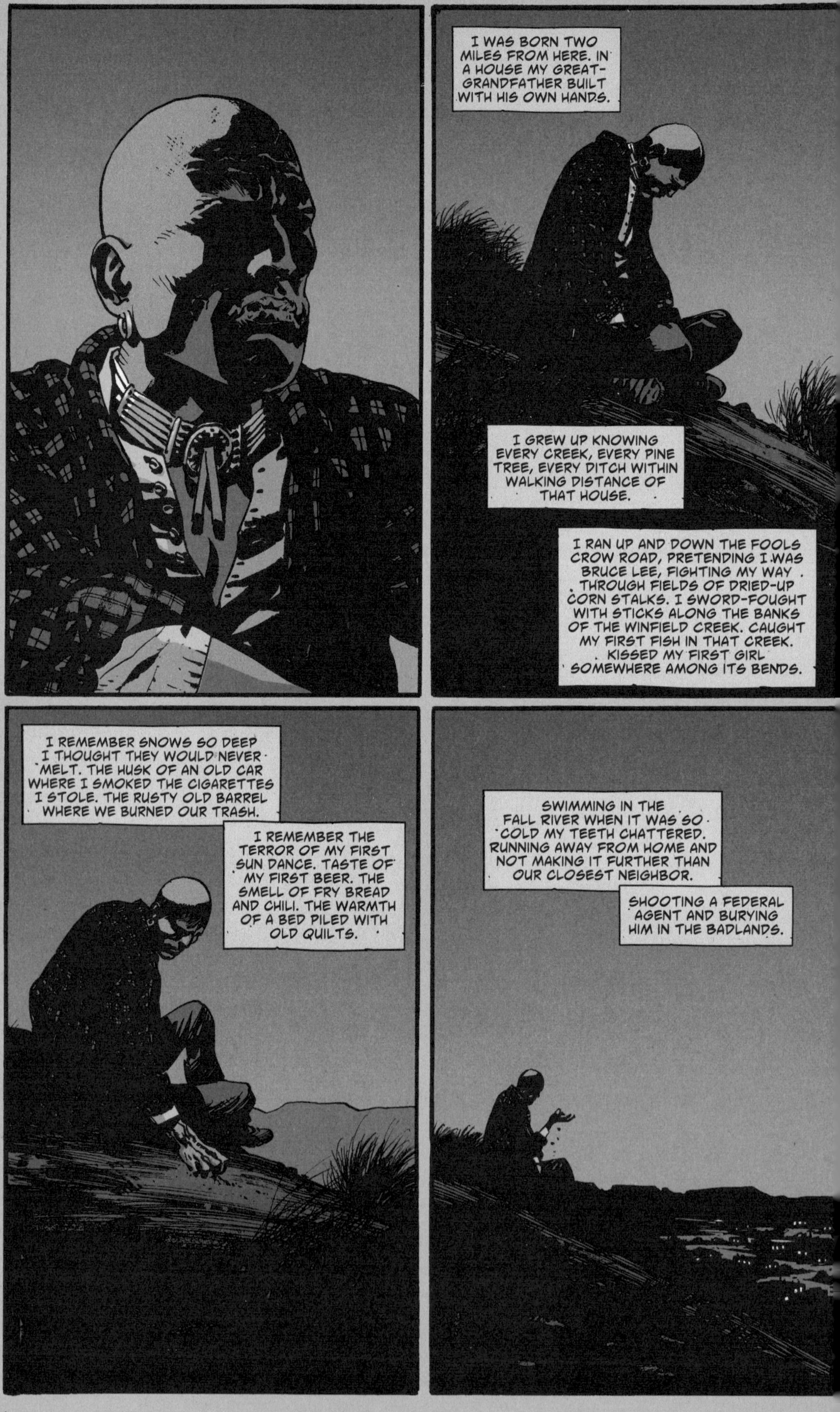
I WAS BORN TWO MILES FROM HERE. IN A HOUSE MY GREAT-GRANDFATHER BUILT WITH HIS OWN HANDS.
I GREW UP KNOWING EVERY CREEK, EVERY PINE TREE, EVERY DITCH WITHIN WALKING DISTANCE OF THAT HOUSE.
I RAN UP AND DOWN THE FOOLS CROW ROAD, PRETENDING I WAS BRUCE LEE, FIGHTING MY WAY THROUGH FIELDS OF DRIED-UP CORN STALKS. I SWORD-FOUGHT WITH STICKS ALONG THE BANKS OF THE WINFIELD CREEK. CAUGHT MY FIRST FISH IN THAT CREEK. KISSED MY FIRST GIRL SOMEWHERE AMONG ITS BENDS.
I REMEMBER SNOWS SO DEEP I THOUGHT THEY WOULD NEVER MELT. THE HUSK OF AN OLD CAR WHERE I SMOKED THE CIGARETTES I STOLE. THE RUSTY OLD BARREL WHERE WE BURNED OUR TRASH.
I REMEMBER THE TERROR OF MY FIRST SUN DANCE. TASTE OF MY FIRST BEER. THE SMELL OF FRY BREAD AND CHILI. THE WARMTH OF A BED PILED WITH OLD QUILTS.
SWIMMING IN THE FALL RIVER WHEN IT WAS SO COLD MY TEETH CHATTERED. RUNNING AWAY FROM HOME AND NOT MAKING IT FURTHER THAN OUR CLOSEST NEIGHBOR.
SHOOTING A FEDERAL AGENT AND BURYING HIM IN THE BADLANDS.

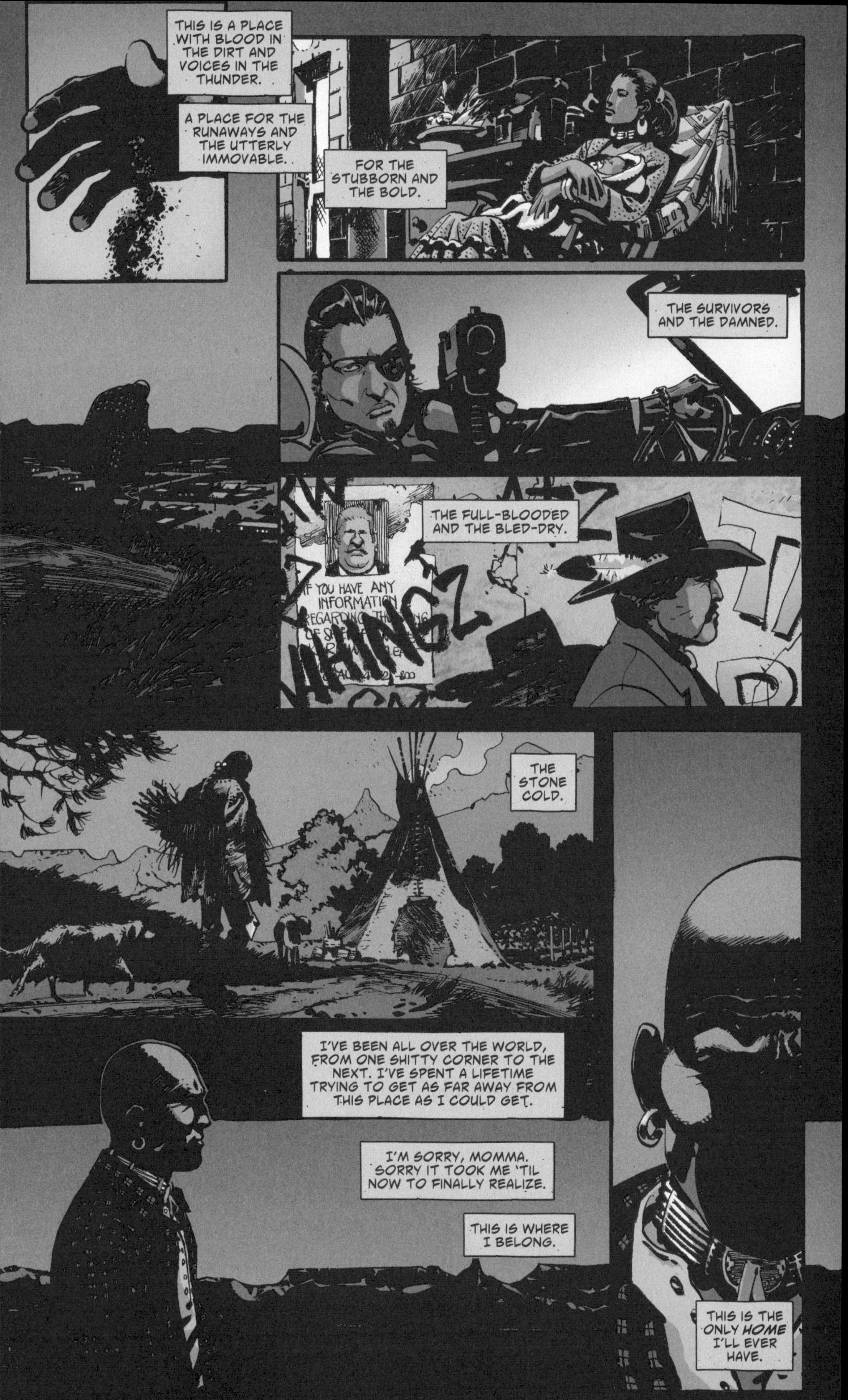
THIS IS A PLACE WITH BLOOD IN THE DIRT AND VOICES IN THE THUNDER.
A PLACE FOR THE RUNAWAYS AND THE UTTERLY IMMOVABLE.
FOR THE STUBBORN AND THE BOLD.
THE SURVIVORS AND THE DAMNED.
THE FULL-BLOODED AND THE BLED-DRY.
THE STONE COLD.
I'VE BEEN ALL OVER THE WORLD, FROM ONE SHITTY CORNER TO THE NEXT. I'VE SPENT A LIFETIME TRYING TO GET AS FAR AWAY FROM THIS PLACE AS I COULD GET.
I'M SORRY, MOMMA. SORRY IT TOOK ME 'TIL NOW TO FINALLY REALIZE.
THIS IS WHERE I BELONG.
THIS IS THE ONLY *HOME* I'LL EVER HAVE.

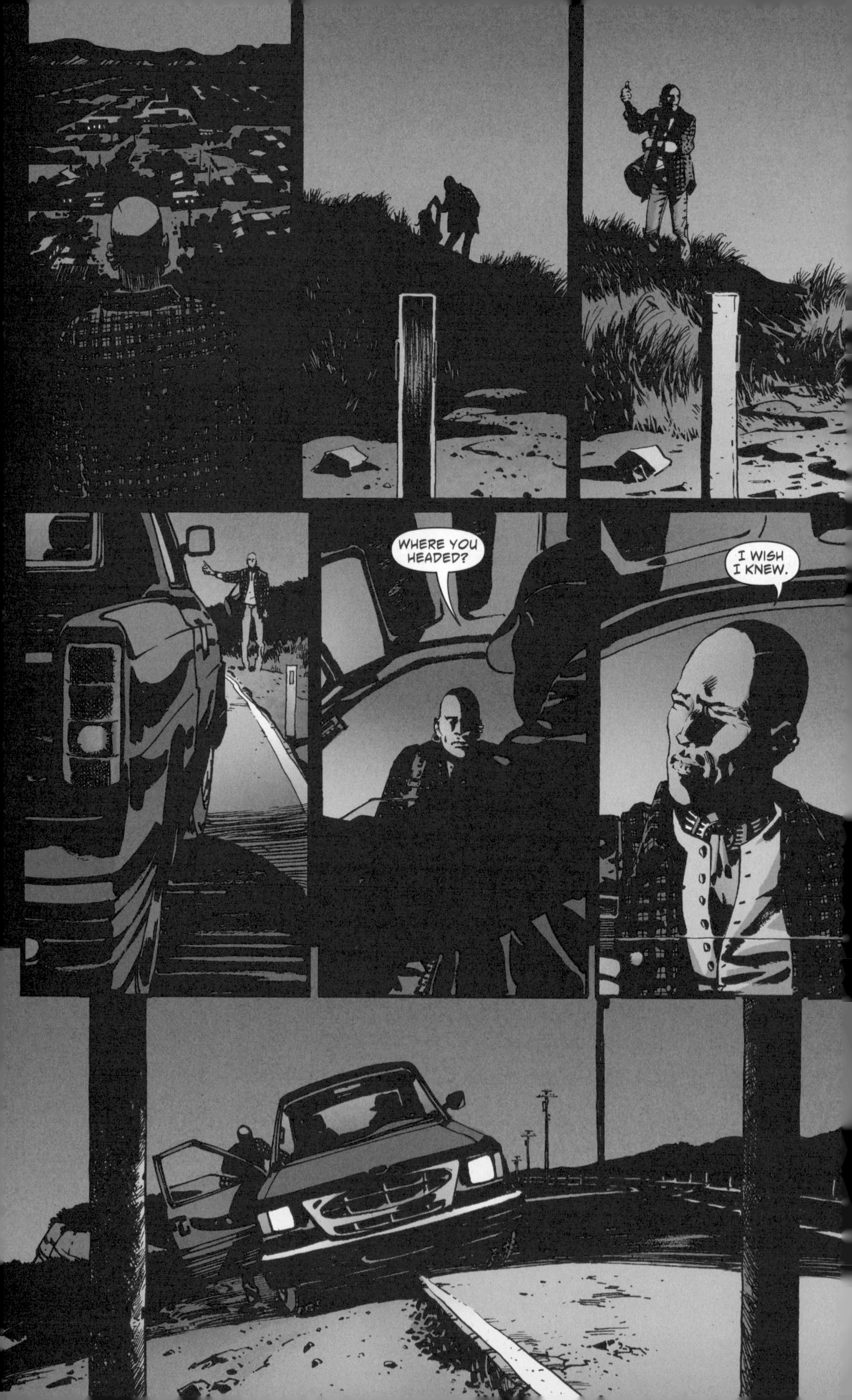
WHERE YOU HEADED?
I WISH I KNEW.

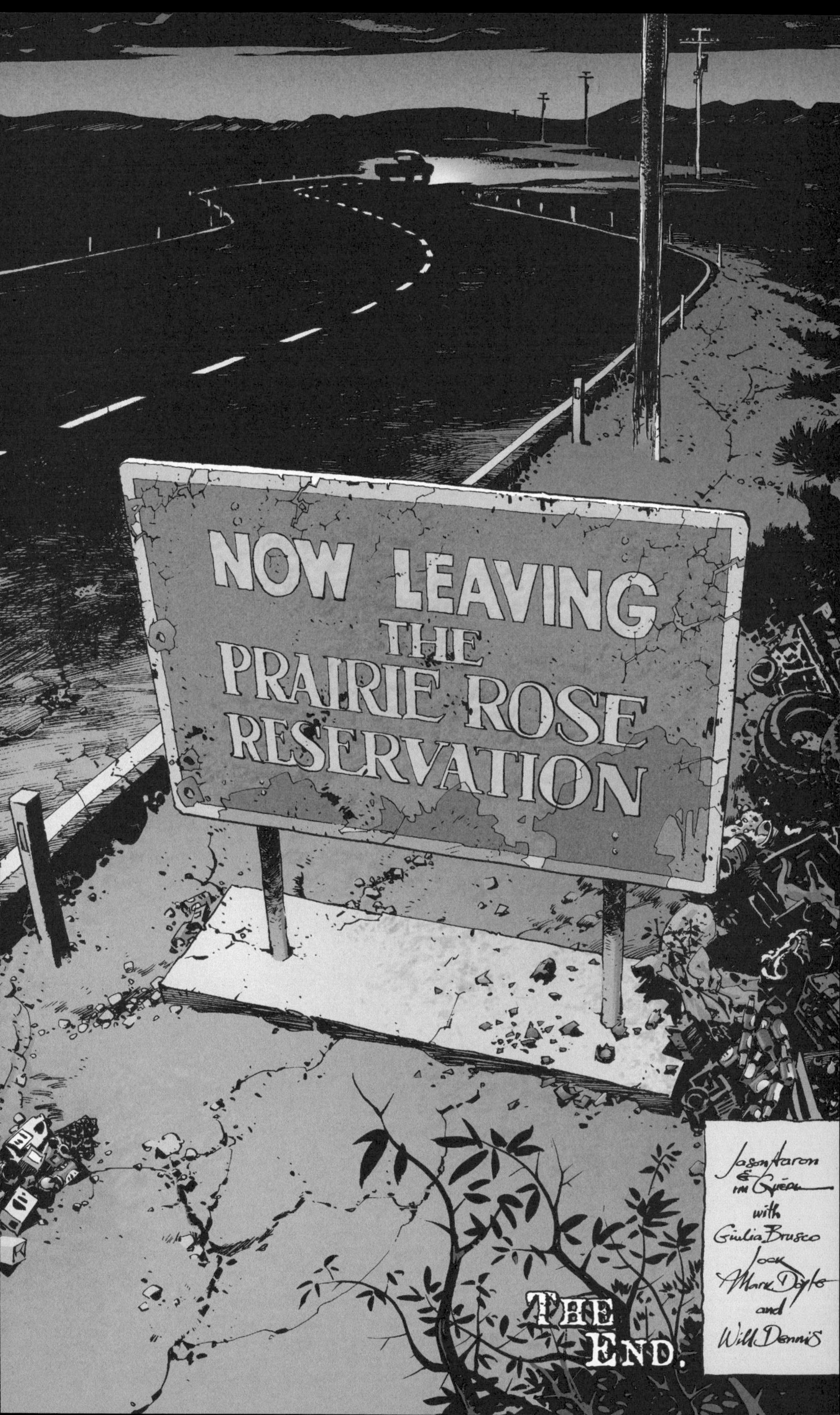
NOW LEAVING
THE
PRAIRIE ROSE
RESERVATION
THE END.
Jason Aaron
& rm Guéra
with
Giulia Brusco
Jock
Mark Doyle
and
Will Dennis

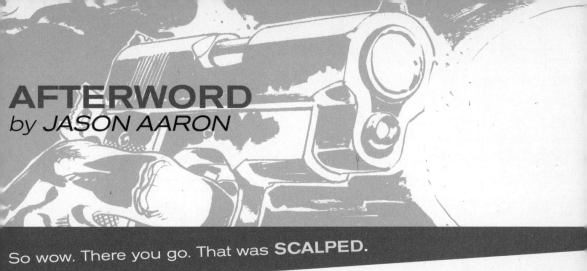

AFTERWORD
by JASON AARON

So wow. There you go. That was **SCALPED.**

Sixty issues. Ten trade paperbacks. More than 1,200 pages. God knows how many shootings, stabbings, betrayals, and bad choices.

There are a lot of different influences tangled up in the story of SCALPED. There's some Italian western, some Cormac McCarthy, some *Deadwood* and *The Wire*. There's Bruce Springsteen and Warren Oates. The Rolling Stones and Sam Peckinpah. Leonard Peltier and James Ellroy. State of Grace. Spanish gypsies. The blues. Garth Ennis. Johnny Cash.

But beyond all that, there's a large chunk of my own past tied up in this story as well. Not in the sense that I've ever lived on a reservation or worked as an undercover fed or smoked heroin. I really don't even like to gamble.

But still, as I look back on this series now that it has wrapped, I can't help seeing all the places where it has intertwined with my life of the last few years. In February 2005 I had just wrecked my (crappy old) car, so I was standing at a bus stop in Kansas City when my phone rang, and editor Will Dennis told me that Vertigo had decided to publish the Native American crime drama I'd pitched them. The next day I got a new car. Or at least a new used car. The day after that, I got married.

Later that year, when our son was born, I quit my day job at a warehouse to stay home with him. His name's Dash, by the way, just like someone else I know. And did I mention that I actually have a cousin named Gina Bad Horse? Suddenly I was a stay-at-home dad and full-time comic book writer, which for quite a while just meant I was working on SCALPED and nothing else. But once the series debuted in January 2007, other job offers started to trickle in.

And now here I am, seven years later, and because of this little series that no one (me included) ever expected to last, I'm still getting to stay home and make up stories for a living.

To say I consider myself the luckiest guy in the world would be an understatement.

So I have SCALPED to thank for how my life has gone, and I have a lot of people to thank for SCALPED.

Karen Berger at Vertigo for pulling the trigger on an ongoing series by a writer and artist she'd never heard of. Richard Bruning and Jack Mahan at DC for being among our earliest and staunchest supporters. Assistant editors Casey Seijas and Mark Doyle for helping shape and guide the story along the way. And the amazing group of creators who've contributed to the series, including colorists Lee Loughridge and Trish Mulvihill, letterers Phil Balsman, Steve Wands and Sal Cipriano and our mind-blowing cavalcade of artists, John Paul Leon, Davide Furno, Dave Johnson, Tim Bradstreet, Francesco Francavilla, Danijel Zezelj, Jason Latour, Igor Kordey, Timothy Truman, Jill Thompson, Jordi Bernet, Denys Cowan, Dean Haspiel, Brendan McCarthy, and Steve Dillon.

Jeez, that's a lot of names. It takes a village to make a comic, doesn't it? And the list doesn't stop there. Instead now we're getting to the folks who've been around for practically the whole ride. The ones who've truly done all the heavy lifting.

SCALPED wouldn't exist without Will Dennis. I wouldn't be writing comics if it weren't for Will Dennis. Once upon a time he plucked my blind submission off his slush pile, read it and decided to give me a shot. That turned into a war book called THE OTHER SIDE, and once that was rolling he asked me to pitch him something else. When Will and I would talk, it was often about crime stories we loved. So I pitched him a crime series called "Scalphunter," which was a reworking of an old west DC hero. It took several more months of work before Will had helped me shape that into SCALPED. I'd written two other comic scripts when I started writing SCALPED. I needed a good editor. Instead I got a great one. Will's been guiding the ship from the get-go, always the calm cool hand at the wheel, even in rough waters when it looked like we might sink. If you at all enjoyed SCALPED, make sure you give thanks to Will sometime. I know I do.

Jock was the cover artist on SCALPED from issue #1. Giulia Brusco was on colors for almost as long. And so much of the look and feel of the world of the Prairie Rose rez is owed to them. Giulia deserves some form of sainthood bestowed upon her for all of the deadline crunches and crazy artist demands (I'll get to him in a minute) she had to endure over the years. And as for Jock, even if he wasn't one of the absolute best cover artists in the business today, he'd still be worth having around for his infectious smile, delightful accent, exemplary taste in Patrick Swayze movies, and predilection for late night air drumming.

And then there's R.M. Guéra. Genius. Madman. Artist extraordinaire. You couldn't ask for a more passionate, more cerebral, more talented co-creator than R.M. Guéra. He and I worked together for four years before we ever met in person, but it never seemed to matter. We were somehow always on the same wavelength. Me, a guy who'd never been further outside the U.S. than Tijuana, and him, a guy who'd never been to the States. Yet somehow it never seemed to matter, thanks to our shared love of spaghetti westerns and Bob Dylan and Peckinpah and everything else that united us even from across the ocean. When we did finally meet a few years ago in New York, it was like seeing an old friend again. And for the first time, we actually got to work on SCALPED together in the same room, as we wrote the last pages of the last issue over some steaks and beers. I can think of no more fitting end and no finer a collaborator.

You may have noticed a bit of an international flavor to the SCALPED team. Guéra is Serbian and lives in Spain. Jock is Scottish, Giulia is Italian, and both live in the UK. Will, Mark and everybody from Vertigo are in New York. And I'm a guy from Alabama who lives in Kansas. Yet somehow we all came together to do a book set in South Dakota. Go figure that one out.

So yeah, like I said, SCALPED has been a huge, important part of my life. And now by reading it, so have you. We never could have made it this far, all the way to sixty issues, if not for an unbelievably fervent group of fans and supporters. All you people who blogged about the series, who forced copies on your friends, who badgered your local retailers into ordering more copies, without you, we wouldn't be here. And for that, I owe you all more drinks than I can ever repay. But catch me at a bar sometime, and we'll give it a try.

I'm going to miss these characters, and all the horrible things I got to put them through. And I'm going to miss working with this crew most of all.

Something tells me we'll all have to do this again sometime.

Cheers.

JASON AARON
Kansas City
July 2012

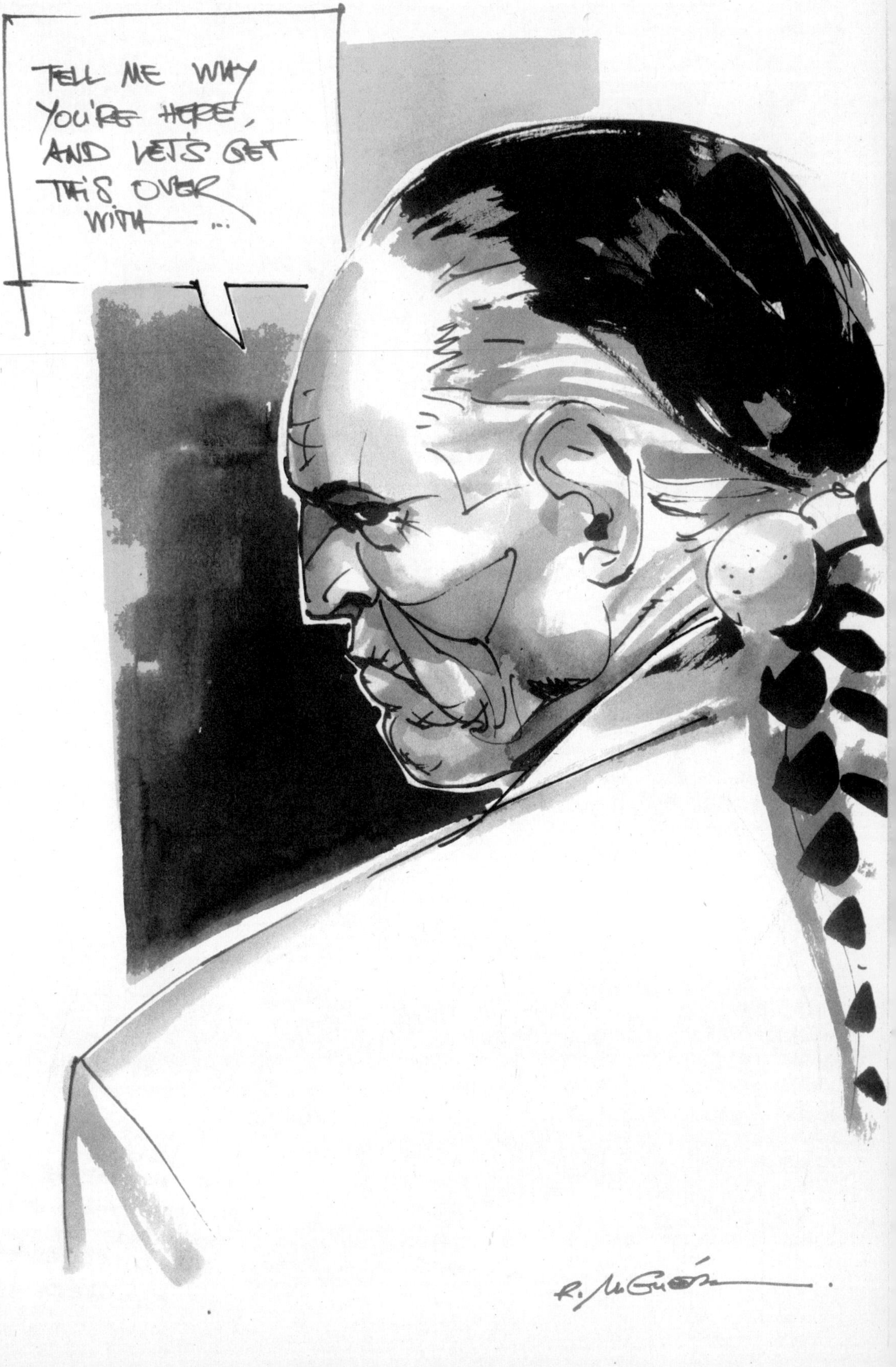
TELL ME WHY
YOU'RE HERE, AND LET'S GET THIS OVER WITH...
R. M. GUÉRA

EARLY ARTWORK **A GIFT FOR JASON 2007**

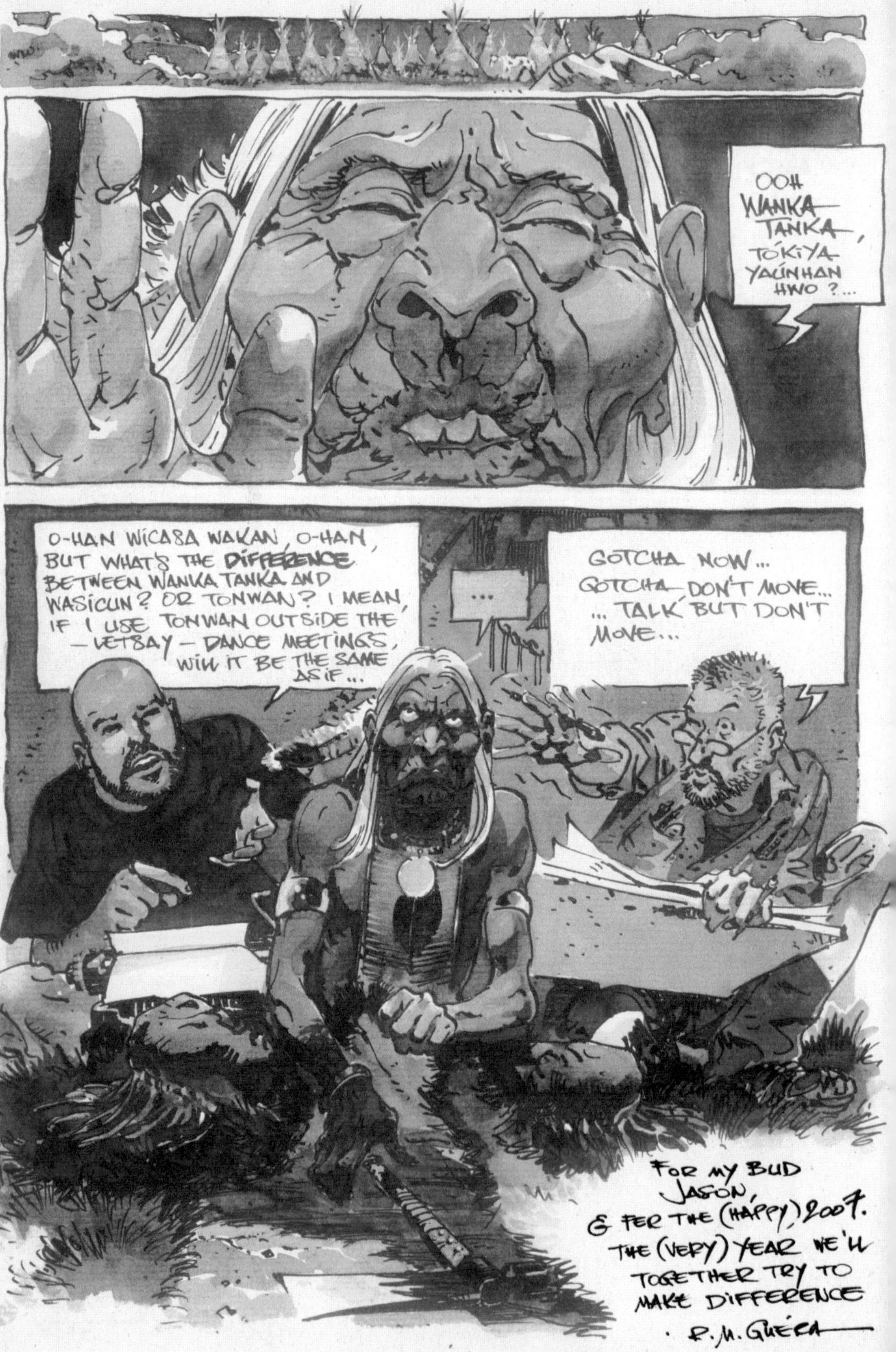
OOH WANKA TANKA, TÓKIYA YAÚNHAN HWO ?...
O-HAN WICASA WAKAN, O-HAN, BUT WHAT'S THE DIFFERENCE BETWEEN WANKA TANKA AND WASICUN? OR TONWAN? I MEAN, IF I USE TONWAN OUTSIDE THE -VETSAY- DANCE MEETINGS, WILL IT BE THE SAME AS IF...
...
GOTCHA NOW... GOTCHA DON'T MOVE... ...TALK BUT DON'T MOVE...
FOR MY BUD JASON, & FOR THE (HAPPY) 2007. THE (VERY) YEAR WE'LL TOGETHER TRY TO MAKE DIFFERENCE
· R.M. GUÉRA

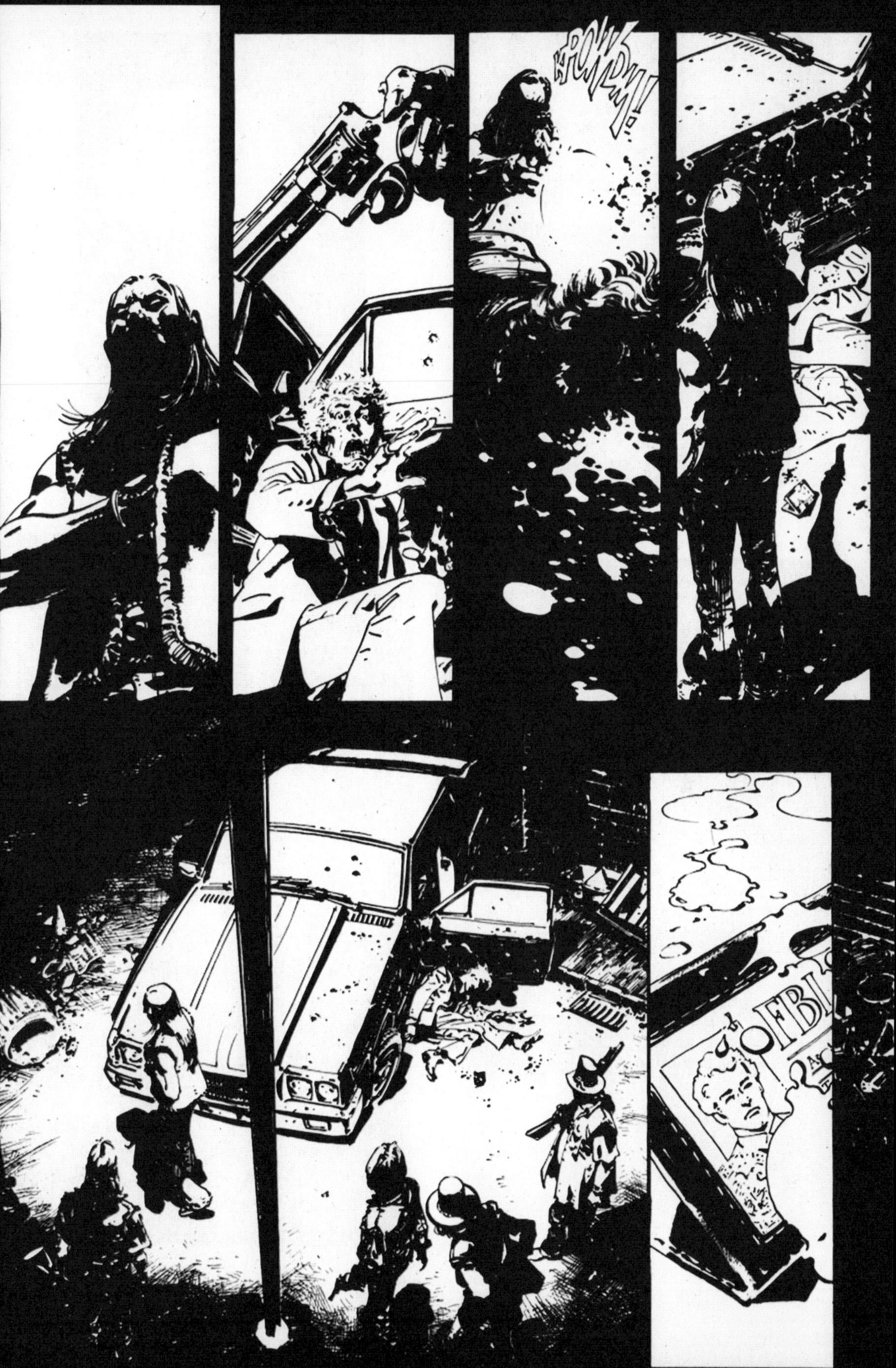
FBI

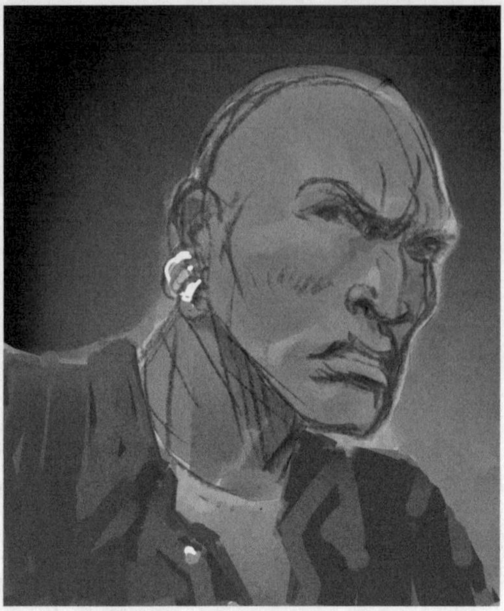

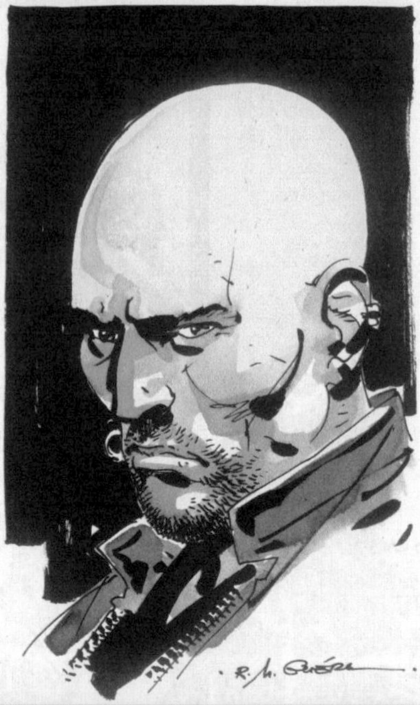

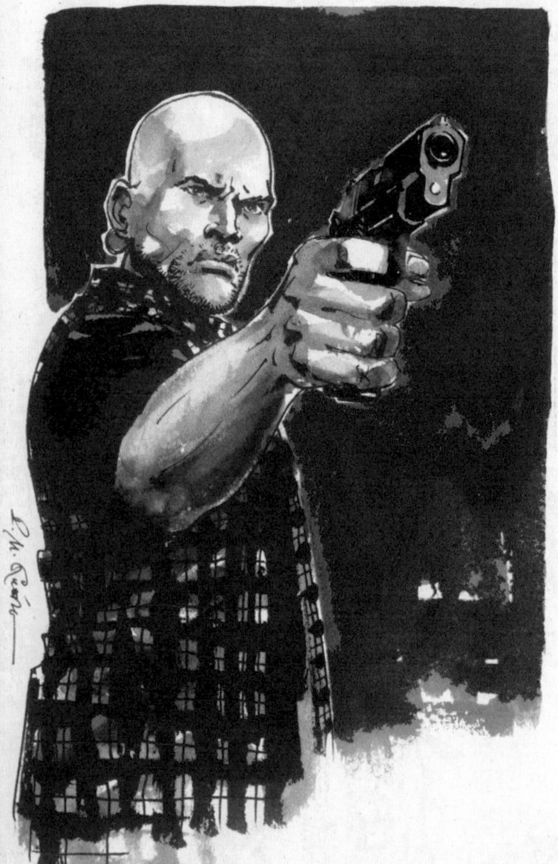

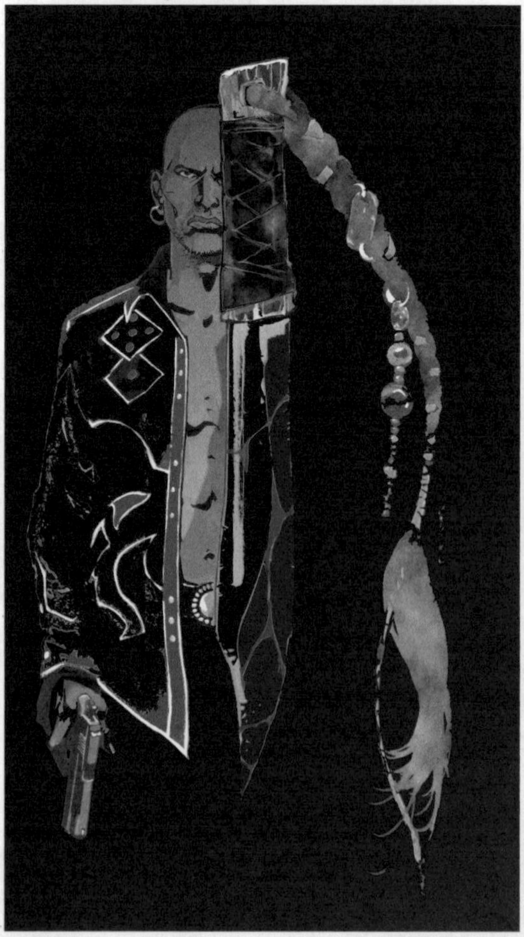

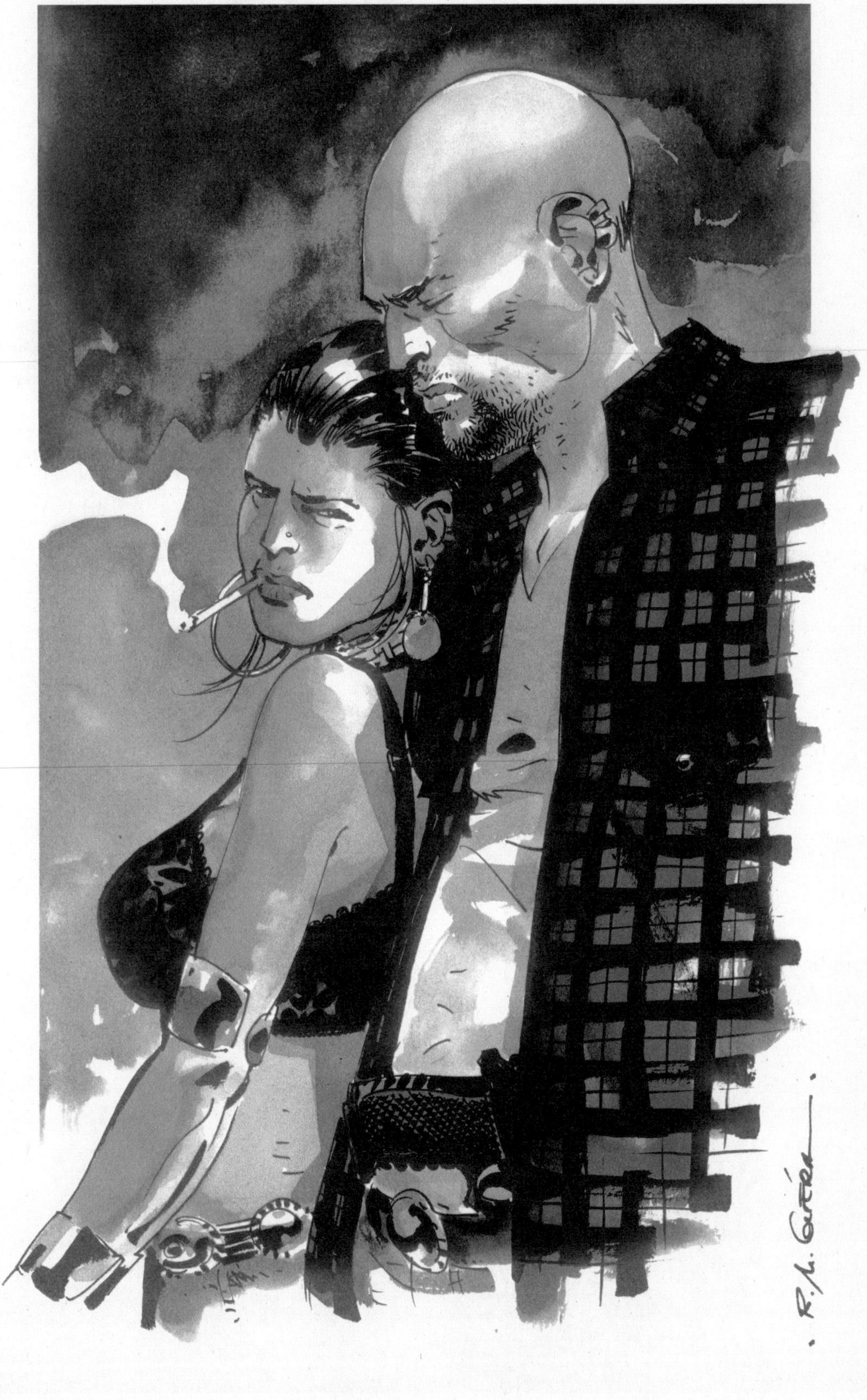

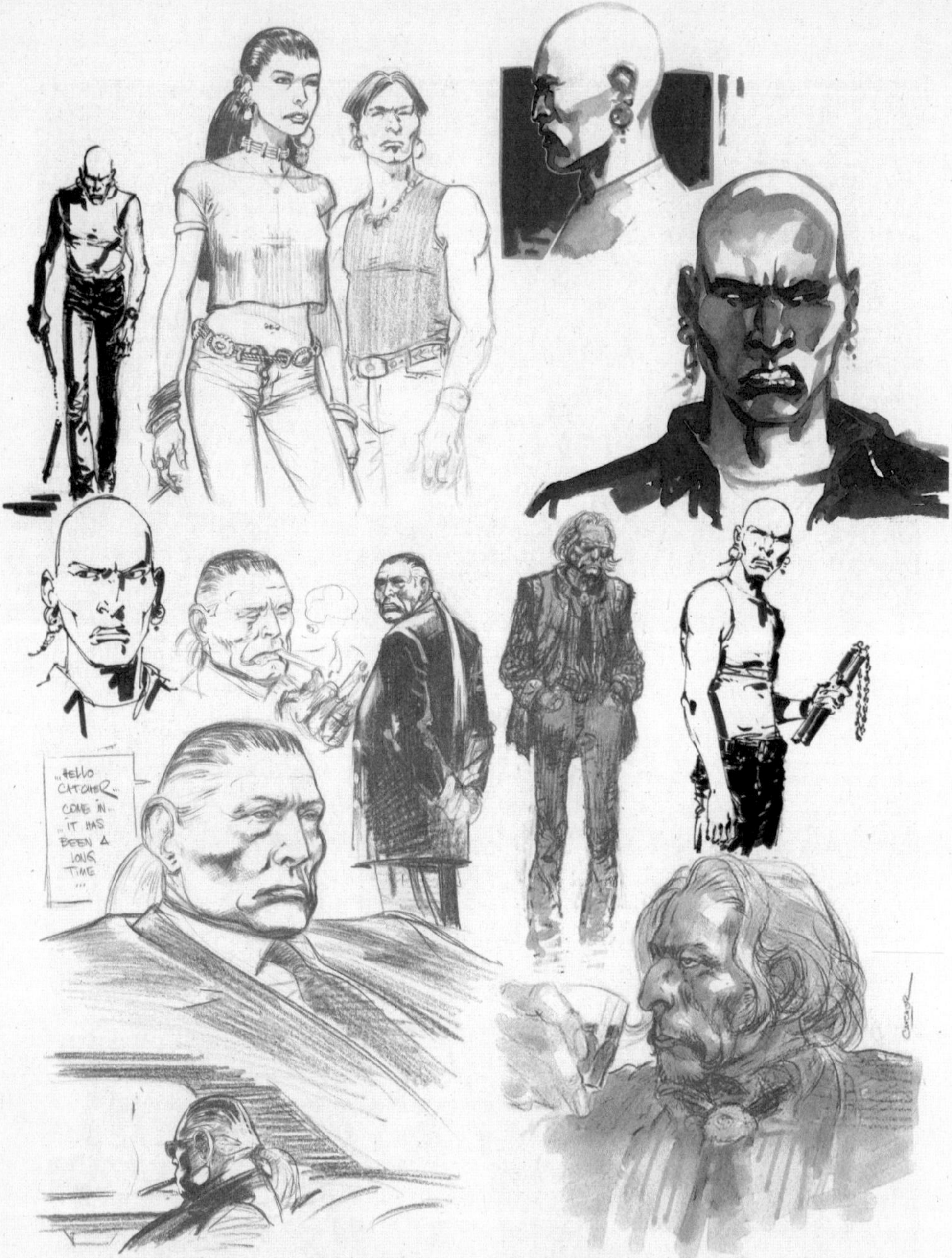
...HELLO CATCHER... COME IN... ...IT HAS BEEN A LONG TIME ...

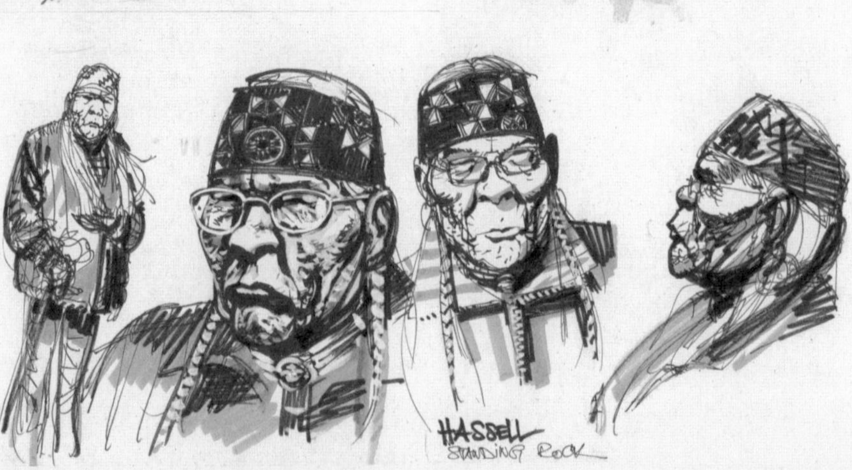
HASSELL
STANDING ROCK

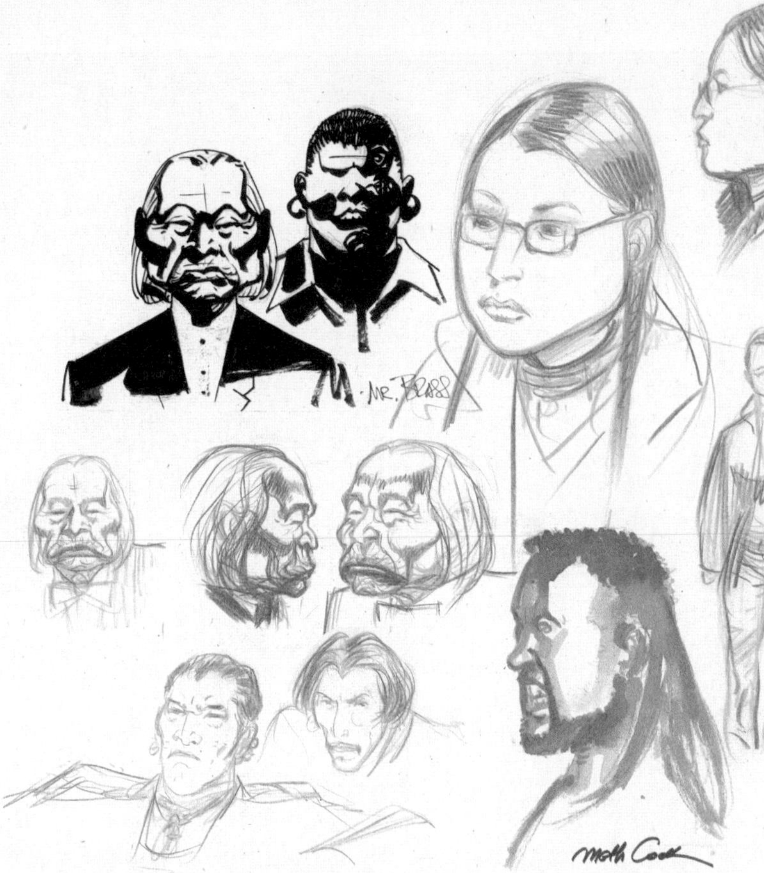
MR. BRASS
MAGGIE STANDING ROCK

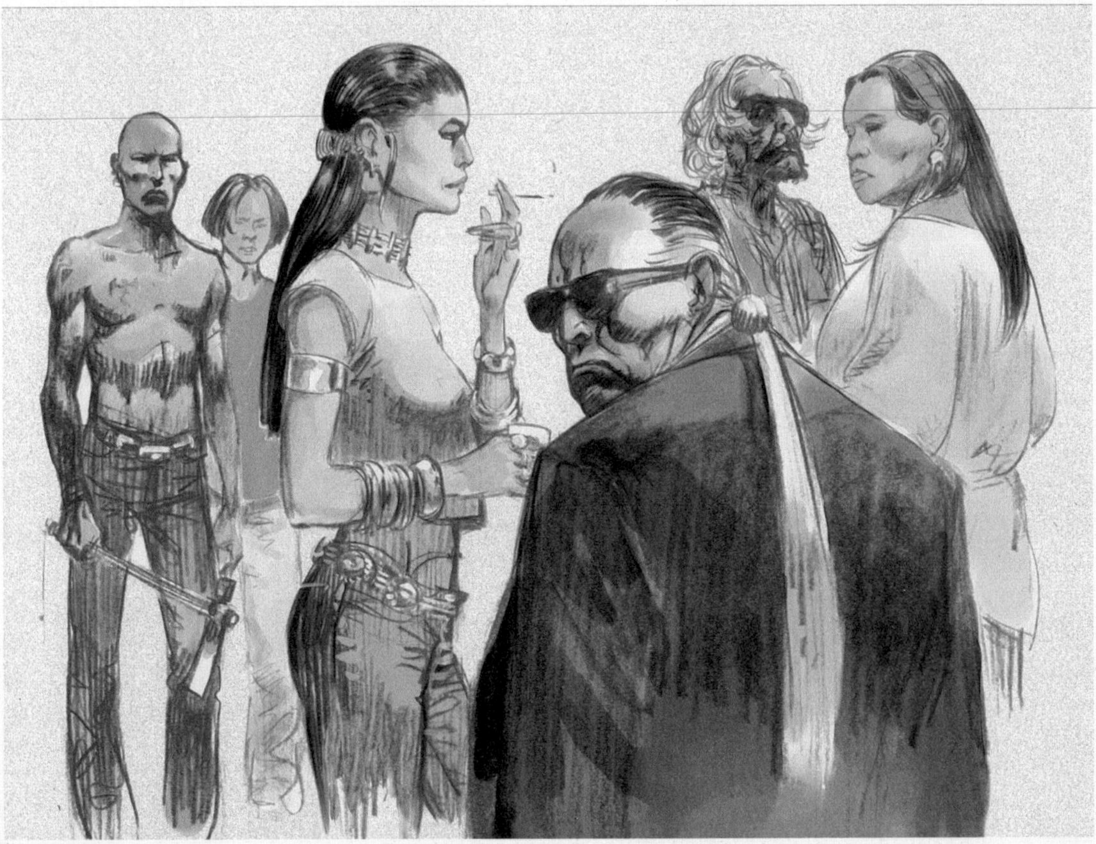

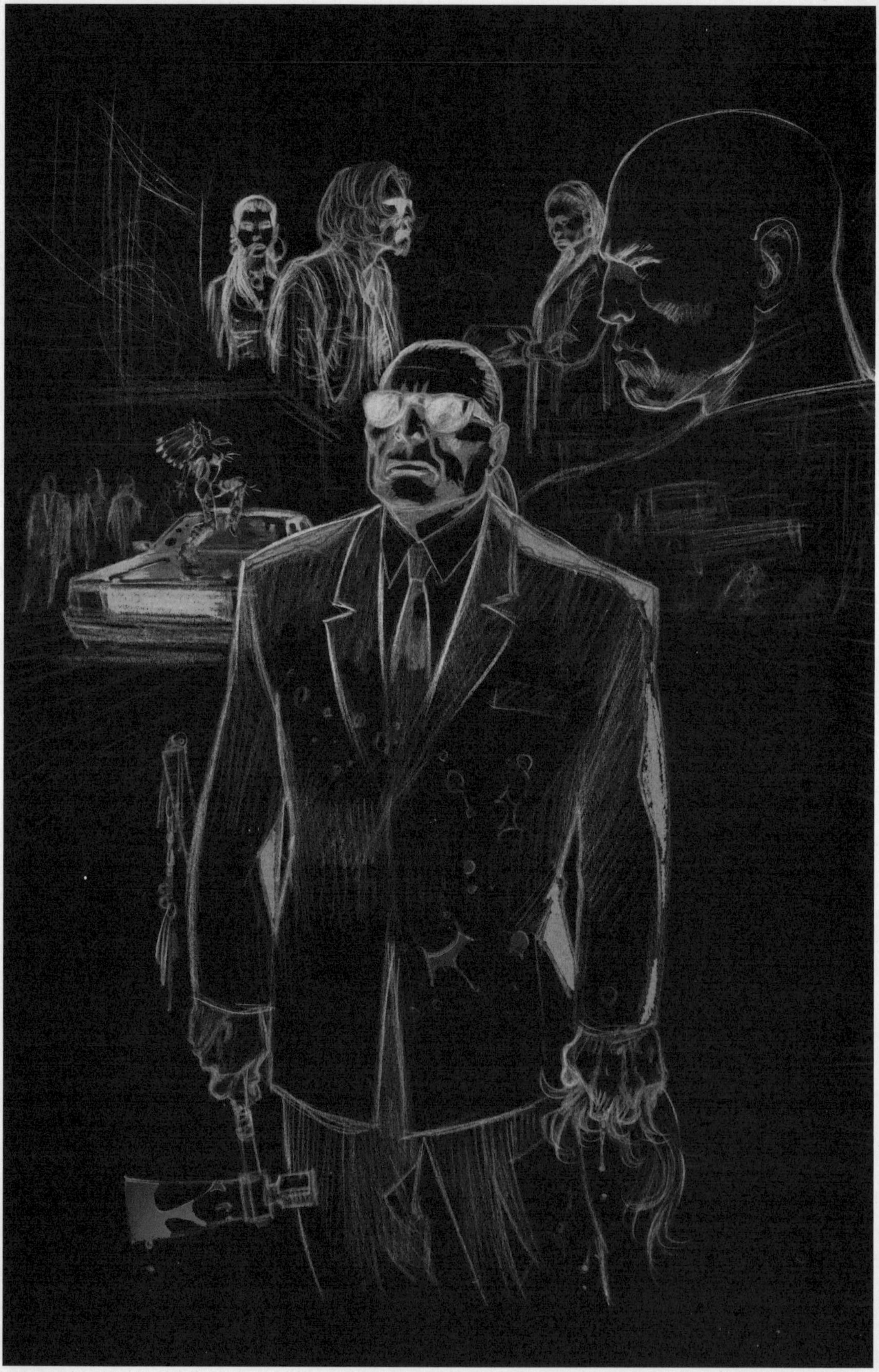

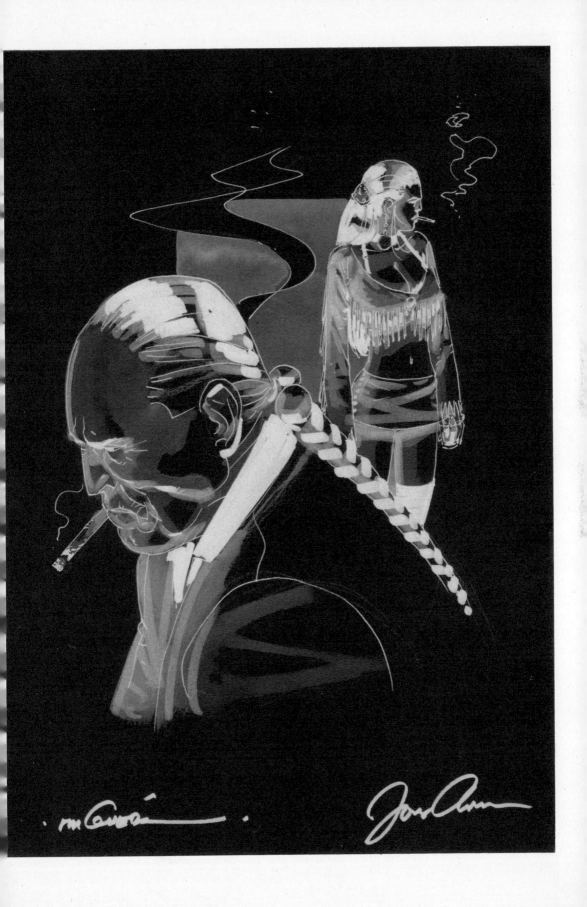

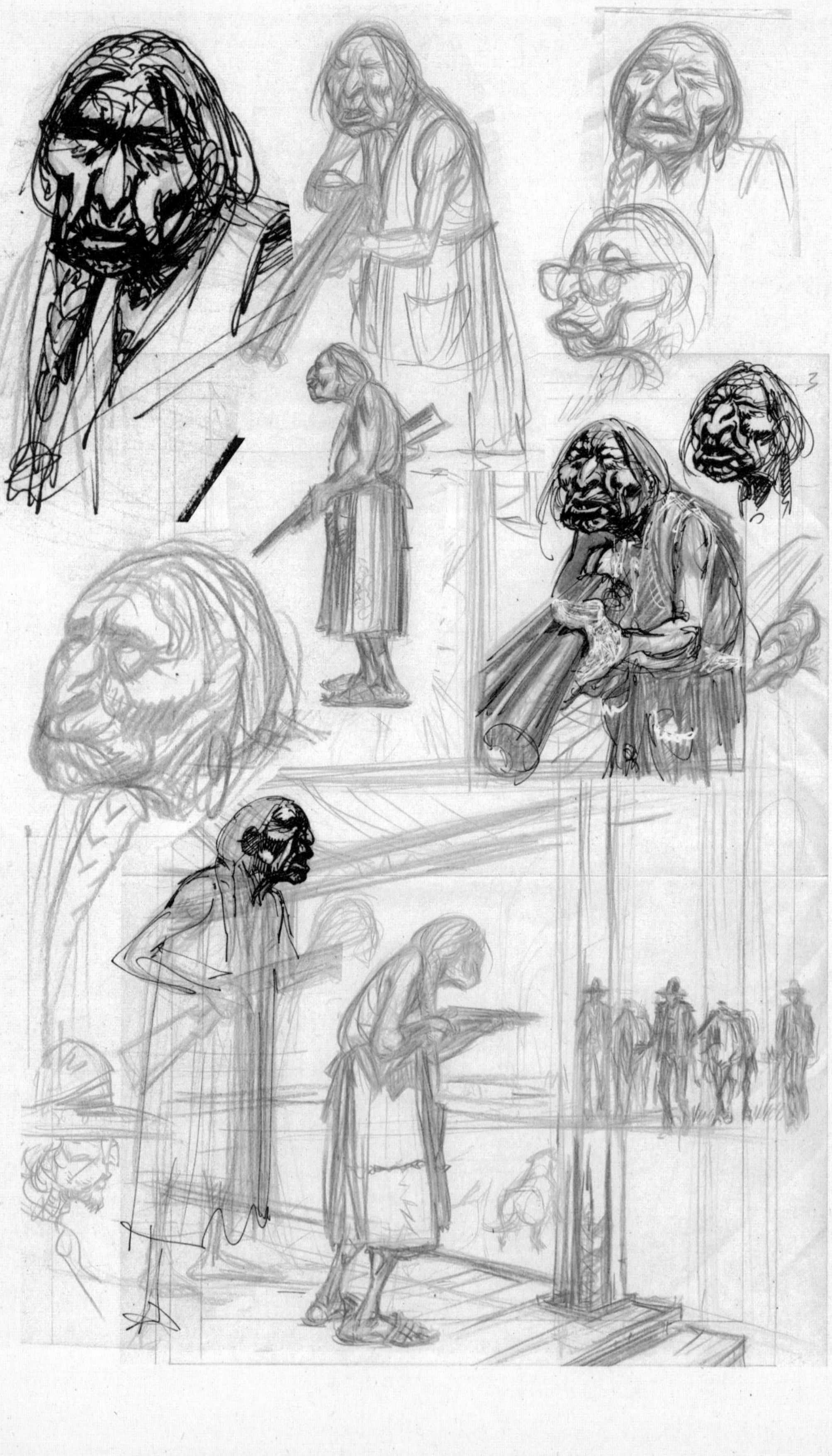

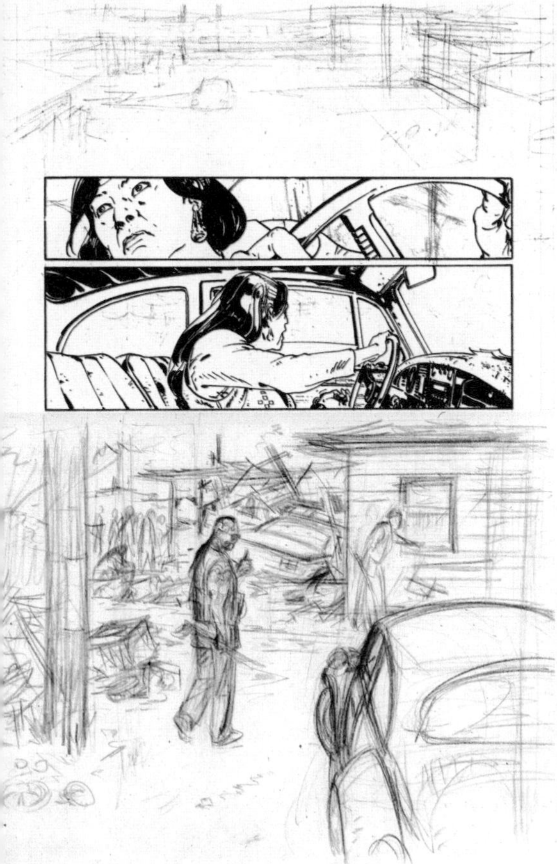

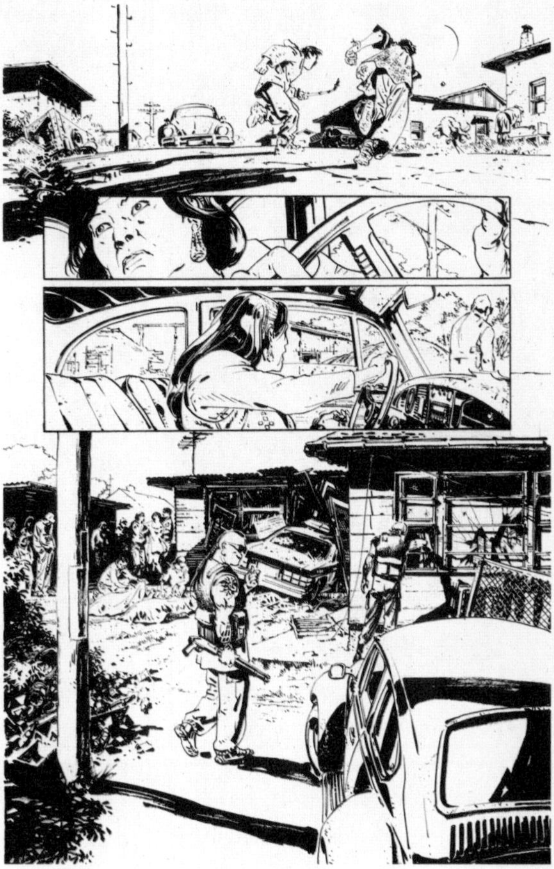

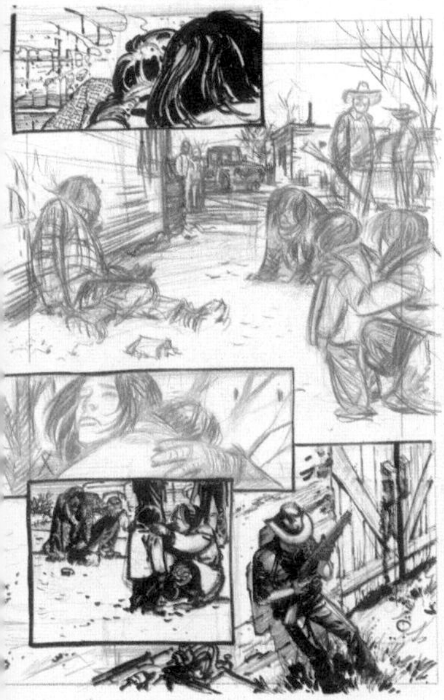

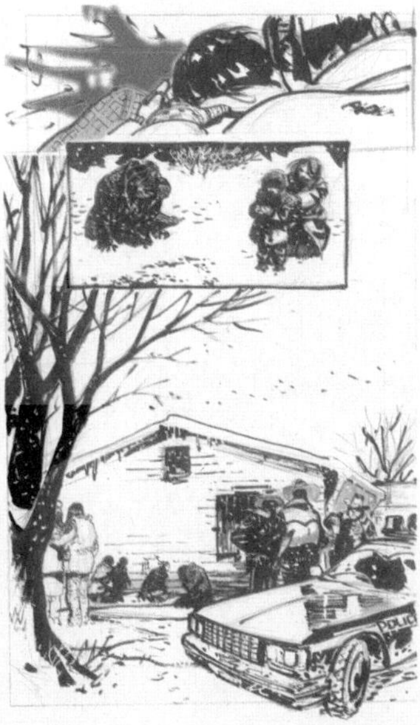

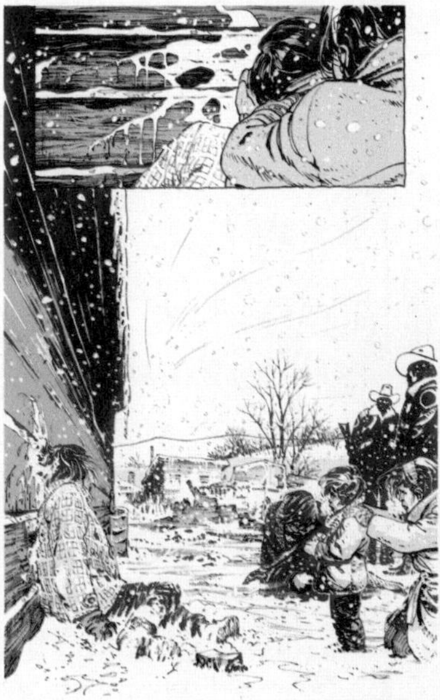

SOMETIMES ONE LAYOUT DEFINES THE WHOLE ISSUE

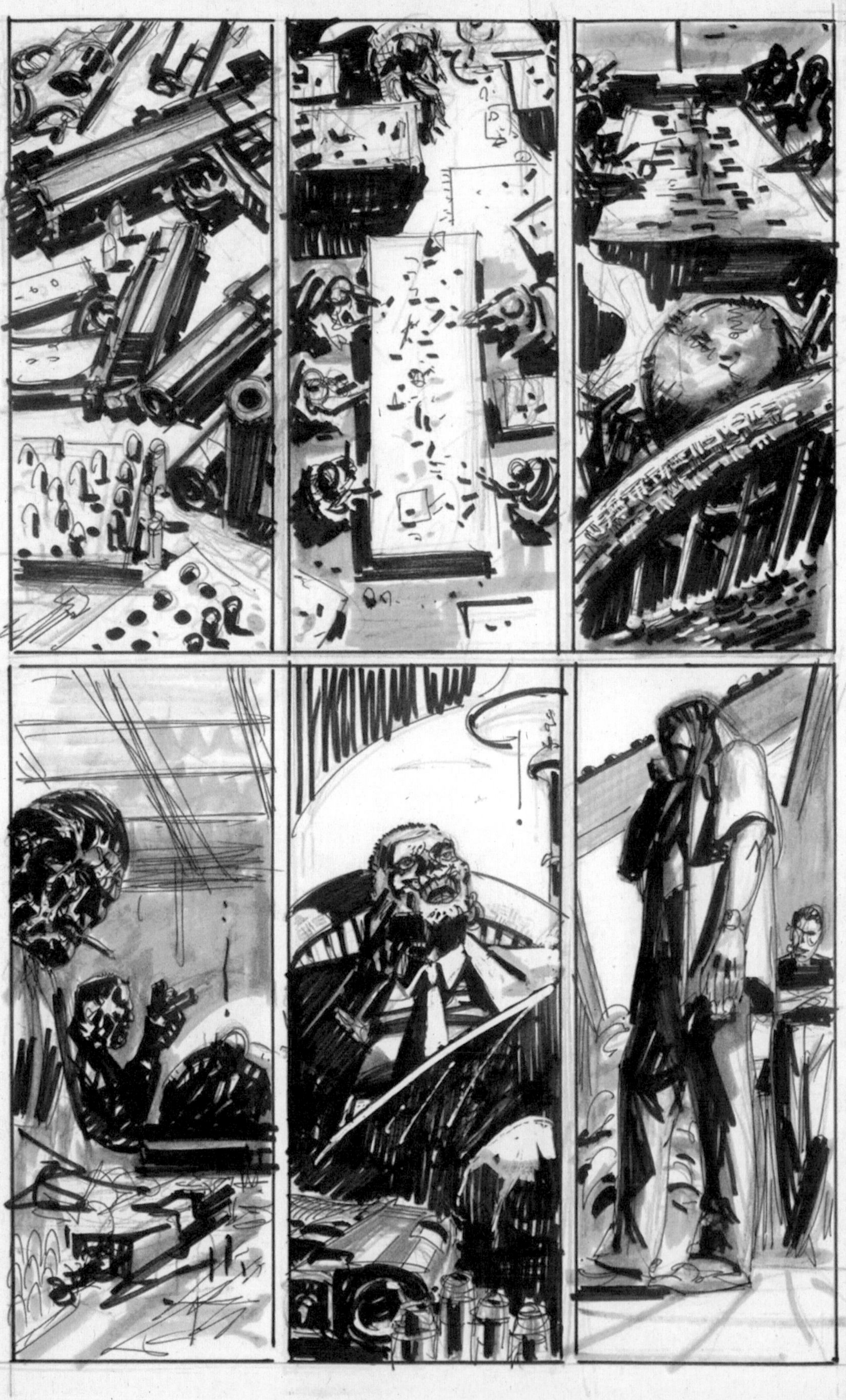

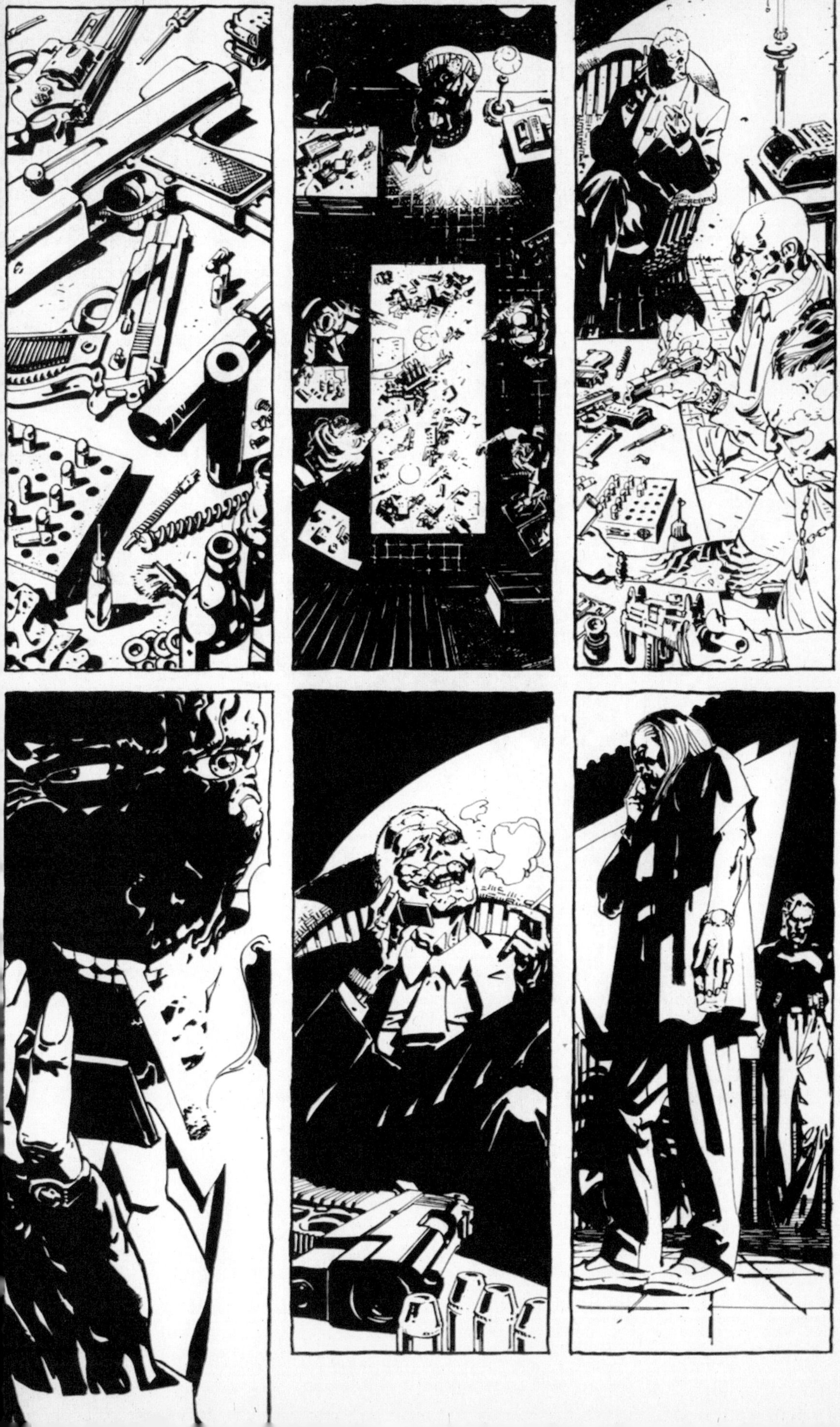

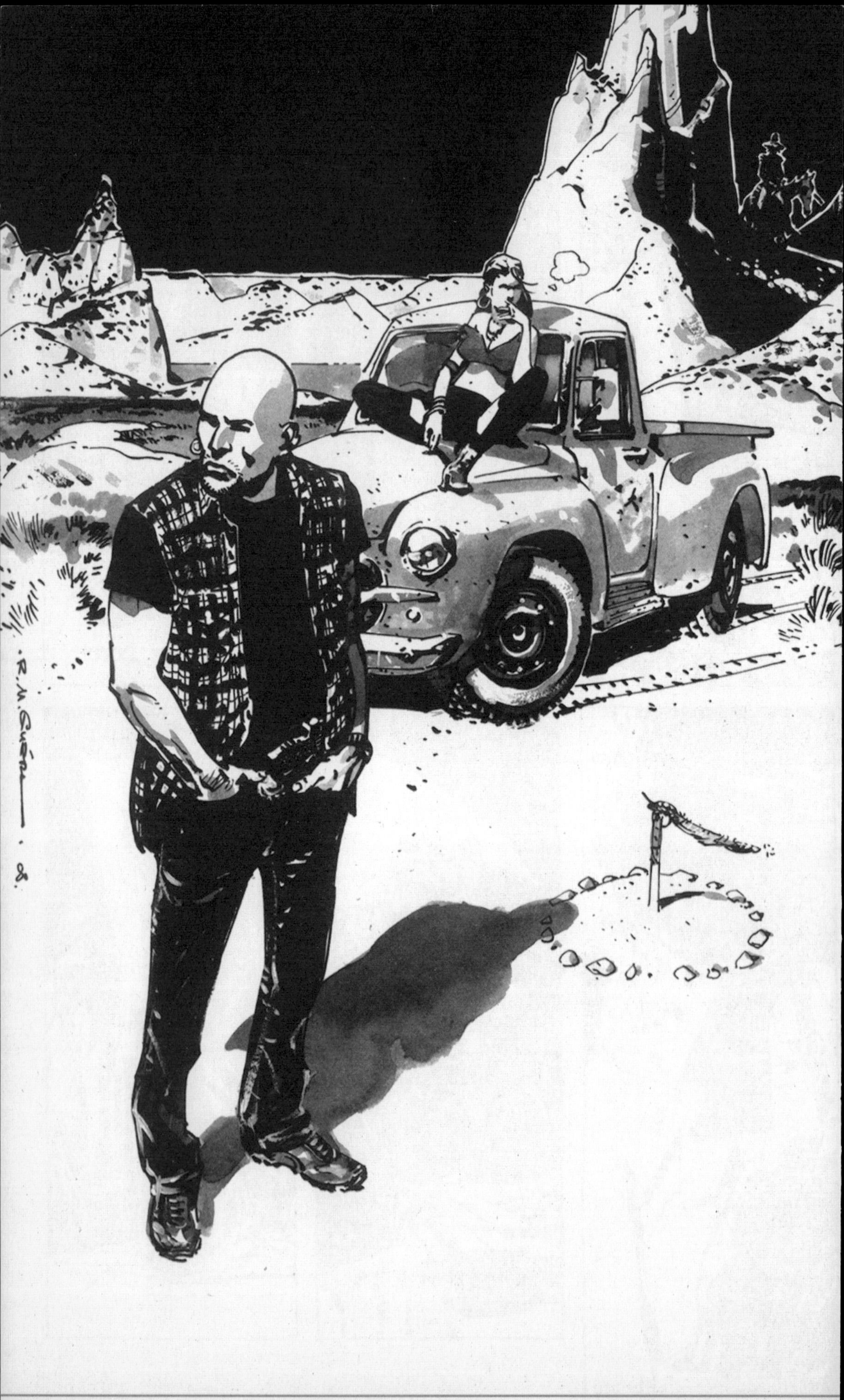